Dominique De Vito
With Heather Russell-Revesz and Stephanie Fornino

Pocket Professional Guide® The Encyclopedia of Dog Breeds

Project Team
Editor: Heather Russell-Revesz, Stephanie Fornino
Indexer: Lucie Haskins
Design, Cover, and Interior: Angela Stanford

T.F.H. Publications
President/CEO: Glen S. Axelrod
Executive Vice President: Mark E. Johnson
Publisher: Christopher T. Reggio
Production Manager: Kathy Bontz

TFH Publications, Inc.
One TFH Plaza
Third and Union Avenues
Neptune City, NJ 07753

Printed and bound in China
11 12 13 14 15 16 1 3 5 7 9 8 6 4 2
Library of Congress Cataloging-in-Publication Data
De Vito, Dominique.
  The encyclopedia of dog breeds / Dominique De Vito, with Heather Russell-Revesz and Stephanie Fornino.
     p. cm.
  Includes index.
  ISBN 978-0-7938-1277-6 (alk. paper)
  1. Dog breeds–Encyclopedias. I. Russell-Revesz, Heather. II. Fornino, Stephanie. III. Title.
  SF422.D43 2011
  636.7'103–dc22

                          2010043863

This book has been published with the intent to provide accurate and authoritative information in regard to the subject matter within. While every reasonable precaution has been taken in preparation of this book, the author and publisher expressly disclaim responsibility for any errors, omissions, or adverse effects arising from the use or application of the information contained herein. The techniques and suggestions are used at the reader's discretion and are not to be considered a substitute for veterinary care. If you suspect a medical problem consult your veterinarian.

Note: In the interest of concise writing, "he" is used when referring to puppies and dogs unless the text is specifically referring to females or males. "She" is used when referring to people. However, the information contained herein is equally applicable to both sexes.

The Leader In Responsible Animal Care For Over 50 Years!©
www.tfh.com

Table of Contents

History of Dog Breeds

Tiny Chihuahua to burly Mastiff, all dogs are one species. Dogs are the most variable animal on the planet, showing so many differences among breeds it's sometimes hard to imagine they are all one species.

What Is a Dog Breed?

Because all dogs are the same biological species, whether purebred or mixed, a breed is a race—a population containing genetically similar animals that differ in certain ways from other races. With dog breeds this is generally an artificial situation, effected by humans' selective breeding.

Origin of Breeds

Through the millennia since their domestication, dogs have been bred in a wide variety of types. Many of today's breeds were established centuries ago, while some were already distinct thousands of years ago. Breeds range in size from tiny teacup purse dogs to mammoth burly animals a child can ride like a horse. Different breeds have short hair, long hair, straight hair, curly hair, or even no hair at all over much of their body. There are dogs with extremely short legs and those with extremely long legs; those with long muzzles and those with squashed-in muzzles; those with powerful, rugged bodies and those with sleek, streamlined bodies. Some breeds come in various colors and patterns, while the dogs of other breeds are all one color or pattern. Behavior also varies from breed to breed, with some dogs excelling at guarding, herding, hunting, retrieving, fighting, carrying loads, or other useful-to-people traits. Dogs of certain breeds are more likely to attach themselves to one particular person, while others are happy for any human companionship, and a few are strictly working dogs with little suitability as house pets.

But a dog breed is more than just a bunch of dogs that look and behave alike. The individuals are genetically similar so that their offspring will also look and behave like the typical specimen of that breed. New breeds are developed when a group of dogs is bred for certain traits, and then the traits are fixed through careful matings until the puppies all fit the standard for the new breed. The breeders then organize, start a studbook, and begin registering dogs in that breed. Registry organizations in various countries divide dog breeds into different groupings. Registries also differ in the breeds that they recognize.

Breed Types

For the purposes of this book, we have grouped the breeds into ten different categories based on their original function: Companion/Toy; Flock Guardian; Herding; Mastiff; Nordic; Pariah; Scenthound; Sighthound; Sporting; and Terrier.

Companion/Toy

Trying to put dog breeds into categories immediately confronts exceptions, and the companion/toy category illustrates this perfectly. Although any dog can be kept as a companion animal, certain breeds are generally kept just as pets. While many of these companion breeds are quite small, not all are. And while many toy breeds are companion breeds, some are not recommended as family pets, especially where there are young children.

Some of the most popular breeds today are toy breeds. The masses who enjoy these animals today are indebted to ancient royalty, as in leaner times only nobles and royal families could afford to keep dogs who did nothing to earn their keep. Various tiny breeds were developed and kept as symbols of authority, rank, and wealth. Many were designed as lapdogs, and they indeed spent much of their time warming the laps of their owners.

Toy Dogs as Pets

Although companionship can be found with just about any dog, it is the principal trait that was selected for in the creation of many toy breeds, so these dogs are often affable to the extreme. Although all dogs are neotonous compared to wolves, toy breeds typically demonstrate even greater neoteny. They constantly seek the companionship of their owners. They often retain the appearance of a puppy into adulthood, and many play like puppies until old age. Other endearing qualities include the comical antics typical of a Pug and the extra-long eyelashes of the Maltese and Shih Tzu.

Flock Guardian

Since the advent of agriculture, people have faced the problem of protecting their domesticated herbivores like goats, sheep, and cattle from wild predators like bears, wolves, and big cats. It must have been readily apparent to prehistoric herdsmen and farmers that a large, fierce dog who felt possessive about his human's flocks was an indispensable asset. Many of these breeds are called sheepdogs, but they can often be used to guard any type of livestock: sheep, goats, cattle, etc. In some parts of the world flocks and predators have lived together for centuries, with guardian dogs keeping the peace between humans and the wild animals.

Flock guards are different from herding dogs, who can precisely direct the herd and are not considered part of the flock. Guardians are large, strong, and protective, but they do not control the movements of their flocks, and the livestock accepts them as part of the group.

Flock Guardians as Pets

Flock guardian breeds are typically large and strong. They have the courage to stand up to a carnivorous predator and the strength to make the threat real, but they can be as gentle with their human families as they traditionally were with their flocks. Because a  be more committed to his charges than to his owner and trainer, the focus on this trait leaves the dog a bit more aloof than other breeds, extremely loyal to his family and territory but r as committed to socialization with humans or other dogs. Flock guardians are also used to m their own decisions and thus are extremely independent, which can make obedience training a challenge.

Herding

At some point long ago, some person must have noticed a dog who particularly enjoyed herding—using his own movements to control the movements of a herd, flock, or group of livestock. (This behavior is part of a dog's wolf ancestry; wolves are very good at directing the movements of their prey.) Eventually dogs were bred who had extremely well-developed herding instincts, and people learned how to train these animals and use them most effectively to control their flocks.

Specific herding instincts differ from breed to breed. For example, Australian Cattle Dogs are heelers—they stay behind the herd animals and nip at their heels to drive them where they are to go. Border Collies, on the other hand, are headers—they stare the herd animals down and direct their movement from the front of the herd. Some dogs use a combination of tactics, and certain breeds are specifically bred to herd one type of livestock, while others are more adaptable and can control various types. In all herding breeds this instinct is so strong that even pets who never received any training will often be found spontaneously herding poultry or other animals or trying to collect and guide the family's children.

HERDERS AS PETS

The intelligence, attention to detail, and ability to learn rapidly from their mistakes that serve these animals so well when dealing with a recalcitrant flock also make them particularly delightful family pets. Herders are typically high-drive dogs who need plenty of exercise and mental stimulation to exist peacefully in a home. They also get bored easily, so training must be made interesting to keep their attention.

Mastiff

It is believed that the original giant dogs who gave rise to the mastiff breeds developed in Tibet many thousands of years ago. As the dogs were traded across the globe, many different types were bred for a variety of purposes, all of which made use of the animals' massive size, heavy bones, and great strength. Mastiffs generally have huge heads, shortened muzzles, smooth coats, loose, wrinkly skin, and an excellent sense of smell. They are very territorial and protective but usually do not herd or hunt, in keeping with their guard-dog origins. Types of Mastiffs include:

- **War Dogs:** Breeders concentrated on aggression, loyalty, and ferocity in addition to size and strength. War dogs, often fitted with spiked, flaming, or bladed collars and full armor, were effective against both foot soldiers and cavalry. With the development of more modern warfare and the demise of the armored knight, some mastiff breeds were developed as guard dogs, but many were turned into sport-fighting dogs.

- **Fighting Dogs:** The size, strength, and fighting ability of war mastiffs were put to the terrible use of developing fighting dogs. Fighters were pitted against each other, against large animals such as bulls and bears, and even against humans. The bloodier the match, the more the crowds approved, and huge amounts of money were wagered. From the Roman Coliseum to the dog pit of an Elizabethan English pub, the practice continued for centuries. Sadly, despite modern sensibilities and legalities, this bloody "sport" persists in some areas.

- **Bull Dogs:** Dogs associated with bulls have a long history, and bull dogs included both the bulldog and mastiff types of the time, which were frequently crossed as breeders perfected their dogs. Large dogs were used to herd and protect bulls as they were driven to market, and their skill and tenacity in dealing with recalcitrant bovines were prized. One specific use of such dogs was behind the development of the Bullmastiff breed, a cross of bulldogs and mastiffs that was widely used to protect game from poachers; the dogs would find and hold poachers until the authorities could catch up with them. They did not attack intruders but used their bulk and strength to prevent escape.

- **Service:** Some mastiff-type breeds avoided a gory history and were developed to serve humankind rather than engage in blood sports. Their size and strength were channeled into guard duty, bearing burdens, and rescue work. Many of these dogs were general-purpose workers, used alternately for guarding herds, carrying loads, pulling carts, and finding avalanche victims. These were often dogs of the common man, able to protect a farmer's livestock from predators and pull his wares to market in a cart, as well as guard the homestead and play with the children.

MASTIFFS AS PETS

As expected with such a diverse group, mastiff breeds vary in their suitability as pets. The breeds that were developed to draw blood from other animals can have problems with aggression, especially to other dogs. Ethical breeders strive to create sound temperament in their dogs, but not all breeders take this task to heart. And there will always be those uninformed owners who choose these dogs based on a desire for their ferocious reputation, which is certainly not good for the future of these dogs. This is most unfortunate, as many of these breeds with terrible origins can today make loving pets. A well-bred dog of this sort is typically intelligent, eager to please his owner, gentle, and devoted. Still, their reputation haunts them, and some are considered so dangerous that in some places, laws have been enacted to prevent their being kept as pets.

The mastiff-type breeds that were developed as guardian, pack, or rescue dogs have avoided such controversy. They combine a natural gentleness and protectiveness with their huge size, and these dogs make excellent (if a bit bull-in-a-china-shop) family pets.

Obviously, obedience training from an early age is necessary to prevent problems when dealing with animals that are larger, heavier, and stronger than their handlers. A drawback to their exceptionally large bones and overall size is the strain placed on the animal's body, which increases the chance of defects like hip dysplasia and shortens the life span.

Nordic

At the top of the globe is a harsh, beautiful land where humans and other animals eke out an existence with little regard for political boundaries. The faithful dog has served humankind here probably as long as humans have braved this difficult life. Typically sporting long double coats and tails that curl forward, these nordic breeds in some cases may have their origins in the last ice age, and they are well adapted for cold weather. The most recognized use for these dogs is as sled dogs, but many were traditionally used for hunting and for herding reindeer. They are quite versatile hunters and have been employed to hunt small game as well as large bears, moose, and mountain lions. Where these breeds are found in more southern regions, they are often used for herding cattle and sheep as well.

Many of these dogs are kept as family pets, but the sport of dog sledding, which can be found in many places around the world, accounts for some of their popularity. In fact, as the native peoples of the Arctic move increasingly to the use of snowmobiles rather than dogsleds, sledding as a sport is becoming the dominant place to find sled dogs.

Nordic Dogs as Pets

These breeds can make intelligent and affectionate pets, but they are independent and can have serious dominance issues. They also cannot be restricted to an apartment and small yard. They often do not tolerate other dogs very well, and they have strong predator instincts that can make them untrustworthy around other animals. They generally do well with older children who understand how to handle them. Some of the newer breeds, like the American Eskimo Dog, were developed primarily as companion dogs and are more suitable pets than the ancient working breeds.

Pariah

With origins in Southeast Asia perhaps as long as 10,000 years ago, pariah dogs are considered by some to be barely changed descendants of the first dogs. Most often yellow or ginger colored, pariahs are medium-sized dogs who have short, erect ears and usually do not bark, although they do howl. Feral populations eat a great variety of foods, including plants, but they excel at hunting. Although they typically hunt small game alone or in pairs, they do come together to hunt larger prey, and in some places they are considered major vermin, killing livestock like sheep and cattle.

Pariah Dogs as Pets

Controversy abounds with regard to pariah dogs. Some people consider them wild dogs, not domesticated companions. In some places it is illegal to possess these animals because they are considered pests and predators on livestock. Sometimes they are labeled as untrainable, and certainly they are the polar opposite of the eager-to-please sporting breeds. On the other hand, many owners of pariah breeds extol their pets' qualities, citing their loyalty and affection. Native Australians reportedly kept warm by sleeping with their Dingoes, which certainly indicates a closeness of sorts!

Scenthound

As a group, hounds are associated with hunting of both small fur-bearing animals and large game, from rabbits and raccoons to wild boars and bears. They were bred to excel at locating, tracking, and containing or treeing their prey, and sometimes they even kill the animals, freeing the human hunter from all tasks. Scenthounds track their prey with their nose. Most breeds have long, droopy ears; long noses with large nasal passages; and loose, drooling lips. These traits are said to help them detect scents. The incredible olfactory abilities of these dogs are difficult to comprehend.

Most scenthounds have a deep baying they utter while tracking and a different vocalization once they have their prey cornered or treed. This enables the hunters to follow the pack, either literally on foot or horseback or auditorily from a central waiting location, from which they proceed to the hounds once the quarry is treed.

Descended from mastiff-type dogs, scenthounds are rugged and strong, not especially fast runners but able to keep tracking for long periods. In some cases sighthounds were used in breeding programs to increase the speed and agility of these breeds. A hunt often continues for a couple of hours or more, and the pack performs tirelessly, running and baying continuously until the quarry is obtained.

SCENTHOUNDS AS PETS

The ability of scenthounds to socialize with humans and with other dogs makes them a good choice as a family pet. They are generally kind and loving, and they usually get along well with other animals, children, and strangers. They often loyally follow their owners wherever they go. Scenthounds tend to take naturally to the hunt, but teaching basic obedience can be a struggle for their owners, as they prefer to follow their noses than repeat training commands.

Sighthound

There is evidence of sighthounds going back about 10,000 years, making them arguably among the oldest-known dogs. Like the scenthounds, sighthounds are associated with hunting game, but they are built for speed because they had to keep their quarry in sight during the chase. These breeds were developed with acute eyesight and a graceful body ideal for speed. A lean physique and a small head with a long muzzle give the dog agility and superior stereoscopic vision to detect motion and follow prey.

Sighthounds hold the speed record for all dogs—and perhaps for all land mammals. Officially the cheetah is faster, but some sighthounds are anecdotally reported to be even faster. After all, they were bred to pursue and bring down all types of game, including deer and antelopes.

Sighthounds as Pets

Sighthounds have an ancient legacy of being working dogs who hunted alone, locating, chasing, and bringing down their prey. They have a tradition of working independently of humans and may be difficult to recall at a dog park. On the other hand, they are typically extremely affectionate "shadows." For the most part, these dogs attach themselves to one person, to whom they remain close. Sometimes called "cat-like," sighthounds, although engineered for speed, are peaceful and sedentary. They will take every opportunity to chase just about any moving object, but the rest of the time they will be curled up at their owner's feet—or on the couch.

Sporting/Gun

Sporting or hunting breeds are also known as gundogs and bird dogs, although they were used before the advent of gunpowder weapons, when birds and other game were netted or clubbed. They are traditionally used for hunting birds, either upland game birds (quails, pheasants, etc.) or waterfowl. Sporting or hunting breeds are in many cases extremely old. While hunting for game has always been a behavior of the human species, hunting as a pastime or a social activity also has its origins more than 1,000 years ago, and many dog breeds were developed to assist in both subsistence and recreational hunting.

All sporting breeds have in common that they work well with humans and with other dogs. Besides this sociability, they are strong and have great stamina. Although a dog of any sporting breed can be trained to some extent to perform any of the desired hunting behaviors, each breed excels at one of them. The various jobs of gundogs may include locating game, signaling its location, flushing the birds, and retrieving the downed ones. These types include:

- **Flushers:** These dogs are used to locate and flush birds so that the hunter can shoot them. Extremely useful when hunting birds like pheasants that otherwise would tend to run away through the brush, these dogs force the birds to take flight, making them easy targets. A well-trained flusher will note where shot birds fall and wait for a command from his handler to go retrieve them. Flushing breeds are primarily spaniels, but retrievers can also be employed on upland game. They work quite close

to their handlers—within shotgun distance—because it is useless for them to flush birds farther away than that.

- **Pointers and Setters:** In contrast to flushers, these breeds work at a great distance from their handlers, locating birds and then pointing or crouching to signal. Birds like quail, which tend to bunch together and wait quietly, are best hunted by this method. Rather than startle the birds into flight, the pointers and setters scare the game into hiding and keep an eye on them until their handlers arrive. At this point trainers differ. Some have the dog remain still while the hunter flushes the game and fires, while others train the dog to remain in position until given the signal to flush the game.

- **Retrievers:** Although retrievers are successfully used for upland bird hunting, their forte is retrieving downed waterfowl. They often must wait quietly and patiently for long periods and then follow their handler's shots, taking note of where each bird lands. Next, when given the command, they must swim out and retrieve the birds. A retriever's training includes staying on the mark and not getting distracted when other birds are shot while the dog is retrieving and staying out of the way of another dog's retrieving.

SPORTING DOGS AS PETS

Loyal, gentle, obedient, and eager to please their owners, sporting dogs make excellent pets. They are typically good watchdogs, but their friendliness makes them poor guard dogs in most cases—the worst an intruder can expect is a sloppy kiss. They do need plenty of exercise and can excel at all types of organized sports.

Terrier

DNA analysis shows that the terrier breeds are relatively new, developing in Europe in the 19th century. Much of the proliferation of terriers took place in the United Kingdom. Both long- and short-legged breeds exist, depending on whether they were bred to chase prey above ground or into burrows. Terriers are sometimes described as being 20-pound (9-kg) dogs with a 200-pound (90-kg) attitude. Indeed, they are intelligent, alert, and fearless. Their traditional function was as varmint killers, and many of the breeds were developed to dig right into animals' burrows to root them out. These were not hunting dogs who went on the hunt with their owners but dogs who were always on patrol, ready to take on rats, foxes, or badgers—often vicious animals considerably larger than the feisty dogs. The bravery of terriers is legendary, but it is a vital part of their behavioral repertoire. Even a small rodent is a formidable adversary when cornered, and terriers often have to confront larger, fiercer prey like foxes and badgers. Standing up to such a foe at the end of a burrow in the dark certainly requires true courage, and the fact that these dogs routinely do this successfully attests to their strength, agility, and killing instincts as well.

TERRIERS AS PETS

Almost all terriers today are kept as pets, not as working dogs. Some of the toy terrier breeds were developed specifically as companion animals. The relatively small size of most terriers is one attraction, but their perky independence also endears them to people, and their energetic attentiveness is easily channeled into a variety of games, making them pint-sized playmates. Some terriers can be a bit feisty for homes with small children, and they tend to view smaller pets as prey.

About the Profiles

With any attempt at compiling an encyclopedic reference work, the first decision is what to include; it then necessarily follows that something must be excluded. How to arrive at both a fair representation of dog breeds of the world and an executable book took months of debate. In the end, the profiles included in this work are a selection of popular recognized breeds from the following organizations: American Kennel Club (AKC); Australian National Kennel Council (ANKC); Canadian Kennel Club (CKC); Fédération Cynologique Internationale (FCI); Kennel Club (KC); and United Kennel Club (UKC). This in no way implies that a breed not represented on these pages is not a "real" breed; nor is it an indication of the quality of any certain breed.

Color-Coded Header Bar

The breed name is enclosed in a colored header bar, based on "Breed Types."

Companion		Pariah
Flock Guard		Scenthound
Herding		Sighthound
Mastiff		Sporting
Nordic		Terrier

Breed Names

The names of the breeds appear with the most prevalent North American spelling based on the applicable registries. Varieties are listed by using commas after the breed name (e.g., Poodle, Standard).

Breed Facts

A statistics box appears on the first page of every profile. It includes the following information.

Country of Origin

This indicates where the breed originated but may also indicate where it was developed or refined.

Height

The height of a breed represents a range of numbers based on those provided by all applicable breed organizations. All empirical measurements are converted to metric, following in parentheses and rounded to the nearest half number.

Often, a breed's height differed by a small amount across the given organizations. When this occurred, both the lowest and highest numbers for both males and females are presented in a range and separated by a "/":

- **Example:** Males 19–20.5 in (48–52 cm)/females 17–18.5 in (43–47 cm)

When some breed organizations listed both a male and female range separately but others just presented an overall range, in most cases the former takes precedence due to its specificity and is listed first. The latter is listed second, separated by a "|" to indicate that it is an exception, and the corresponding breed organization is listed in brackets.

- **Example:** Males 10 in (25.5 cm)/females slightly smaller|8–11 in (20–28 cm) [AKC]

In instances where no breed organization listed specific numbers for height, the numbers are based on the editors' research and denoted by "[est.]" to signify that they are an estimate only.

- **Example:** 12–13 in (30–33 cm) [est.]

Weight

The weight of a breed represents a range of numbers based on those provided by all applicable breed organizations. All empirical measurements are converted to metric, following in parentheses and rounded to the nearest half number.

Often, a breed's weight differed by a small amount across the given organizations. When this occurred, both the lowest and highest numbers for both males and females are presented in a range and separated by a "/":

- **Example:** Males 66–88 lb (30–40 kg)/females 55–77 lb (25–35 kg)

When some breed organizations listed both a male and female range separately but others just presented an overall range, in most cases the former takes precedence due to its specificity and is listed first. The latter is listed second, separated by a "|" to indicate that it is an exception, and the corresponding breed organization is listed in brackets.

- **Example:** Males 16–18 lb (7.5–8 kg)/females 15–17 lb (7–7.5 kg)|3.5–7 lb (1.5–3 kg) [UKC]

In instances where no breed organization listed specific numbers for weight, the numbers are based on the editors' research and indicated by "[est.]" to indicate that they are an estimate only.

- **Example:** 35–45 lb (16–20.5 kg) [est.]

Coat

Each breed's coat description is based on what is considered acceptable by all applicable breed organizations.

- **Example:** Double coat with hard, wiry, dense outercoat and short, soft undercoat; beard

When some breed organizations recognized more than one coat type but others recognized just one, the majority consensus takes precedence. Each coat type is separated by a "/." The minority coat type is listed second, separated by a "|" to indicate that it is an exception, and the corresponding breed organization is listed in brackets:

- **Example:** Two varieties—shorthaired has short, strong, very dense, smooth-lying outercoat and no or sparse undercoat/longhaired has long, flat or slightly wavy, soft outercoat and may or may not have undercoat|one variety—short, smooth, sleek [AKC][UKC]

In instances where no breed organization provided a description of the coat, it is based on the editors' research and denoted by "[est.]" to signify that this is an estimate only.

- **Example:** Short, smooth, firm, close [est.]

Color

Each breed's listed coat colors are based on what are considered acceptable by all applicable breed organizations.

- **Example:** Red to yellow with black saddle or mantle; white markings

When the breed organizations listed different colors for a particular breed, the lowest common color denominators are presented first; then, the remaining colors are listed, separated by a "|," in descending order of recognizing organizations. The corresponding breed organizations are listed in brackets.

- **Example:** Black, wheaten, brindle of any color|also steel or iron gray, sandy [CKC]

When multiple organizations recognize a breed but list completely different colors, all are presented and the exception, separated by a "|," is the least-inclusive registry.

- **Example:** Any color, pattern, or combination except black, solid blue, and tricolor|solid white, pied, white with brindle or red patches [ARBA]

In instances where no breed organization provided a coat color, it is based on the editors' research and denoted by "[est.]" to signify that this is an estimate only.

- **Example:** Black, tan [est.]

Other Names

Some breeds are commonly known by a variety of other formal names, which are presented in this section, if applicable, in alphabetical order.

Registries

The selected breeds are recognized by at least one registry, which include the American Kennel Club (AKC); Australian National Kennel Council (ANKC); Canadian Kennel Club (CKC); Fédération Cynologique Internationale (FCI); Kennel Club (KC); and United Kennel Club (UKC).

(The FCI is technically not a registry, but for the intents and purposes of this book, it functions as a breed classification tool nonetheless.) In addition, each registry classifies its breeds into groups (e.g., Working, Herding, Guardian) based on their origin and/or what they were bred to do.

This section alphabetically lists the applicable registries for the breeds, along with their group classifications, which follow in parentheses. The spelling of a group is based upon the registries' classifications and may vary from registry to registry (e.g., "Gundog" versus "Gun Dog").

History and Personality

Many breeds have painstaking records of their creation—famous breeders, renowned foundation dogs, and the like. However, the history of some breeds has been lost to time—this inevitably leads to speculation and downright legend when it comes to their origins. This section includes the most current research about a breed's history, and when exact facts are not known, the prevailing theory about where a breed may have originated.

Although "personality" may seem a bit anthropomorphic, it's merely a fun way of listing typical behavior traits and temperament for a breed. Of course, dogs are individuals—anyone who spends time with dogs understands this fact. However, there are some generalizations one can make based on breed type.

Exercise, Training, Grooming, and Health

This section provides specific information on exercise, grooming, and training, plus health information as they apply to each breed.

Exercise

All dogs need exercise—it is an absolute necessity for their physical and mental well-being. What may vary is the amount and intensity certain breeds require, and even this will change with age. This section gives an idea of how much exercise certain breeds need, as well as ideas on what types of activities might fulfill this requirement.

Training

Just like exercise, training should not be an option for a dog—it's a necessity. From the smallest toy to the largest mastiff, every dog benefits from training and socialization. This section takes note of any special training challenges (such as difficulty housetraining or an independent nature) and tasks that the breed may excel at or find challenging.

It's important to note that a dog's ability to be trained is not a reflection of intelligence. Some extremely smart breeds may be harder to train because they tend to be independent or high drive and not focused on following basic obedience commands.

Grooming

This section attempts to cover the time needed, difficulty level, and particular coat care for a breed. It typically reflects grooming a pet dog; if a dog is being groomed for show, it is likely to take more time and effort than noted here.

Health

Each breed's average life span is noted in this section. This range can vary among individuals and is dependant upon a variety of factors, including the care they have received throughout their lifetime.

Every breed is prone to certain health problems, especially those related to old age. What this section also attempts to provide is an overview of breed-specific health concerns related to the genetics, structure, or function of a particular breed. This does not mean that a breed will get any of the noted problems, and in fact, most breeders work hard to stamp out the health concerns of their breed. The best way to ensure a healthy dog is to go to an ethical breeder and ask for health clearances.

Breed Facts

- **Country of Origin**: Germany

- **Height**: 9–12 in (23–30 cm)

- **Weight**: 6.5–13 lb (3–6 kg)

- **Coat**: Dense, rough, harsh; longer hair on head, eyebrows, beard

- **Colors**: Black|and black and tan, gray, silver [AKC][CKC] [UKC]|and red [CKC][UKC]|and beige [UKC]|may have mask [AKC][CKC]

- **Registries (With Group)**: AKC (Toy); ANKC (Toys); CKC (Toys); FCI (Pinscher and Schnauzer); KC (Toy); UKC (Companion)

History and Personality

Small black dogs looking somewhat like the Affenpinscher, although slightly larger, were bred in Germany and Eastern

Europe around 1600 for the purpose of hunting rats and mice in people's homes. It is believed that the Pug, German Pinscher, and Schnauzer all contributed to what is now known as the Affenpinscher. The breed was refined in Germany in the 17th and 18th centuries and has changed little since. Works of art from that time and place often feature small, black-bearded dogs, valued both for their superior ratting skills and for their fine companionship.

The Affenpinscher is noted for his willful personality. A natural charmer and clown, he cannot be ignored; in fact, not paying him enough attention can bring out the worst in him, from erratic behavior to excessive barking. The Affenpinscher is curious, alert, and quick to learn—and don't underestimate his need for mental stimulation!

Exercise, Training, Grooming, and Health

- A couple vigorous walks a day, interactive playtime, and a busy social schedule keep the Affenpinscher in shape.

- The Affenpinscher requires patient and persistent training done with enthusiasm and lots of rewards.

- The Affenpinscher's dense, harsh coat has a natural scruffiness to it, but it requires brushing several times a week and trimming to keep it looking its finest.

- Average life span is 11 to 14 years. Breed health concerns may include eye problems; heart problems; hernias; hip dysplasia; hypothyroidism; Legg-Calve-Perthes disease; liver shunts; oligodontia; patellar luxation; sebaceous cysts; and von Willebrand disease.

Breed Facts

- **Country of Origin**: Afghanistan

- **Height**: Males 26–29 in (66–73.5 cm)/females 24–27 in (61–69 cm)

- **Weight**: Males approx. 60 lb (27 kg)/females approx. 50 lb (22.5 kg)

- **Coat**: Thick, silky, fine, with topknot of long hair, may have beard on lower jaw [FCI]

- **Colors**: All colors

- **Other Names**: Balkh Hound; Baluchi Hound; Barutzy Hound; Galanday Hound; Kabul Hound; Ogar Afgan; Sage Baluchi; Shalgar Hound; Tazi; Tāzī

- **Registries (With Group)**: AKC (Hound); ANKC (Hounds); CKC (Hounds); FCI (Sighthounds); KC (Hound); UKC (Sighthound & Pariah)

History and Personality

This ancient sighthound was developed in Afghanistan, India, and Pakistan to be both a guardian to the people and their livestock and a protector. Part kindly shepherd and part lethal weapon, the Afghan Hound has always needed to be an independent thinker, as well as a dog who could handle the harsh environment of that part of the world. Afghans were used to hunt everything from gazelles to hares, yet they also did double duty as the guardians of sheep.

The elegant and independent Afghan may fool you with his looks—on the outside, it's all flash and style; on the inside is a dog with a silly streak, a fast friend who will follow you to the ends of the earth and quietly and faithfully be there for you.

Exercise, Training, Grooming, and Health

- Afghans need to get outside, as they have an innate speed that must be appropriately directed. These dogs thrive on several walks a day and some quality playtime in a securely fenced-in yard.

- Do to their independent nature, Afghan Hounds can be difficult to train and they must be socialized from puppyhood to cut down on their strong prey drive.

- Their thick, flowing coats require intensive grooming and must be washed first, as brushing the dry hair will damage it. A professional groomer is a must for a first-time Afghan owner.

- Average life span is 12 to 14 years. Breed health concerns may include allergies; anesthesia sensitivity; bloat; cancer; cataracts; chylothorax; and hip dysplasia.

Breed Facts

- **Country of Origin**: England

- **Height**: Males 23–24 in (58–61 cm)/females 22–23 in (56–59 cm)

- **Weight**: Males 50–65 lb (22.5–29.5 kg)/females 40–45 lb (18–20.5 kg) [est.]

- **Coat**: Double coat with wiry, hard, dense outercoat and soft, downy undercoat; coat lies straight and close to body; especially hard coats crinkling or slightly waved

- **Colors**: Body saddle—tan with black or dark grizzle on sides and upper body

- **Other Names**: Bingley Terrier; Waterside Terrier

- **Registries (With Group)**: AKC (Terrier); ANKC (Terriers); CKC (Terriers); FCI (Terriers); KC (Terrier); UKC (Terrier)

History and Personality

A relatively "young" breed, the Airedale Terrier was developed in the Aire Valley in West Riding, Yorkshire, in the mid-19th century. Working-class citizens, who wanted a hunting and companion dog, crossed the extinct Old English Rough-Coated Black-and-Tan Terrier with the Otterhound to create the Airedale, a large, tenacious terrier who can also work in water. The breed was used to hunt foxes, weasels, otters, badgers, water rats, and small game in the valleys of the rivers Colne, Calder, Warfe, and Aire.

The intelligent, energetic, and curious Airedale has become today's "King of Terriers," the largest of all the terrier breeds—a proficient hunter, watchdog, athlete, and companion.

Exercise, Training, Grooming, and Health

- The Airedale Terrier needs a good deal of daily exercise, including several brisk walks a day and a securely fenced-in area where he can run off lead. This breed can become destructive if it doesn't receive adequate exercise.

- When it comes to training, the smart, quick-thinking Airedale becomes bored with repeated requests given in a monotone; the trick is to have reasonable expectations and make training interesting.

- If being shown in a conformation event, the Airedale's coat must be stripped, something that's often best left to a professional groomer. If not being shown, the coat can be clipped instead. He needs to be brushed daily or his coat will become shaggy and unkempt.

- Average life span is 10 to 13 years. Breed health concerns may include cancer; hip dysplasia; hypothyroidism; skin problems; and urologic problems.

Breed Facts

- **Country of Origin**: Japan

- **Height**: Males 26–28 in (66–71 cm)/females 24–26 in (61–66 cm)

- **Weight**: Males 100–130 lb (45.5–59 kg)/females 70–100 lb (31.5–45.5 kg) [est.]

- **Coat**: Double coat with straight, harsh outercoat and thick, soft, dense undercoat; coat most prominent on tail

- **Colors**: Any color, including white, brindle, fawn, red, pinto; may have mask

- **Other Names**: American Akita

- **Registries (With Group)**: AKC (Working); ANKC (Utility); CKC (Working); FCI (Spitz and Primitive); KC (Utility); UKC (Northern)

History and Personality

The Akita is an ancient Japanese dog, relative to the Ainu and the Shiba Inu. The largest of the spitz breeds, it was originally developed as a guard dog and fighting dog. As dog fighting lost favor, the nobility found new uses for this brave breed in their hunts for deer, wild boars, and even black bears. After World War II, American servicemen who became fond of the breed while stationed in Japan smuggled some home with them, establishing the American lines of the Akita.

Fearless, brave, strong, independent, and intelligent are all apt descriptions of this tough, somewhat obstinate, robust dog. He is aggressive with other animals (and particularly dogs of the same sex) and will defend his territory against all intruders, human or otherwise, yet he is an affectionate and intensely loyal companion to his family.

Exercise, Training, Grooming, and Health

- Akitas appreciate and eagerly anticipate their walks and should have several of them a day.

- A working dog, the Akita is by nature an independent thinker, but if worked with properly from an early age, the Akita is certainly trainable. Socialization from an early age is critical for this breed.

- The Akita's lush double coat needs regular and consistent care. He doesn't shed regularly, but he blows his undercoat a couple times a year and will need daily brushing so that large clumps of fur are properly displaced.

- Average life span is 10 to 12 years. Breed health concerns may include bloat; elbow dysplasia; hip dysplasia; hyperkalaemia; hypothyroidism; juvenile-onset polyarthritis syndrome; myasthenia gravis (MG); pemphigus; progressive retinal atrophy (PRA); sebaceous ad⟨ (SA); uveodermatological syndrome (UDS); and von Willebrand disease.

Breed Facts

- **Country of Origin**: United States

- **Height**: Males 25–28 in (64–71 cm)/females 23–26 in (58–66 cm)

- **Weight**: Males approx. 85 lb (38.5 kg)/females approx. 75 lb (34 kg)|84–123.5 lb (38–56 kg) [KC]

- **Coat**: Double coat with thick, coarse outercoat and dense, oily, woolly undercoat

- **Colors**: Solid white, mostly white with shadings from light gray to black, sable, red

- **Registries (With Group)**: AKC (Working); ANKC (Utility); CKC (Working); FCI (Spitz and Primitive); KC (Working); UKC (Northern)

History and Personality

In the harsh environment of northeastern Alaska, Malamute Eskimos—now known as the Kobuk—needed a dog who could withstand the cold and literally "pull his weight" to find and put food on the table. These selective breeders were renowned for producing intelligent, reliable, and strong dogs and for taking excellent care of them.

With a better temperament than some other spitz breeds, the large, boisterous Malamute is a loyal, devoted companion who is affectionate and playful.

Exercise, Training, Grooming, and Health

- The Alaskan Malamute must be exercised often. He was originally bred for pulling sleds over great distances, hunting, and protecting his family, so he has a lot of energy that must be expended.

- The Malamute's sensitivity and smarts make him most receptive to positive, motivational, and creative training, preferably from an early age. However, he can be more of a challenge to train than other breeds.

- The Alaskan Malamute needs regular brushing, as his thick undercoat sheds almost constantly, and about twice a year he blows his undercoat.

- Average life span is 10 to 12 years. Breed health concerns may include autoimmune hemolytic anemia (AIHA); bloat; cancer; chondrodysplasia; coat funk; diabetes; epilepsy; eye problems; hemeralopia; hip dysplasia; hypothyroidism; immune diseases; polyneuropathy; a skin problems.

American English Coonhound

Breed Facts

- **Country of Origin**: United States
- **Height**: Males 22–27 in (56–68.5 cm)/females 21–25 in (53.5–63.5 cm)
- **Weight**: In proportion to height|40–65 lb (18–29.5 kg) [est.]
- **Coat**: Hard, protective; medium length
- **Colors**: Blue and white ticked, red and white ticked, tricolor ticked, red and white, white and black|also white and lemon [UKC]
- **Other Names**: English Coonhound; Redtick Coonhound
- **Registries (With Group)**: AKC (FSS); UKC (Scenthound)

History and Personality

The breed is a descendant of the English and Virginia Foxhounds, as well as the Treeing Walker Coonhound and Bluetick

Coonhound. In fact, the breed was initially bred to adapt to the rougher American climate and terrain. The American English Coonhound was selectively bred to be fast, hot on a trail, and wide ranging, and to have an exceptional voice—qualities that make him a competitive coon hunter.

The American English Coonhound is outgoing and sociable. He is confident and loves, above all, to hunt, but he is also a pleasant companion. This breed loves to bark.

Exercise, Training, Grooming, and Health

- The American English Coonhound needs a lot of exercise. A passionate hunter, he is best exercised doing what he loves.

- The only training this hound may have any interest in is for coon hunting—an activity at which he excels. He is responsive when properly motivated.

- The American English Coonhound is an easy-to-care-for breed with a short wash-and-wear coat.

- Average life span is 11 to 12 years. Breed health concerns may include hip dysplasia.

Breed Facts

- **Country of Origin**: United States

- **Varieties**: Standard, Miniature, Toy

- **Height**: *Standard*: 15–19 in (38–48 cm)/females over 14 in (35.5 cm) up to and including 18 in (45.5 cm) [UKC]; *Miniature*: 12–15 in (30.5–38 cm)/females 11 in (28 cm) up to and including 14 in (35.5 cm) [UKC]; *Toy*: 9–12 in (23–30.5 cm)

- **Weight**: *Standard*: 18–35 lb (8–16 kg) [est.]; *Miniature*: 10–20 lb (4.5–9 kg) [est.]; *Toy*: 6–10 lb (3–4.5 kg) [est.]

- **Coat**: Double coat with long, straight outercoat and dense, thick, short undercoat; ruff at neck

- **Colors**: Pure white, white with biscuit cream|and cream [UKC]

- **Other Names**: American Deutscher Spitz; American Spitz

- **Registries (With Group)**: AKC (Non-Sporting); CKC (Non-Sporting, Toy); UKC (Northern)

History and Personality

The breed is a close relation of the white Keeshond, white Pomeranian, and white German Spitz. Perhaps because of anti-German sentiment during World War I, the breed's name was changed in 1917 to the American Eskimo Dog. "American Eskimo" was also the kennel name of the first breeders to register the breed with the United Kennel Club (UKC) in the early 1900s.

Playful, charming, affectionate, intelligent, willing to please—all are used to describe the American Eskimo Dog. An energetic, spunky breed, he will develop nuisance behaviors that can be difficult to change if he is left alone too long or is not provided with proper guidance. American Eskimo Dogs are barkers, but this trait has resulted in a big watchdog in a small and loving body.

Exercise, Training, Grooming, and Health

- Regular exercise will help release the American Eskimo Dog's natural energy and stimulate his ever-present curiosity.

- The American Eskimo Dog enjoys and excels at training, where he is a top contender in the obedience, rally, and agility rings.

- Although his double coat sheds quite a bit, it stays clean and white with minimal care—regular brushing and an occasional going-over with a shedding blade are all that's needed.

- Average life span is 12 to 17 years. Breed health concerns may include diabetes; epilepsy; hip dysplasia; juvenile cataracts; Legg-Calve-Perthes disease; patellar luxation; and progressive retinal atrophy (PRA).

Breed Facts

- **Country of Origin**: United States
- **Height**: Males 22–25 in (56–63.5 cm)/females 21–24 in (53–61 cm)
- **Weight**: 65–75 lb (29.5–34 kg) [est.]
- **Coat**: Close, hard hound coat; medium length
- **Colors**: All colors
- **Other Names**: Foxhound
- **Registries (With Group)**: AKC (Hound); CKC (Hounds); FCI (Scenthounds); UKC (Scenthound)

History and Personality

The American Foxhound's roots can be found in the English Foxhound, thought to have arrived in the United States as early as the mid-1600s. The American Foxhound is a direct descendent of the English hound, crossed with French hounds whom General

Lafayette gave to George Washington. The resulting American Foxhound and his line were bred to be larger and faster than the English hounds, and they still are today.

Although sweet and gentle at home, when out with the pack, the American Foxhound is all business. The field-bred American Foxhound thrives on the pack life; those bred for the show ring are more amenable to life in the home.

Exercise, Training, Grooming, and Health

- This Foxhound needs plenty of exercise—he was bred to be out for six to eight hours on a single hunt, often hunting several times a week.

- The Foxhound is extremely scent driven and could be considered "focus challenged" when it comes to doing what his owner wants him to do. He can be difficult to housetrain as well.

- The American Foxhound's short coat requires only an occasional brushing with a stiff brush and bathing only if absolutely necessary.

- Average life span is 10 to 13 years. Breed health concerns may include deafness; eye problems; hip dysplasia; and thrombocytopathy.

Breed Facts

- **Country of Origin**: United States

- **Height**: Males 18–19 in (45.5–48 cm)/females 17–18 in (43–46 cm)

- **Weight**: In proportion to height|57–67 lb (26–30.5 kg) [est.]

- **Coat**: Short, close, stiff, glossy

- **Colors**: All colors; solid, particolor, patched|excludes solid white, black and tan, liver [ANKC][CKC][FCI]

- **Registries (With Group)**: AKC (Terrier); ANKC (Terriers); CKC (Terriers); FCI (Terriers)

History and Personality

Until 1936 the American Staffordshire Terrier ("AmStaff") was known by the name "American Pit Bull Terrier" and was, in fact, the same breed. It was becoming increasingly important to the new breed image to avoid breed names associated with fighting pits, but the new name "Staffordshire Terrier" was unpopular with some owners, who ultimately decided to stay with the original name. The word "American" was added to the AmStaff's name in 1972 to differentiate him from the AKC's newly recognized Staffordshire Bull Terrier. The American Staffordshire Terrier and the American Pit Bull Terrier have been bred independently for more than half a century; the modern AmStaff has a slightly stockier build than his cousin.

The American Staffordshire Terrier is a confident, stable, good-natured, and loving dog toward people—as long as he is socialized from an early age. Intelligent and easily trained, his keen personality soon wins people over. However, he is often aggressive toward other dogs and may see smaller animals as prey.

Exercise, Training, Grooming, and Health

- The high-energy AmStaff needs several walks a day to keep him physically fit and mentally challenged.

- Responsive and smart, the American Staffordshire Terrier is a relatively easy breed to train and has excelled in many areas that demand a high level of aptitude.

- The AmStaff's short, smooth coat is easily managed with regular brushing with a firm-bristled brush and an occasional bath.

- Average life span is 10 to 12 years. Breed health concerns may include allergies; cancer; cataracts; congenital heart disease; hip dysplasia; hives; hypothyroidism; progressive retinal atrophy (PRA); and spinocerebellar ataxia.

American Water Spaniel

Breed Facts

- **Country of Origin**: United States
- **Height**: 15–18 in (38–45.5 cm)
- **Weight**: Males 28–45 lb (12.5–20.5 kg)/females 25–40 lb (11.5–18 kg)
- **Coat**: Double coat with outercoat that varies from uniformly wavy to closely curled and dense, weather-resistant undercoat
- **Colors**: Dark chocolate, liver|also solid brown [AKC][FCI]
- **Registries (With Group)**: AKC (Sporting); CKC (Sporting); FCI (Water Dogs); KC (Gundog); UKC (Gun Dog)

History and Personality

The American Water Spaniel is descended from water dogs and spaniels who accompanied immigrants and settlers to the United States. The breed was used as a jump-shooting retriever, and the dog would retrieve the ducks whether they fell on land or in the water. Although this breed is rare, it still enjoys moderate but steady favor among hunters and as family pets.

This charming dog is happy, energetic, and trainable, and most love to work the field or waterways. He tends to bark quite a bit.

Exercise, Training, Grooming, and Health

- The American Water Spaniel is happiest with several outings a day, especially if they are to areas where he can use his hunting instincts. An athletic and energetic dog, he will also enjoy other activities—as long as they involve time spent with his owner.

- Eager to please, training the American Water Spaniel is easy and enjoyable. Lessons should be positive and motivational, and if they are, he will be quick to learn and sure to respond.

- The curly double coat requires routine brushing and occasional trimming to keep it clean and neat. His long, furry ears make him susceptible to ear infections and should be cleaned regularly.

- Average life span is 10 to 12 years. Breed health concerns include diabetes; epilepsy; eye problems; heart problems; hip dysplasia; and hypothyroidism.

Anatolian Shepherd Dog

Breed Facts

- **Country of Origin**: Turkey

- **Height**: Males 29–32 in (73.5–81 cm)/females 27–31 in (68.5–78.5 cm)

- **Weight**: Males 110–150 lb (50–68 kg)/females 80–130 lb (36.5–59 kg)

- **Coat**: Double coat with short- or medium-length, dense outercoat and thick undercoat

- **Colors**: All colors, patterns, markings

- **Other Names**: Anadolu Kopek; Anatolian Karabash Dog; Anatolian Shepherd; Coban Köpegi; Karabas; Turkish Guard Dog; Turkish Sheepdog

- **Registries (With Group)**: AKC (Working); ANKC (Utility); CKC (Working); FCI (Molossoid); KC (Pastoral); UKC (Guardian)

History and Personality

The Anatolian Shepherd Dog was once used as a combat dog and for hunting big game, such as lions and horses. He was bred to withstand extremes of weather, serving as an unerring protector. The breed stems directly from ancient flock-guarding and mastiff dogs of the Middle East, and his strength and speed are legendary.

Bred to be fiercely loyal, the Anatolian Shepherd can be highly possessive toward anything he considers "his," including family, property, and livestock. His strong guarding and protective instincts must be properly channeled, which requires socialization and lots of it from an early age and well into adulthood.

Exercise, Training, Grooming, and Health

- The Anatolian Shepherd Dog doesn't need huge amounts of exercise compared with other dogs his size, but he does need a long walk and active playtime every day. He thrives on being outdoors so that he can explore and sniff around.

- The Anatolian Shepherd Dog needs a trainer who understands and respects who he is. Only a strong, positive, and consistent leader will do.

- Whether rough or smooth coated, the Anatolian Shepherd Dog is generally a low-maintenance breed, requiring regular brushing and an occasional bath. He blows his coat twice a year.

- Average life span is 11 to 13 years. Breed health concerns may include anesthesia sensitivity; cancer; ear infections; entropion; hip dysplasia; and hypothyroidism.

Breed Facts

- **Country of Origin**: Switzerland

- **Height**: Males 20.5–23 in (52–58.5 cm)/females 18.5–21 in (47–54 cm)

- **Weight**: 49–70 lb (22–31.5 kg) [est.]

- **Coat**: Firm, close double coat with thick, shiny outercoat and thick undercoat

- **Colors**: Black with white and tan markings|Havana brown with rust and white markings [FCI][UKC]

- **Other Names**: Appensell Cattle Dog; Appensell Mountain Dog; Appenzell Cattle Dog; Appenzeller Mountain Dog; Appenzeller Sennenhund; Swiss Mountain Dog

- **Registries (With Group)**: AKC (FSS); FCI (Swiss Mountain and Cattle Dogs); UKC (Guardian)

History and Personality

The Appenzeller Sennenhunde is one of the four Swiss sennenhundes—the others being the Bernese Mountain Dog, Entlebucher Mountain Dog, and Greater Swiss Mountain Dog—and was most likely developed through crossing with smaller herding dogs like the Puli. As sure-footed in the mountains as the goats they watched, when market day came, Appenzellers were harnessed to carts and hauled goat milk and cheese to town. They also serve as a rescue dogs in avalanches and other catastrophes.

This hardy Swiss cattle dog has the physical and mental stability and strength to be a versatile herding, guarding, cart-pulling, and almost all-purpose family dog. He is self-assured, reliable, and fearless.

Exercise, Training, Grooming, and Health

- In his native land, the Appenzeller thrives on an exercise regime of outdoor living that includes doing the things for which he was bred. This is what satisfies him most. These active herding dogs need lots of regular exercise and thrive best when given a job to do.

- A trusting companion, the Appenzeller responds well to positive training and quickly masters what's expected of him.

- His short, dense coat needs only regular brushing to keep shedding under control.

- Average life span is 12 to 13 years. Breed health concerns may include bloat; ectropion; elbow dysplasia; entropion; epilepsy; hip dysplasia; and thyroid problems.

Argentine Dogo

Breed Facts

- **Country of Origin**: Argentina
- **Height**: Males 24.5–27 in (62–68.5 cm)/females 23.5–25.5 in (60–65 cm)
- **Weight**: 80–100 lb (36.5–45.5 kg) [est.]
- **Coat**: Short, thick, glossy, smooth, uniform
- **Color**: Solid white; may have black patch at eye
- **Other Names**: Argentinian Mastiff; Dogo Argentino
- **Registries (With Group)**: AKC (FSS); FCI (Molossoid); UKC (Guardian)

History and Personality

The Argentine Dogo is the only dog developed exclusively in Argentina. It originated in the 1920s as a tough guardian—a hunter of wild boar, puma, and jaguar that was also a trustworthy and stable family dog. Today's Argentine Dogos are still used to hunt big game in packs and to guard. They are also reliable home protectors, family dogs, and police dogs.

The Argentine Dogo is a warrior with the heart of a child. His stamina and longevity are remarkable, with some dogs still hunting at 16 years of age. This sometimes sweet breed can turn dangerous, and he needs a clear signal from his owner to determine the severity or potential threat of a situation before he takes it upon himself to figure it out.

Exercise, Training, Grooming, and Health

- Regular, vigorous exercise is best for the Argentine Dogo, who needs to be active and given plenty to explore in the course of a day.

- Experienced trainers are best for this protective breed. Socialization from an early age is critical.

- The Argentine's short, smooth coat is easy to care for with brushing and an occasional bath. Because of its sleek white coat, the breed is susceptible to sunburn.

- Average life span is 10 to 12 years. Breed health concerns may include bloat; deafness; and hip dysplasia.

Australian Cattle Dog

Breed Facts

- **Country of Origin**: Australia
- **Height**: Males 18–20 in (45.5–51 cm)/females 17–19 in (43–48 cm)
- **Weight**: 33–50 lb (15–22.5 kg)
- **Coat**: Smooth double coat with close, straight, hard, weather-resistant outercoat and short, dense undercoat
- **Colors**: Blue (solid or with markings), red speckle
- **Other Names**: Australian Heeler; Blue Heeler; Hall's Heeler; Queensland Heeler; Red Heeler
- **Registries (With Group)**: AKC (Herding); ANKC (Working); CKC (Herding); FCI (Cattle Dogs); KC (Pastoral); UKC (Herding)

History and Personality

The name says it all: This is an Australian breed developed to work alongside the cattlemen of this rugged continent. Derived through intensive and careful crossbreeding over a 60-year period, the Australian Cattle Dog was the result of the deliberate introduction of various breeds—including the Dingo, Australian Kelpie, and Blue Smooth Highland Collie—serving specific purposes. He came to be because imported herding dogs were not capable of controlling the tough cattle on long treks to market. The Australian Cattle Dog, on the other hand, could move livestock over any terrain and in almost any weather.

He is extremely intelligent, courageous, and ever alert. These dogs are described as having two speeds: extremely fast and comatose. They take things seriously, consider themselves almost indestructible, and consider their person the center of their universe.

Exercise, Training, Grooming, and Health

- This is a breed that can go all day and that truly needs a job. Without sufficient physical and mental stimulation, the Australian Cattle Dog will direct his vast reserves of energy into potentially destructive and harmful pursuits.

- Alert and intelligent, the Australian Cattle Dog is a quick study, equally eager to learn and to please. His strong herding instinct must be tempered with training or it can get him into trouble when he wants to chase cars, animals, and even people.

- Regular brushing is necessary to keep his dense undercoat in check, particularly when he blows his coat, but otherwise he is a fairly wash-and-wear breed.

- Average life span is 10 to 13 years. Breed health concerns may include deafness; hip dysplasia; patellar luxation; and progressive retinal atrophy (PRA).

Australian Shepherd

Breed Facts

- **Country of Origin**: United States
- **Height**: Males 20–23 in (51–58 cm)/females 18–21 in (45.5–53 cm)
- **Weight**: Males 50–65 lb (22.5–29.5 kg)/females 40–55 lb (18–25 kg) [est.]
- **Coat**: Double coat with outercoat of medium texture and length, straight or wavy, weather resistant; undercoat varies with climate; moderate mane and frill
- **Colors**: Black, blue merle, red, red merle; may have white markings
- **Registries (With Group)**: AKC (Herding); ANKC (Working); CKC (Herding); FCI (Sheepdogs); KC (Pastoral); UKC (Herding)

History and Personality

The Australian Shepherd is not an Australian breed at all but rather was developed in the United States by cattle and sheepherders who lived in the western states. He was a hardworking stock dog and sometimes the only companion for an isolated shepherd. He was adept not only at herding and guarding livestock but also at almost any duty a farm family could ask of him. He is still the breed of choice for many ranchers.

Smart and friendly, he works with enthusiasm and style, whether it is tending to livestock, running an agility course, participating in competitive obedience, or making someone's day as a therapy dog.

Exercise, Training, Grooming, and Health

- The Australian Shepherd absolutely must have both physical and mental exercise. He needs a meaningful job and a purpose toward which to direct his abundant energy.

- With a can-do attitude—and aptitude—there is almost nothing an Aussie can't be taught to do, as long as his instruction is positive, inspiring, and purposeful.

- His double coat needs consistent care to keep shedding under control and to keep him looking his best.

- Average life span is 12 to 15 years. Breed health concerns include allergies; autoimmune diseases; cancer; cataracts; chryptorchidism; Collie eye anomaly (CEA); corneal dystrophy; dental problems; distichiasis; epilepsy; hip dysplasia; iris coloboma; osteochondritis dissecans (OCD); patellar luxation; patent ductus arteriosus (PDA); and persistent pupillary membrane.

Australian Terrier

Breed Facts

- **Country of Origin**: Australia

- **Height**: Males approx. 10 in (25.5 cm)/females slightly smaller|10–11 in (25.5–28 cm) [AKC]

- **Weight**: Males 14 lb (6.5 kg)/females slightly less|approx. 14 lb (6.5 kg) [CKC][KC]|in proportion to height [AKC]

- **Coat**: Double coat with harsh, straight, dense outercoat and short, soft undercoat; topknot; neck ruff

- **Colors**: Solid red, solid sandy, various shades of blue and tan; light-colored topknot

- **Registries (With Group)**: AKC (Terrier); ANKC (Terriers); CKC (Terriers); KC (Terrier); FCI (Terriers); UKC (Terrier)

History and Personality

The Australian Terrier was developed in the 19th century, using various British terrier breeds. In fact, the likely descent of the Australian Terrier was from terriers of Scotland and northern

England brought to Australia with settlers. The resulting breed served many purposes for his family, from being an exceptional ratter and vermin hunter to being a keen watchdog and devoted companion—jobs he still tends to with pride in households around the world.

Plucky, intelligent, and always up for an adventure, this relatively small dog can stand up to just about anything. Friendly and gentle with his family, he can seem aloof to strangers.

Exercise, Training, Grooming, and Health

- The active Australian Terrier will want to go everywhere and do everything with his owner, which is one way of getting exercise. He's small enough that he is easily brought along. This shouldn't preclude regular walks and outings during which he can explore and dig.

- He has a strong desire to please that makes him a quick study for training.

- The Australian Terrier is a relatively fuss-free terrier in regard to grooming. Regular brushing and trimming will keep him looking good.

- Average life span is 12 to 15 years. Breed health concerns may include allergies; diabetes; itchy skin; Legg-Calve-Perthes disease; patellar luxation; and thyroid problems.

Breed Facts

- **Country of Origin:** Republic of Mali

- **Height:** Males 25–29 in (64–73.5 cm)/females 23.5–27.5 in (60–70 cm)

- **Weight:** Males 44–55 lb (20–25 kg)/females 33–44 lb (15–20 kg)

- **Coat:** Short, fine; fades to none at belly

- **Colors:** All shades of fawn; may have white markings; may have dark mask|black, brindle, chocolate, cream to dark red, grizzle, grizzle, particolor, white [UKC]

- **Other Names:** Idii n' Illeli; Tuareg Sloughi

- **Registries (With Group):** AKC (FSS); FCI (Sighthounds); KC (Hound); UKC (Sighthound & Pariah)

History and Personality

Bred for more than 1,000 years by the Tuareg tribes of the southern Sahara as hunting and guard dogs, the Azawakh was developed for the chase and will course any game. A hunting sighthound, he was also used to defend goats and camels, vigorously protecting the herds against jackals, hyenas, and wild dogs.

Typical of the sighthounds, the Azawakh is cat-like: He prefers things on his terms, and his instinctively touchy behavior—like jumping away from something that startles him—has been described as similar to that of large cats like cheetahs. The Azawakh can be aloof, but he's affectionate with his family. He is often reserved with strangers.

Exercise, Training, Grooming, and Health

- Although the Azawakh can reach high speeds—as high as 40 mph (65 kph)—his outings don't need to be that intense. Regular exercise will keep him in shape.

- This is an independent-minded breed that is not especially concerned with honoring someone else's requests, though he is generally a well-mannered and gentle hound.

- The Azawakh's short coat is easy to keep clean with a soft cloth or hound glove to remove dirt, debris, and dead hair. His thin skin is prone to cuts and should be checked regularly.

- Average life span is 12 years. Breed health concerns may include anesthesia sensitivity; autoimmune-mediated diseases, including autoimmune thyroiditis, eosinophilic myositis (EM), and generalized demodectic mange; bloat; cardiac problems; hypothyroidism; seizures; and skin allergies.

Barbet

Breed Facts

- **Country of Origin**: France
- **Height**: Males 22–25.5 in (56–65 cm)/females 20–24 in (51–61 cm)
- **Weight**: 33–55 lb (15–25 kg) [est.]
- **Coat**: Long, profuse, woolly, curly, forming cords
- **Colors**: Chestnut brown, gray, red fawn, pied, sandy, solid black, white
- **Other Names**: French Water Dog; Griffon d'Arrêt à Poil Laineux
- **Registries (With Group)**: AKC (FSS); CKC (Sporting); FCI (Water Dogs); UKC (Gun Dog)

History and Personality

The Barbet is an ancient breed of water dog that through the centuries has served man as a retriever of waterfowl, a herding dog, and an exceptionally even-tempered companion. He is still an excellent water dog, able to withstand hours in water and chilly marshes. His webbed feet give him an advantage in swimming, and he can work for hours without tiring. Almost unknown outside his native France, the breed is promoted by a few enthusiasts around the world.

The Barbet is gentle, loyal, playful, and affectionate—truly devoted to his people. He enjoys a swim in all kinds of weather.

Exercise, Training, Grooming, and Health

- Like all sporting dogs, the Barbet needs a healthy dose of outdoor activity or exercise every day. He is happiest when that includes going somewhere to swim or work in the water.

- Eager to please, the Barbet trains easily.

- Left unbrushed, the Barbet's thick, woolly coat will start to form cords. Many opt to shave the Barbet to minimize the amount of coat care needed. A thick coat on an active dog like the Barbet needs regular attention.

- Average life span is 12 to 15 years. Breed health concerns may include allergies; cataracts; and hip dysplasia.

Breed Facts

- **Country of Origin**: Democratic Republic of the Congo (formerly Zaire)

- **Height**: Males 17 in (43 cm)/females 16 in (40.5 cm)

- **Weight**: Males approx. 24 lb (11 kg)/females approx. 21–22 lb (9.5–10 kg)

- **Coat**: Short, sleek, close, fine

- **Colors**: Brindle, chestnut red, black, tricolor (black and chestnut red); white markings|also black and tan, tan and white [ANKC] [FCI][KC]

- **Other Names**: African Barkless Dog; African Bush Dog; Ango Angari; Avuvi; Congo Bush Dog; Congo Dog; Congo Terrier; Zande Dog

- **Registries (With Group)**: AKC (Hound); ANKC (Hounds); CKC (Hounds); FCI (Spitz and Primitive); KC (Hound); UKC (Sighthound & Pariah)

History and Personality

The Basenji is an ancient breed from the Democratic Republic of the Congo (formerly Zaire) in Africa, believed to descend from the very earliest types of pariah dogs. The breed's keen nose and sharp eyesight were useful to hunters, who used the dogs to drive game into nets or to track wounded prey. Basenjis are quick, inquisitive hunters and protectors of the homestead.

One look at a Basenji and you can tell he's smart, playful, inquisitive, and independent-minded. Called the "barkless dog" because he does not vocalize like other dogs, he is far from quiet! His unique larynx creates yodels, chortles, whines, howls—and even sounds similar to screams or crows. He is typically aloof with strangers but very friendly with his family.

Exercise, Training, Grooming, and Health

- The Basenji is very active and needs regular activity that should not only exercise his body but also allow his inquisitive nature to be satisfied. He is capable of great speeds and should never be left off lead in an unsecured area.

- The Basenji's can be responsive when properly motivated, but his independent nature and intelligence mean that his attention will quickly lag with overly repetitive or heavy-handed training. He should be socialized with a variety of other animals and people from a young age to lessen his predatory and possessive instincts.

- The Basenji is a neat dog—known to groom himself like a cat by licking his paws and wiping his face. His short coat will shine when regularly tended to with a hound glove.

- Average life span is 10 to 14 years. Breed health concerns may include cataracts; coloboma; corneal dystrophy; Fanconi syndrome; hemolytic anemia; hip dysplasia; immunoproliferative small intestinal disease (IPSID); persistent pupillary membrane (PPM); progressive retinal atrophy (PRA); thyroid problems; and umbilical and inguinal hernias.

Basset Hound

Breed Facts

- **Country of Origin**: Great Britain

- **Height**: 13–15 in (33–38 cm)

- **Weight**: 50–70 lb (22.5–31.5 kg)

- **Coat**: Hard, smooth, short, dense

- **Colors**: Generally tricolor (black, white, tan) or bicolor (lemon, white), but any hound color acceptable

- **Registries (With Group)**: AKC (Hound); ANKC (Hounds); CKC (Hounds); FCI (Scenthounds); KC (Hound); UKC (Scenthound);

History and Personality

The Basset is a hunting dog from antiquity. This scenthound was developed to stand low to the ground in order to hunt game such as rabbits, foxes, squirrels, and pheasants in heavy ground cover. The Basset Hound became popular in the late 1800s, and his characteristic low, long body, droopy ears, and sad expression won him admirers from all over Europe and America.

He is always friend, never foe—sweet, gentle, kind, naturally well behaved, and devoted. Though he thrives on finding and tracking scents, he is not so single-minded that he forgets where he is or who he's with. He has a deep, melodic voice, which he is not shy to use.

Exercise, Training, Grooming, and Health

- The Basset is content to take short strolls that occupy his nose more than the rest of his body. He isn't interested in getting anywhere particularly quickly, but if requested or required, he has significant stamina.

- He can be stubborn and may need some extra time learning basic training, but he is highly food motivated, and training that seems like fun and involves rewards is right up his alley.

- While the Basset's coat is easy to care for, his skin is less so and is susceptible to abrasion and infection. His ears are highly prone to infection, as their length and weight keep air from getting to the canal.

- Average life span is 10 to 12 years. Breed health concerns may include allergies; back and joint problems; bloat; ear infections; eyelid and eyelash problems; glaucoma; intervertebral disk disease; obesity; panosteitis; thrombopathia; and von Willebrand disease.

Breed Facts

- **Country of Origin**: Great Britain

- **Height**: 13–16 in (33–40 cm)|two varieties—no more than 13 in (33 cm)/over 13 in (33 cm) up to and including 15 in (38 cm) [AKC][CKC]|not to exceed 15 in (38 cm) [UKC]

- **Weight**: 22–35 lb (10–16 kg) [est.]

- **Coat**: Close, dense, hard, weatherproof, medium length

- **Colors**: Any hound color|no liver [ANKC][FCI][KC]|no solid colors acceptable [UKC]

- **Other Names**: English Beagle

- **Registries (With Group)**: AKC (Hound); ANKC (Hounds); CKC (Hounds); FCI (Scenthounds); KC (Hound); UKC (Scenthound)

History and Personality

The Beagle is a distinctly British breed, dating as far back as the Celts, where small hounds similar to the Beagle were used for hunting hares in the British Isles and Wales. He has always been hunted in packs and is prized for his ability to find and stick with a trail, working the quarry back to the hunter.

Attracted to the Beagle because he's so cute, people soon respond to his other endearing characteristics: his playfulness, his curious nature, his self-assuredness. He doesn't particularly like to be alone, and when upset he likes to use his voice.

Exercise, Training, Grooming, and Health

- The Beagle is always up for an expedition. It doesn't need to last for hours, but it should be interesting for him—meaning he's allowed to sniff whatever might catch his nose along the way.

- He can be stubborn and easily distracted when it comes to training, but he will pay attention and learn if his owner is offering something he really wants—like food.

- His short, hard coat is simple to keep clean, and he is compact to boot, so grooming is really a breeze with the Beagle.

- Average life span is 12 to 14 years. Breed health concerns may include back and musculoskeletal problems; Beagle Pain Syndrome (BPS); Chinese Beagle Syndrome; corneal dystrophy; epilepsy; glaucoma; heart disease; hypothyroidism; and obesity.

Bearded Collie

Breed Facts

- **Country of Origin**: Scotland

- **Height**: Males 21–22 in (53–56 cm)/females 20–21 in (51–53 cm)

- **Weight**: 40–60 lb (18–27 kg) [est.]

- **Coat**: Double coat with flat, harsh, strong, shaggy overcoat and soft, furry close undercoat; beard

- **Colors**: Black, blue, brown, fawn, all of which tend to lighten with age; with or without white and tan markings|also gray [ANKC][CKC][KC]|also sandy [ANKC][KC]

- **Other Names**: Hairy Mou'ed Collie; Highland Collie; Mountain Collie

- **Registries (With Group)**: AKC (Herding); ANKC (Working); CKC (Herding); FCI (Sheepdogs); KC (Pastoral); UKC (Herding)

History and Personality

The Bearded Collie evolved from Polski Owczarek Nizinnys—dogs who were left on the shores of Scotland in the 1500s and bred to native herding dogs. They were developed to work independently, able to make decisions about their flock without the help of a shepherd who may be far away. He gets his name from the trademark beard that flows between his lower jaw and chest.

The Beardie is bouncy, bubbly, and boisterous—a clown, charmer, and con artist. He makes a loving family pet and an enthusiastic therapy dog.

Exercise, Training, Grooming, and Health

- Beardies enjoy being out and treasure their walks and excursions. They can stay out for hours and don't mind the rain or the cold.

- The Bearded Collie's stubborn streak can sometimes interrupt training, but his desire to please brings him back around, and training will seem simple again.

- His thick, long coat needs regular weekly brushing to keep from getting tangled and matted. The hair will need to be pushed back from his eyes, mouth, and ears so these areas can be thoroughly inspected and kept clean.

- Average life span is 12 to 14 years. Breed health concerns may include allergies; auto-immune disease; eye problems; hip dysplasia; and hypothyroidism.

Breed Facts

- **Country of Origin**: France
- **Height**: Males 25.5–28 in (65–71 cm)/females 24–27 in (61–68.5 cm)
- **Weight**: Up to 110 lb (50 kg) [est.]
- **Coat**: Double coat with coarse, dense, close-lying outercoat and short, fine, dense, downy undercoat
- **Colors**: Black and tan, harlequin (gray, black, tan)
- **Other Names**: Bas Rouge; Beauce Shepherd; Berger de Beauce
- **Registries (With Group)**: AKC (Herding); FCI (Sheepdogs); KC (Working); UKC (Herding)

History and Personality

The Beauceron is an ancient French herding dog, used to herd and protect sheep and cattle as well as guard his family. He was an integral part of the French armies in both world wars, where he was used as a messenger, guard, mine detector, and deliverer of goods to the front lines of battle. Today his work includes that of police dog, military dog, tracking dog, and of course, herding dog.

He is strong, versatile, courageous, resilient, and even-tempered, but also affectionate, spirited, and great with children. He excels at learning new things and will want to continue to be challenged. The Beauceron is an outstanding guard dog.

Exercise, Training, Grooming, and Health

- The active and intelligent Beauceron needs a challenging physical regimen that should include as much off lead time as possible.

- The quick and clever Beauceron catches on fast, and experienced trainers may be best for this high-drive breed.

- Outside of periods of heavy shedding of his undercoat, the Beauceron is a dog who's easy to keep clean.

- Average life span is 10 to 12 years. Breed health concerns may include bloat and hip dysplasia.

Breed Facts

- **Country of Origin**: Great Britain

- **Height**: Males 16–17.5 in (40.5–44.5 cm)/females 15–16.5 in (38–42 cm)|16 in (41 cm) [ANKC][FCI][KC]

- **Weight**: 17–23 lb (7.5–10.5 kg)

- **Coat**: Crisp, thick, and linty, with distinctive mixture of hard and soft hair standing away from body; tendency to curl, especially on head and face|topknot [AKC][CKC][UKC]

- **Colors**: Blue, blue and tan, liver, liver and tan, sandy, sandy and tan

- **Other Names**: Rothbury Terrier

- **Registries (With Group)**: AKC (Terrier); ANKC (Terriers); CKC (Terriers); FCI (Terriers); KC (Terrier); UKC (Terrier)

History and Personality

Boasting a longer traceable pedigree than any other terrier, the curly-coated Bedlington Terrier hails from the mining area north of England. He was probably bred from the wire-coated terriers found in the North and may have been crossed with scenthound (Otterhound) and sighthound (Whippet). Reportedly, these terriers were used by gypsies and poachers to catch game on wealthy landowner's properties. In the 1830s, Lord Rothbury, from Bedlington in Northumberland County, became an enthusiast of these "gypsy dogs," and the breed was first known as Rothbury's Terrier (or Rothbury's Lamb). They were capable of everything from ratting and badgering to swimming after otters and running down hares.

The Bedlington is a talented athlete with plenty of energy and intelligence to excel at a variety of sports and activities. He is playful, charming, alert, and spirited and thrives on attention and affection—he loves nothing more than to be the center of attention.

Exercise, Training, Grooming, and Health

- The eager Bedlington needs several brisk walks and plenty of playtime every day, if not a regular sport to compete in.

- He is an adaptable and responsive terrier who enjoys figuring out what you want him to do and learning it quickly.

- He sheds very little; however, his coat grows in curly and can become unmanageable if not clipped back about every six weeks.

- Average life span is 11 to 16 years. Breed health concerns may include cataracts; copper toxicosis; patellar luxation; renal cortical hypoplasia; and retinal dysplasia.

Breed Facts

- **Country of Origin**: Belgium

- **Height**: Males 23–26.5 in (58.5–67.5 cm)/females 21–24.5 in (53–62 cm)

- **Weight**: Males 55–66 lb (25–30 kg)/females 44–55 lb (20–25 kg)

- **Coat**: Double coat with rough, dry, dense, close-fitting outercoat and dense, woolly undercoat

- **Colors**: Fawn with traces of black overlay; small amount of white possible|gray acceptable [CKC]|sable acceptable [UKC]

- **Other Names**: Belgian Sheepdog, Lakenois; Belgian Shepherd Dog (Laeken); Chien de Berger Belge; Laeken; Laekenois

- **Registries (With Group)**: AKC (FSS); ANKC (Working); CKC (Herding); FCI (Sheepdogs); KC (Pastoral); UKC (Herding)

History and Personality

The Laekenois is one of four sheepdogs from Belgium, which also include the Malinois, the Tervuren, and the Belgian Sheepdog (a.k.a Groenendael). The hard-working shepherds' dogs from Belgium have rated raves since the Middle Ages. In those days, type varied widely and breeding was based on herding ability. The Laekenois's original job was to guard the flax fields of Flanders. He went on to prove his worth as a police dog at home and on the front lines of World Wars I and II.

The Laekenois is smart, self-assured, loyal, and honest and can make a wonderful family companion, provided he is given proper training, exercise, and socialization.

Exercise, Training, Grooming, and Health

- The Laekenois will not be satisfied with a few casual strolls around the block every day—he needs to have an active outdoor life to keep him fit and help prevent problem behaviors.

- The Laekenois is a quick and eager learner and will excel in sports or any type of work—this is a breed that needs a job and extensive training and socialization.

- His rough, wiry coat sheds very little and does not need much daily care. Aside from the occasional brushing with a wide-toothed comb to get rid of tangles, he will need to be trimmed twice a year.

- Average life span is 10 to 14 years. Breed health concerns may include allergies; epilepsy; and hip dysplasia.

Breed Facts

- **Country of Origin**: Belgium

- **Height**: Males 23–26.5 in (58.5–67.5 cm)/females 21–24.5 in (53–62 cm)

- **Weight**: Males 55–66 lb (25–30 kg)/females 44–55 lb (20–25 kg)

- **Coat**: Double coat with short, straight, hard, dense, close-fitting, weather-resistant outercoat and dense, woolly undercoat

- **Colors**: Rich fawn to mahogany; black mask; may have white markings|only fawn with black overlay and mask; may have white markings [FCI]

- **Other Names**: Belgian Sheepdog, Malinois; Chien de Berger Belge; Malinois

- **Registries (With Group)**: AKC (Herding); ANKC (Working); CKC (Herding); FCI (Sheepdogs); KC (Pastoral); UKC (Herding)

History and Personality

The Belgian Malinois is one of four sheepdogs from Belgium, which also include the Laekenois, the Tervuren, and the Belgian Sheepdog (a.k.a Groenendael). The short-coated Malinois was a sheepherder par excellence. His abilities and tenacity became prized by the military, and he continues to be used as a police dog. His high level of trainability earns him top prizes in many types of canine competitions today.

The Malinois is smart, self-assured, loyal, and honest—keenly sensitive and very family-oriented. He is a quick and eager learner and excels at herding, tracking, obedience, agility, and schutzhund.

Exercise, Training, Grooming, and Health

- The Malinois is very high-energy, and many owners find the breed almost impossible to wear out. If they are not given the opportunity for plenty of activity, they can become destructive.

- The Belgian Malinois has a desire to please his owner and respond to positive, reward-based training methods.

- The short coat of the Malinois is easier to maintain than his double-coated brethren—just brushing with a bristle brush a few times a week. He sheds lightly through most of the year, with a twice yearly heavier shed.

- Average life span is 10 to 14 years. Breed health concerns may include elbow dysplasia; epilepsy; hip dysplasia; and progressive retinal atrophy (PRA).

Belgian Sheepdog (Groenendael)

Breed Facts

- **Country of Origin**: Belgium
- **Height**: Males 23–26.5 in (58.5–67.5 cm)/females 21–24.5 in (53–62 cm)
- **Weight**: Males 55–66 lb (25–30 kg)/females 44–55 lb (20–25 kg)
- **Coat**: Double coat with long, abundant, well-fitting, straight guard hairs and very dense, woolly undercoat; very long and profuse hair around the neck, where it forms a collarette
- **Colors**: Black; may have white markings
- **Other Names**: Belgian Sheepdog, Groenendael; Belgian Shepherd Dog; Chien de Berger Belge; Groenendael
- **Registries (With Group)**: AKC (Herding); ANKC (Working); CKC (Herding); FCI (Sheepdogs); KC (Pastoral); UKC (Herding)

History and Personality

The Belgian Sheepdog (also known as Groenendael) is one of four sheepdogs from Belgium, which also include the Malinois, the Tervuren, and the Laekenois. During World War I, the Belgian Sheepdog served his country by helping find wounded soldiers and carrying messages to the front.

The Belgian Sheepdog is intelligent, courageous, and devoted, is very protective of his family and can be possessive about having their attention. He thrives when given a job to do and excels at activities like herding trials, agility, and obedience.

Exercise, Training, Grooming, and Health

- The Belgian Sheepdog needs plenty of exercise—he is the very definition of a high-energy dog. Plenty of intense activity and daily sessions of play are needed to keep him from becoming bored and destructive.

- The Belgian Sheepdog is a quick and eager learner who excels in all types of sports and activities. Early socialization is essential.

- The double coat of the longhaired Belgian Sheepdog needs regular attention—daily brushing is essential, or the fine fur will mat.

- Average life span is 10 to 14 years. Breed health concerns may include elbow dysplasia; epilepsy; hip dysplasia; hypothyroidism; and progressive retinal atrophy.

Breed Facts

- **Country of Origin**: Belgium

- **Height**: Males 23–26.5 in (58.5–67.5 cm)/females 21–24.5 in (53–62 cm)

- **Weight**: Males 55–66 lb (25–30 kg)/females 44–55 lb (20–25 kg)

- **Coat**: Double coat with long, abundant, well-fitting, straight guard hairs and very dense, woolly undercoat; very long and profuse hair around the neck, where it forms a collarette

- **Colors**: Rich fawn to russet mahogany, with black overlay; may have white markings|gray acceptable [CKC][KC]|only fawn with black overlay or gray with black overlay; both with black mask; may have white markings [FCI]

- **Other Names**: Belgian Sheepdog, Tervuren; Chien de Berger Belge; Tervuren

- **Registries (With Group)**: AKC (Herding); ANKC (Working); CKC (Herding); FCI (Sheepdogs); KC (Pastoral); UKC (Herding)

History and Personality

The Tervuren is one of four sheepdogs from Belgium, which also include the Malinois, the Laekenois, and Belgian Sheepdog (a.k.a Groenendael). The Tervuren distinguishes himself through his beauty and trainability, excelling in events as diverse as conformation showing, obedience, rally, agility, tracking, and herding. He works as a search-and-rescue dog, in the military, as a therapy dog, and even as an entertainer.

The Belgian Tervuren is smart, self-assured, loyal, and honest. Watchful and protective of his family, he is happiest when he has a job to do. Tervurens are elegant and alert and form strong bonds with their owners.

Exercise, Training, Grooming, and Health

- All the Belgian shepherds need lots of exercise, and the Tervuren is no exception. He needs to work hard and play hard—every day.

- The Tervuren is eager to please and a quick learner who requires require positive, reward-based training, as harsh methods will cause this sensitive breed to shut down. Tervurens require early socialization.

- His longhaired double coat needs regular attention. He is a heavy seasonal shedder, and the fine fur will mat if neglected.

- Average life span is 10 to 14 years. Breed health concerns may include allergies; cataracts; elbow dysplasia; epilepsy; hip dysplasia; hypothyroidism; and progressive retinal atrophy.

Breed Facts

- **Country of Origin**: Italy

- **Height**: Males 23–24.5 in (58–62 cm)/females 21–23 in (54–58 cm)

- **Weight**: Males 70–84 lb (31.5–38 kg)/females 57–71 lb (26–32 kg)

- **Coat**: Three types of hair—*woolly*, very long, very abundant outercoat/*long*, straight, rough "goat hair"/*short*, dense, greasy undercoat; various parts of coat form strands or loose mats

- **Colors**: Solid gray or gradations of gray up to and including solid black; may have white markings

- **Other Names**: Bergamaschi; Bergamasco Shepherd Dog; Bergamese Shepherd; Cane da Pastore Bergamasco; Italian Bergama Shepherd

- **Registries (With Group)**: AKC (FSS); ANKC (Working); FCI (Sheepdogs); KC (Pastoral); UKC (Herding)

History and Personality

These shaggy, corded sheepdogs were brought into Italy by ancient Phoenician merchants. A large, robust herding dog with flock-guarding ability, he served his masters well over the centuries by developing keen independent problem-solving abilities as well as the ability to work closely with his shepherd.

Devoted and loyal, patient and tolerant, the Bergamasco is a great family dog for those who can provide a suitable environment for him. He is happiest when he knows what his job is, and he enjoys time outside.

Exercise, Training, Grooming, and Health

- A day in the outdoors spent watching his flock or his human family is all the exercise the Bergamasco needs. If that's not possible, a few intriguing excursions a day will satisfy him; he doesn't need a lot of exercise, just enough to keep him fit and mentally acute.

- The Bergamasco knows his place in the family and settles in with little training. He learns quickly but has an independence that means he will never follow direction blindly.

- His corded coat was meant to protect him from the elements and from wild animals—it should be left in its natural state.

- Average life span is 12 to 15 years. There are no reported breed-specific health concerns.

Berger Picard

Breed Facts

- **Country of Origin**: France

- **Height**: Males 23.5–25.5 in (60–65 cm)/females 21.5–23.5 in (55–60 cm)

- **Weight**: 50–70 lb (22.5–31.5 kg) [est.]

- **Coat**: Double coat with hard, fairly long, shaggy, crisp outercoat and fine, dense undercoat

- **Colors**: Gray, gray-black, gray with black highlights, gray-blue, gray-red, light or dark fawn, or mixture these shades; may have white markings

- **Other Names**: Berger de Picard; Berger de Picardie; Picardy Sheepdog; Picardy Shepherd

- **Registries (With Group)**: AKC (FSS); CKC (Herding); FCI (Sheepdogs); UKC (Herding)

History and Personality

Believed to be one of the oldest French sheepherding dogs, the Berger Picard was probably introduced to France by the Celts in the 9th century. For many years, the breed has been a flock worker in the Pas-de-Calais region by the Somme in the north of France. He is rarely seen outside of France.

The Picard can be moody and difficult to generalize, but he is especially sensitive to the voice and body language of his family and may mirror what's happening with them. He needs lots of human companionship, exercise, and a job to do. Owners soon become smitten with his versatility, good humor, and complicated nature.

Exercise, Training, Grooming, and Health

- The Berger Picard enjoys vigorous activity. He loves to swim and makes a happy biking or jogging companion.

- Because he is sensitive, intelligent, and somewhat unpredictable, training should be approached in as positive a manner possible and from an early age.

- The Berger Picard's unique coat is a dog owner's dream for ease of care—he sheds only seasonally, has no real doggy odor, and comes clean with a simple wipe. Brushing can be restricted to a couple of times a month, and baths are discouraged.

- Average life span is 13 to 14 years. Breed health concerns may include hip dysplasia and progressive retinal atrophy (PRA).

Bernese Mountain Dog

Breed Facts

- **Country of Origin**: Switzerland

- **Height**: Males 25–27.5 in (63.5–70 cm)/females 23–26 in (58.5–66 cm)

- **Weight**: Males 85–110 lb (38.5–50 kg)/females 80–105 lb (36.5–47.5 kg) [est.]

- **Coat**: Thick, soft, silky, fairly long; slightly wavy or straight|seasonal undercoat [CKC]

- **Colors**: Tricolor (black, rust, white)

- **Other Names**: Berner Sennenhund

- **Registries (With Group)**: AKC (Working); ANKC (Utility); CKC (Working); FCI (Swiss Mountain and Cattle Dogs); KC (Working); UKC (Guardian)

History and Personality

During the Roman invasion of Helvetia (Switzerland) 2,000 years ago Caesar's legions brought mastiff-type dogs prized for their guarding ability who crossed with native flock-guarding dogs able to withstand the severe weather of the Alps. The Bernese Dog became a general farm worker and flock guardian and was used by the weavers of the Berne district as a draft dog. The Bernese Mountain Dog is one of four varieties of Swiss Mountain Dogs, which also include the Appenzeller Sennenhunde, the Entlebucher Mountain Dog, and the Greater Swiss Mountain Dog.

The Bernese Mountain Dog ("Berner") looks like a black bear from a distance, but up close he's really a teddy bear—friendly, easygoing, and extremely huggable. He retains his watchdog instincts and is alert to anyone or anything that may be moving in on his family, but he is never fierce or aggressive. He loves children and makes an excellent family dog.

Exercise, Training, Grooming, and Health

- The playful yet lumbering Berner needs his exercise but is content with several strolls around the block.

- The Bernese Mountain Dog is quick to learn and takes well to training.

- His double coat sheds—and sheds a lot seasonally. He needs to be brushed several times a week, and he looks great after a bath, although his double coat takes time to dry.

- Average life span is 7 to 10 years. Breed health concerns may include arthritis; autoimmune disease; bloat; cancer; elbow dysplasia; hip dysplasia; kidney disease; and progressive retinal atrophy (PRA).

Bichon Frise

Breed Facts

- **Country of Origin**: France
- **Height**: 9–11.5 in (23–29 cm)|less than 12 in (30 cm) [ANKC]|height should not exceed 12 in (30 cm) [FCI]
- **Weight**: 7–12 lb (3–5.5 kg) [est.]
- **Coat**: Double coat with coarse, curly outercoat and soft, dense undercoat|fine, silky coat with corkscrew curls [ANKC][FCI][KC]
- **Colors**: Solid white|also shadings permissible [AKC][ANKC][CKC][KC][UKC]
- **Other Names**: Bichon à Poil Frisé; Bichon Tenerife
- **Registries (With Group)**: AKC (Non-Sporting); ANKC (Toys); CKC (Non-Sporting); FCI (Companion and Toy); KC (Toy); UKC (Companion)

History and Personality

The Bichon Tenerife of the Canary Islands was popular with visiting sailors, who traded the small, fluffy dog in their ports of call. He became a favorite of the 16th-century French royals, including King Henry III. With the French Revolution, Bichons were tossed out on the streets and soon became a pet of the commoner. The breed became known in France as *Bichon a Poil Frise* (Bichon Frise), or "Bichon with the curly coat."

Affectionate and gentle, he will want to be with his owner as often as possible. The perky Bichon loves to be the center of attention and will often think up fun games to entertain his family. He is well mannered and loves to be around people, children, and other pets. He is often used as a trick or performance dog because he has the added charm of being so irresistibly cute.

Exercise, Training, Grooming, and Health

- The Bichon is happy to have his exercise needs met by playing with the family and accompanying his owner everywhere.

- Eager to please, the Bichon responds well to training, although housetraining can be a challenge.

- Though he sheds very little, his coat requires daily brushing and combing in order to prevent matting as well as monthly coat trimmings—usually cut to appear square and compact, with the hair on the face and ears and at the end of their tail left rather fluffy.

- Average life span is 13 to 16 years. Breed health concerns may include allergies; cataracts; dental disease; ear infections; patellar luxation; and skin allergies.

Black and Tan Coonhound

Breed Facts

- **Country of Origin**: United States
- **Height**: Males 23–27 in (58.5–68.5 cm)/females 21–26 in (53–66 cm)
- **Weight**: Males 50–75 lb (22.5–34 kg)/females 40–65 lb (18–29.5 kg)
- **Coat**: Short, dense|smooth, fine, glossy [UKC]
- **Colors**: Black with rich tan markings
- **Other Names**: American Black and Tan Coonhound
- **Registries (With Group)**: AKC (Hound); CKC (Hounds); FCI (Scenthounds); UKC (Scenthound)

History and Personality

A southern gentleman through and through, the Black and Tan Coonhound can trace his ancestry to the American Foxhound and Virginia Foxhound of Colonial days, but the breed's development was for the purposes of hunters in the American South. Raccoon hunters, who were after a dog with exceptional scenting and tracking abilities, probably crossed the Foxhounds with Bloodhounds, which would account for some of the breed's coloring, as well as its stockiness and long ears. His long, pendulous ears are one of his hallmarks; like a Bloodhound's, they help capture and hold scent.

A kind, confident, bright, and courageous hound, the Black and Tan Coonhound is in his glory when working an open trail and treeing a raccoon. While he's big and ready, he's also mellow when he's not on the trail—an excellent hunter and an excellent fireside companion. His favorite pastime is hunting, and he is a quick study.

Exercise, Training, Grooming, and Health

- Vigorous walks are necessary for this fellow, who was bred to work all night if necessary. He's an athletic dog for his size, and if he's not going out hunting with you, he'll need an alternately stimulating way to release his energy.

- The Black and Tan Coonhound responds well to training and learns quickly, as long as his handler is positive and patient.

- His short, sleek coat comes clean with a once-over with a hound glove. It's his pendulous ears that need regular attention, as they can harbor infections.

- Average life span is 10 to 14 years. Breed health concerns may include ear infections and hip dysplasia.

Black Russian Terrier

Breed Facts

- **Country of Origin**: Russia

- **Height**: Males 26–30.5 in (66–77 cm)/females 25–29 in (64–73.5 cm)

- **Weight**: 80–143 lb (36.5–65 kg) [est.]

- **Coat**: Double coat with hard, rough, ample, broken outercoat and thick, soft undercoat; rough, brushy mustache and beard

- **Colors**: Black, black with gray hairs

- **Other Names**: Black Terrier; Chornyi; Russian Bear Schnauzer; Russian Black Terrier; Tchiorny Terrier

- **Registries (With Group)**: AKC (Working); ANKC (Utility); CKC (Working); FCI (Pinscher and Schnauzer); KC (Working); UKC (Guardian)

History and Personality

In the 1930s Russian breeders began working to create a large working terrier to be part of the national security force. Giant

Schnauzers were crossed with Airedales, Rottweilers, and other working breeds to create the Black Russian Terrier ("BRT")—a total of 17 breeds going into making this large, agile, tough, and weather-resistant dog. He is still an all-purpose working and protection dog who can withstand the variety of environments found in Russia.

He has a strong protective instinct but a balanced temperament. He loves children and is sensitive and enthusiastic, thriving on the contact with his human family and not doing well without it.

Exercise, Training, Grooming, and Health

- As a large, athletic dog, the BRT needs several daily jaunts to stay in shape. He is playful and boisterous outdoors, particularly loving the snow.

- This is a very smart and sensitive breed, and his training works best with an experienced hand. Obedience training and early socialization are necessary to help curb any overly protective instincts.

- The BRT's distinctive mop of hair over his eyes and under his chin need to be brushed so they don't tangle, but they should never be cut. The coarse fur on his body is typically hand-stripped (like that of most terriers), and professional grooming is advised to keep him looking his best.

- Average life span is 10 to 12 years. Breed health concerns may include bloat and hip dysplasia.

Bloodhound

Breed Facts

- **Country of Origin**: Belgium

- **Height**: Males 25–27 in (63.5–68.5 cm)/females 23–25 in (58.5–63.5 cm)

- **Weight**: Males 90–119 lb (41–54 kg)/females 79.5–106 lb (36–48 kg)

- **Coat**: Short, smooth, close lying, weatherproof|harsh [FCI]

- **Colors**: Black and tan, liver and tan, red; may have white markings

- **Other Names**: Chien de Saint-Hubert; St. Hubert Hound; St. Hubert's Hound

- **Registries (With Group)**: AKC (Hound); ANKC (Hounds); CKC (Hounds); FCI (Scenthounds); KC (Hound); UKC (Scenthound)

History and Personality

The modern Bloodhound traces its history back over 1,000 years and were bred to be slow, deliberate, heavy-skinned tracking dogs with persistence, exquisite noses, and melodious voices. They originally cold-trailed game such as wolves, big cats, or deer or followed the trail of wounded game. His name did not derive from his ability to track a blood trail, however, but because he was used exclusively by the nobility. His reputation for cold-trailing, or tracking, is why many law enforcement officials put his nose on trails thought to be especially difficult to detect.

He is a kind-souled hound who gets along with everyone. Large and loose-skinned, he is a gentle and loving presence wherever he goes. Bred to be single-minded and persistent, the Bloodhound is often more interested in what's on the ground than what his owner is trying to show or tell him. They do not thrive if left alone.

Exercise, Training, Grooming, and Health

- While the Bloodhound doesn't need vigorous exercise, he is a large dog who needs regular exercise to keep his mind and body sharp. Going for walks on a long leash in a park where he can find and track scents make him happiest.

- This independent-minded dog is inclined to think training commands are not that important—it takes patience and consistency to train a Bloodhound.

- It's not the fur on a Bloodhound that demands the attention of a groomer, though it does need brushing to keep off the dead hairs and stimulate the skin. Instead, it's the wrinkles on his face and his large, droopy ears that keep a groomer busy with this breed.

- Average life span is 10 to 12 years. Breed health concerns may include bloat; ear infections; entropion; and hip dysplasia.

Bluetick Coonhound

Breed Facts

- **Country of Origin**: United States
- **Height**: Males 22–30 in (56–76 cm)/females 21–28 in (53–71 cm)
- **Weight**: Males 55–100 lb (25–45.5 kg)/females 45–85 lb (20.5–38.5 kg)
- **Coat**: Smooth, glossy, fairly coarse, lying close to the body
- **Colors**: Dark blue, thickly mottled with black spots; may have tan markings, red ticking
- **Registries (With Group)**: AKC (Miscellaneous); ANKC (Hounds); UKC (Scenthound)

History and Personality

French hounds had been brought to America even before Colonial times. These patient, persistent, beautifully voiced hounds were bred to relatively pure form in remote parts of the South. These dogs, mainly of the heavily ticked blue color, were often referred to as Blue Gascons or French Staghounds. Crossed with Foxhounds and curs, they formed the basis for the Bluetick Coonhound recognized today.

Devoted and intelligent, the Bluetick is a fine family member. His easygoing nature allows him to fit into home life, and he forms deep, loyal bonds with his owner. Although he has a lot of energy, he is also content to lay at his owner's feet while off the hunt. Because of his strong predator drive, he has a tendency to chase small animals and must be socialized from an early age to accept other small pets, but he thrives in the company of other dogs. He is very friendly with children.

Exercise, Training, Grooming, and Health

- The Bluetick needs vigorous daily exercise and preferably the opportunity to hunt. This is a dog that does best with a job to do.

- Intelligent and sensitive, the Bluetick can have a tendency toward stubbornness when not in the field, so early obedience training is key to getting the best out of this breed.

- His coat is relatively easy to keep clean with occasional brushing, and his ears need to be regularly checked for infection.

- Average life span is 10 to 12 years. Breed health concerns may include ear infections.

Boerboel

Breed Facts

- **Country of Origin**: South Africa
- **Height**: Males 25–28 in (63.5–71 cm)/females 23–25.5 in (58.5–65 cm) [est.]
- **Weight**: 154–200 lb (70–90.5 kg) [est.]
- **Coat**: Short, dense, sleek [est.]
- **Colors**: Brindle, brown, red-brown, red, fawn, yellow-cream, black; may have white markings; may have mask [est.]
- **Other Names**: South African Boerboel; South African Mastiff
- **Registries (With Group)**: AKC (FSS)

History and Personality

Dutch settlers in South Africa brought large, strong dogs with them from the 1600s on, and the dogs most likely to survive the demanding circumstances were strong, hardy, loyal, versatile, and adaptable. The families had to rely on these multipurpose working dogs to protect the homestead from a variety of dangers. Isolated from the rest of the world, the dogs eventually interbred, and the Boerboel (literally, "farmer's dog") type was established.

This large, steadfast, intelligent working dog is loving and affectionate while possessing the courage and self-confidence to protect his family to the death. He needs human companionship and will automatically bond to his family; he should not be kept solitary and isolated from them. Socialization as early as possible to a variety of people and situations is essential in raising a large, protective dog like the Boerboel.

Exercise, Training, Grooming, and Health

- The Boerboel's exercise needs are moderate; care should be taken with puppies and young dogs, so that they do not overstress growing bones.

- He needs a firm but fair leader able to handle his dominant tendencies and should be taught his basic obedience commands as early as possible. Training should be ongoing throughout his life.

- His short coat requires very minimal grooming; brushing every two weeks should suffice. He drools, so attention should be paid to keeping his mouth area clean.

- Average life span is about 12 years. Breed health concerns may include bloat; ectropion; elbow dysplasia; entropion; and hip dysplasia.

Breed Facts

- **Country of Origin:** Italy
- **Height:** Males 10.5–12 in (27–30.5 cm)/females 9.5–11 in (24–28 cm)
- **Weight:** 5.5–9 lb (2.5–4 kg)
- **Coat:** Long, fluffy, flocked
- **Colors:** Pure white
- **Other Names:** Bichon Bolognese
- **Registries (With Group):** AKC (FSS); FCI (Companion and Toy); KC (Toy); UKC (Companion)

History and Personality

The existence of the Bolognese has been recorded since the year 1200, most likely a descendent of the bichon-type dogs of southern Italy and Malta. They belong to the family of Bichon dogs, who include the Maltese, Havanese, and Coton de Tulear. Named for the city of Bologna in northern Italy, these small white dogs became a favorite of the nobility during the Renaissance.

Intelligent, faithful, and companionable, but not hyperactive or high-strung, the Bolognese is described as more serious and docile than his close cousin the Bichon Frise. He loves people above all and follows his owner like a shadow.

Exercise, Training, Grooming, and Health

- The Bolognese doesn't need much exercise. A jaunt around the block and the activity he gets while following his owner everywhere suits him just fine.

- The Bolognese will readily respond to requests for good manners and obedience. He can be slow in the housetraining department, where perseverance pays off.

- He doesn't have the grooming requirements of the Bichon Frise, but he does have daily grooming needs. To prevent tangling, the Bolognese's coat needs almost daily brushing.

- Average life span is 13 to 15 years. Breed health concerns may include patellar luxation.

Breed Facts

- **Country of Origin**: Great Britain

- **Height**: Males 21 in (53 cm)/females slightly less|males 19–22 in (48–56 cm)/females 18–21 in (45.5–53 cm) [AKC][ANKC]

- **Weight**: In proportion to height|males 30–45 lb (13.5–20.5 kg)/females 27–42 lb (12–19 kg) [est.]

- **Coat**: Two varieties—moderately long double coat is close, dense, weather resistant, with coarse, straight or wavy, moderately long outercoat and soft, short, dense undercoat/smooth double coat, short and coarser than rough variety|double coat with moderately long, dense, medium-textured overcoat and soft, short, dense undercoat [ANKC]|varied lengths—long, medium, smooth [UKC]

- **Colors**: All colors, combinations, markings|black and white, blue and white, chocolate and white, red and white, blue merle, tricolor (black, tan, white) [ANKC]|black and red, gray, blue

merle, red merle, lemon, sable; may have white, tan markings
[UKC]

- **Registries (With Group)**: AKC (Herding); ANKC (Working); CKC (Herding); FCI (Sheepdogs); KC (Pastoral); UKC (Herding)

History and Personality

The Border Collie is a sheep herder developed in the border country between Scotland, England, and Wales. Modern breeding programs started to favor the quality of "eye" (a hypnotic stare that wills the sheep to move and turn) and a more trainable nature in order to win herding trials. Besides working as exceptional farm dogs, he is renowned for his prowess in the fast-paced sport of agility and also serves as a service dog, narcotics and bomb detection dog, and able athlete in a number of sports.

Border Collies are considered one of the most intelligent breeds of dog on the planet. Energetic, sturdy, sensitive, and able to make snap decisions on their own, they are workaholics—driven to herd anything and everyone continuously. They tend to be friendly with familiar people and standoffish with strangers.

Exercise, Training, Grooming, and Health

- The Border Collie needs lots of vigorous physical exercise to keep him content. He needs mental stimulation as well—chores, activities, attention, and tasks.

- The Border Collie's intense drive, desire, and intelligence make him exceptionally trainable.

- Both varieties need regular brushing to keep their coats free of dead hair and looking their best. Bred to withstand extremes of weather, their coats can be muddy one moment, then shake out to be clean the next.

- Average life span is 12 to 15 years. Breed health concerns may include Collie eye anomaly; epilepsy; and hip dysplasia.

Border Terrier

Breed Facts

- **Country of Origin**: Great Britain
- **Height**: 11–16 in (28–40.5 cm) [est.]
- **Weight**: Males 13–15.5 lb (6–7 kg)/females 11–14 lb (5–6.5 kg)
- **Coat**: Double coat with very wiry, somewhat broken, close-lying outercoat and short, dense undercoat
- **Colors**: Blue and tan, grizzle and tan, red, wheaten|may have white markings [AKC][CKC]
- **Registries (With Group)**: AKC (Terrier); ANKC (Terriers); CKC (Terriers); FCI (Terriers); KC (Terrier); UKC (Terrier)

History and Personality

In the Scottish-English border country (the same area where the Border Collie emerged) the Border Terrier was developed to keep vermin at bay—particularly sheep-stealing foxes. He needed legs that were long enough to move quickly and cover ground but short enough that he could easily go to ground after vermin. He has retained his rough-and-tumble good looks and working attributes to this day.

A small dog with a large amount of pluck and verve, he makes an excellent watchdog. Hard as nails in the field, he is less fiery than other terriers at home, and his affectionate, obedient nature makes him easy to live with. An all-weather, all-conditions companion, the Border Terrier is happy-go-lucky and companionable.

Exercise, Training, Grooming, and Health

- Bred to be a worker, the Border Terrier needs to get outside and move. He is happiest investigating the tree lines, rock walls, and other areas in which he may find small animals hiding.

- Smart, responsive, and eager to please, the Border Terrier is a quick study when it comes to training.

- His close, rough coat can be left in its natural state—kept tidy with occasional brushing, and using a slicker brush to remove some of the dead hair. Unlike other terriers, he does not need to be stripped to keep the proper texture (unless he is being shown in the conformation ring).

- Average life span is 13 to 16 years. Breed health concerns may include allergies; Canine Epileptoid Cramping Syndrome (CECS); heart defects; hip dysplasia; juvenile cataracts; and progressive retinal atrophy (PRA).

Breed Facts

- **Country of Origin**: Russia

- **Height**: Males 28–33.5 in (71–85 cm)/females 26–30.5 in (66–78 cm)

- **Weight**: Males 75–105 lb (34–47.5 kg)/females 15–20 lb (7–9 kg) less

- **Coat**: Long, silky coat can be flat, wavy, curly; neck has large, curly frill

- **Colors**: Any color or combination of colors|but never blue, brown, and any derivatives of these colors [FCI]

- **Other Names**: Barzoï; Borzaya; Russian Hunting Sighthound; Russian Wolfhound; Russkaya Psovaya Borzaya

- **Registries (With Group)**: AKC (Hound); ANKC (Hounds); CKC (Hounds); FCI (Sighthounds); KC (Hound); UKC (Sighthound & Pariah)

History and Personality

The Borzoi has been used in its motherland for coursing wolves since the early 1600s. Wolf hunting was a monied sport in which hunters would go out with their hounds (whose colors ideally matched) and set a pair loose upon a wolf so that the dogs could attack from two sides while the hunter approached on horseback and killed the wolf with a sword. To add to their appeal, Borzois were exotic-looking and had excellent temperaments, making them sought-after gifts among nobles.

Remarkably calm and cat-like indoors, the Borzoi is self-aware and dignified and doesn't take well to boisterousness or rough-housing. He is extremely loyal and affectionate but has a stubborn streak due to his independent nature. He whole-heartedly takes to the chase when given the opportunity.

Exercise, Training, Grooming, and Health

- Though capable of reaching great speeds, the Borzoi doesn't require a great deal of exercise. Daily walks or running in a safely enclosed area will keep him fit.

- The Borzoi is intelligent, but his independent streak can make basic obedience a challenge.

- His soft, wavy coat is easy to care for and should be brushed every day or two. During a seasonal shed, brushing should be more frequent. The hair between his toes needs to be kept short, and the thin skin on the face should be tended to with a soft, damp cloth.

- Average life span is 11 to 14 years. Breed health concerns may include bloat; hip dysplasia; osteochondritis dissecans; and progressive retinal atrophy (PRA).

Boston Terrier

Breed Facts

- **Country of Origin**: United States
- **Height**: 15–17 in (38–43 cm) [est.]
- **Weight**: Three classes—under 15 lb (7 kg)/15 lb (7 kg) to under 20 lb (9 kg)/20–25 lb (9–11.5 kg); 20 lb (9 kg) and under 25 lb (11.5 kg) [FCI][KC]|not to exceed 25 lb (11.5 kg) [ANKC]|under 15 lb (7 kg) up to and including 25 lb (11.5 kg) [UKC]
- **Coat**: Short, smooth, bright, fine
- **Colors**: Black, brindle; white markings|also seal; white markings [AKC][ANKC][FCI][UKC]
- **Other Names**: Boston Bull; Boston Bull Terrier
- **Registries (With Group)**: AKC (Non-Sporting); ANKC (Non Sporting); CKC (Non-Sporting); FCI (Companion and Toy); KC (Utility); UKC (Companion)

History and Personality

The Boston Terrier is as American as apple pie and baseball. In 1865 a resident of Boston, purchased an English Bulldog–white English Terrier cross, probably for the horrific sports of dog fighting and bullbaiting. Luckily, Mother Nature had other intentions, and several generations of dogs later Boston Terrier was born. He possessed a fine disposition and was free of his ancestors' fighting temperament, gaining the nickname "The American Gentleman."

Keen, intelligent, and biddable, he is a dog who can adapt to almost any situation and thrive in it. He has a sense of humor and can be quite playful, yet he will settle down nicely at home with his family, a friend and playmate to people of all ages.

Exercise, Training, Grooming, and Health

- The Boston loves to get out and about, but his exercise needs aren't great. A few walks around the block to stretch his legs and satisfy his curiosity will suit him fine.

- The Boston Terrier is a quick and eager learner who takes well to training and is a frequent competitor in all manner of dog sports and activities, from agility to therapy.

- His short, sleek, coat is easy to keep clean with a fine brush and a brisk rub with a soft cloth. The wrinkles and fine skin on his face need regular attention.

- Average life span is about 15 years. Breed health problems may include brachycephalic syndrome; corneal ulcers; eye problems; hemivertebrae; patellar luxation; and sensorineural deafness.

Bouvier des Flandres

Breed Facts

- **Country of Origin**: France/Belgium

- **Height**: Males 24.5–27.5 in (62–70 cm)/females 23–26.5 in (59–67 cm)

- **Weight**: Males 77–100 lb (35–45.5 kg)/females 59.5–85 lb (27–38.5 kg)

- **Coat**: Tousled, weather-resistant double coat with rough, harsh, dry outercoat and fine, soft, dense, waterproof undercoat; thick mustache and beard

- **Colors**: Shades of fawn to black; may have white marking

- **Other Names**: Belgian Cattle Dog; Flanders Cattle Dog; Vlaamse Koehond

- **Registries (With Group)**: AKC (Herding); ANKC (Working); CKC (Herding); FCI (Cattle Dogs); KC (Working); UKC (Herding)

History and Personality

Like his close relative the Bouvier des Ardennes, the Bouvier des Flandres was developed from a rough-coated cattle dog native to northern France and Belgium. He was a messenger and ambulance dog during World War I. Today, he is on the job in places all over the world, where he is also treasured as a first-rate companion.

He is affectionate and loyal, obedient and even-tempered. A genuine working breed, the Bouvier's herding and guarding instincts are keen, and he can be intimidating; in fact, he makes an exceptional watchdog.

Exercise, Training, Grooming, and Health

- A large, intent dog, the Bouvier should receive plenty of exercise but doesn't require a heavy workout. He enjoys long hikes where he can cover some ground at a natural pace.

- The Bouvier des Flanders is a highly versatile and trainable breed who needs a fair, consistent, and experienced handler to bring him to his fullest potential.

- He isn't much of a shedder, his thick, wavy coat needs regular attention—brushing several times a week and trimming several times a year. The hair around his face and his "vuilbaard" (beard) need to be kept clean; the same is true for his feet.

- Average life span is 10 to 12 years. Breed health concerns may include autoimmune disease; cancer; glaucoma; hip dysphasia; subaortic stenosis (SAS); and thyroid dysfunction.

Breed Facts

- **Country of Origin**: Germany
- **Height**: Males 22–25 in (56–63.5 cm)/females 21–23.5 in (53–60 cm)
- **Weight**: Males 66–70.5 lb (30–32 kg)/females 55–62 lb (25–28 kg)|males over 66 lb (30 kg) when height 23.5 in (60 cm)/females over 55 lb (25 kg) when height 22 in (56 cm) [FCI]
- **Coat**: Short, hard, shiny, lies smooth and tight against body
- **Colors**: Fawn shades, brindle; may have white markings; black mask
- **Other Names**: Deutscher Boxer; German Boxer
- **Registries (With Group)**: AKC (Working); ANKC (Utility); CKC (Working); FCI (Molossoid); KC (Working); UKC (Guardian)

History and Personality

A descendant of Assyrian war dogs 4,000 years ago, the modern Boxer evolved into a do-most-anything breed, working as a guardian, herder, and even a trick dog. The Boxer began his development as a distinct breed around Munich, Germany, beginning in the late 1800s and was refined by three Germans: Friedrich Robert, Elard Konig, and R. Hopner, who brought the Boxer to world prominence.

The Boxer is handsome, athletic, and tractable, excelling in everything from service work to competitive obedience. When he plays with other dogs or people, he "puts up his dukes" and appears to box his playmate. He is playful, curious, energetic, high-spirited, and wonderful with children. He is a smart-looking and smart-acting companion who worships his family, but is naturally suspicious of strangers. Early socialization will help bring out the best in him.

Exercise, Training, Grooming, and Health

- The Boxer is a high-energy, athletic dog who needs a physical outlet for his energy every day—long walks, lots of active play, and activities that include mental as well as physical challenges.

- The Boxer's high intelligence and problem-solving ability allows him to thrive on obedience training. His strength and energy can make him a challenge to manage, and he needs a firm but fair leader.

- His short, smooth, and sleek coat is easy to keep clean and neat with a simple rubdown and a soft bristle brush. His face needs extra attention to keep the wrinkles and flews free of dirt and debris.

- Average life span is 11 to 14 years. Breed health concerns may include allergies; bloat; Boxer cardiomyopathy (BCM); brachycephalic syndrome; deafness; ear infections; epilepsy; hip dysplasia; hypothyroidism; and subaortic stenosis (SAS).

Breed Facts

- **Country of Origin**: United States
- **Height**: Males 15.5–18 in (39–45.5 cm)/females 14–16.5 in (35.5–42 cm)
- **Weight**: Males 30–40 lb (13.5–18 kg)/females 25–35 lb (11–16 kg)
- **Coat**: Double coat with fairly long, flat to slightly wavy outercoat and short, dense undercoat|flat to fairly curly [UKC]
- **Colors**: Dark chocolate, liver; may have white markings|also brown [AKC]
- **Registries (With Group)**: AKC (Miscellaneous); UKC (Gun Dog)

History and Personality

Just after the turn of the 20th century, the Boykin Spaniel was developed as a first-rate turkey dog and waterfowl retriever. His brown coloring was the perfect camouflage in the areas of South Carolina where he was—and still is—used for hunting. He is now the official state dog of South Carolina.

He is notably docile, pleasant, and obedient with a keen desire to please, a go-everywhere, do-anything dog. He is an excellent swimmer and loves the water. He gets along well with people and other pets, and socializing him is easy, as he is friendly to all he meets.

Exercise, Training, Grooming, and Health

- His athleticism and energy demand that the Boykin receive regular and consistent exercise. He needs long walks and romps in the yard to satisfy his exercise requirements.

- The Boykin is easy to train and eager to learn. He gets along well with people and other pets, and socializing him is easy, as he is friendly to all he meets.

- His soft, wavy fur needs but a weekly brushing, though many hunters clip the coat to avoid briar damage when hunting.

- Average life span is 14 to 16 years. Breed health concerns may include cataracts; corneal dystrophy; ear infections; eyelid distichiasis; hip dysplasia; patellar luxation; and retinal dysplasia.

Bracco Italiano

Breed Facts

- **Country of Origin**: Italy
- **Height**: Males 23–26.5 in (58–67 cm)/females 22–24.5 in (55–62 cm)|22–26.5 in (55–67 cm) [FCI][UKC]
- **Weight**: 55–88 lb (25–40 kg)
- **Coat**: Short, dense, glossy
- **Colors**: White, white with orange or amber patches, white with pale orange patches, white speckled with chestnut patches, white speckled with pale orange patches; may have mask
- **Other Names**: Italian Pointer; Italian Pointing Dog
- **Registries (With Group)**: AKC (FSS); ANKC (Gundogs); FCI (Pointing Dogs); KC (Gundog); UKC (Gun Dog)

History and Personality

The Bracco Italiano is very old and hound-like, long valued and utilized as an all-purpose gun dog. The breed was well established by the Middle Ages and thrived in the Renaissance. His numbers decreased significantly in the 1800s and 1900s, but the efforts of Ferdinando Delor de Ferrabouc revived and sustained the breed. He is still rare outside of Italy, where he makes a fine family dog and hunting companion.

He is a people-loving hound who thrives on companionship and forms strong bonds with his owners. He loves to play and gets along well with other dogs and pets. The Bracco is affectionate and loyal and thrives when given a job to do, especially if that job is hunting.

Exercise, Training, Grooming, and Health

- The Bracco is a hunting dog who needs ample exercise and mental stimulation. He needs daily walks and makes a fine jogging partner. He also loves to swim.

- The Bracco is fairly easy to train and wants to please, although he can be stubborn. He will turn off if you use sharp tones with him, but for a fair and pleasant trainer, he will do anything.

- What demands the most attention in the grooming department is the Bracco's head. He has long, pendulous ears that need to be kept clean lest they harbor infection. The droopy skin around his eyes and his flews needs to be kept clean. His coat needs just a simple going-over with a hound glove to loosen dirt and dead hair.

- Average life span is 10 to 14 years. Breed health concerns may include ear infections; ectropion; elbow dysplasia; enostosis; entropion; hip dysplasia; panosteitis; and umbilical hernia.

Breed Facts

- **Country of Origin**: France
- **Height**: Males 23–27 in (58.5–68.5 cm)/females 22–25.5 in (56–65 cm)
- **Weight**: 65–100 lb (29.5–45.5 kg) [est.]
- **Coat**: Double coat with long, coarse, shiny, hard, dry outercoat lying flat against body with slightly wavy locks and fine, tight undercoat; mustache and beard
- **Colors**: Black, shades of gray, shades of tawny|also all uniform colors except white; may have white marking [AKC][UKC]
- **Other Names**: Berger de Brie
- **Registries (With Group)**: AKC (Herding); ANKC (Working); CKC (Herding); FCI (Sheepdogs); KC (Pastoral); UKC (Herding)

History and Personality

The need for a large herding dog who could both control and protect the flock led to the development of the Briard, a French herder who has been around since at least the Middle Ages. He and the short-coated Beauceron (Berger de Beauce) are closely related, with the coat being the major difference between the two. The Briard was so valuable to French war efforts—carrying supplies to the front lines, finding wounded soldiers, transporting ammunition—that he was named the official dog of the French army.

The Briard is a big dog with a big personality. He can be reserved with strangers, but his loyalty and bravery make him a natural guardian of home and family. He is a sensitive soul, and unkind or unjust treatment can make the Briard skittish and even aggressive. However, enthusiastic and appreciative training and care will yield an even-tempered, affectionate dog. A natural herder, the Briard likes to keep his family close and if socialized to a variety of people and animals, gets along fine with everyone.

Exercise, Training, Grooming, and Health

- The Briard needs regular outings that include some vigorous form of exercise. He loves to be near his family, so walking, jogging, or backyard play with his owners will help keep him satisfied.

- A smart, willing dog, the Briard is a quick study. However, a stern or harsh manner or tone will backfire and bring out his stubborn nature. He will respond to and thrive only with positive training.

- The long, double coat of the Briard needs to be brushed several times a week to prevent tangling. The coarseness of the coat keeps dirt from sticking to it, and the Briard sheds very little.

- Average life span is 10 to 12 years. Breed health concerns may include bloat; cataracts; congenital stationary night blindness (CSNB); hip dysplasia; hypothyroidism; and lymphoma.

Breed Facts

- **Country of Origin**: France
- **Height**: 17.5–20.5 in (44.5–52 cm)
- **Weight**: 30–45 lb (13.5–20.5 kg)
- **Coat**: Dense, flat or wavy
- **Colors**: Liver and white or orange and white with clear or roan patterns, tricolor (liver and white with orange markings); may have ticking|also black and white [UKC]
- **Other Names**: Brittany Spaniel
- **Registries (With Group)**: AKC (Sporting); CKC (Sporting); UKC (Gun Dog)

History and Personality

The Brittany is named for the area in France with which he's associated: Brittany, the province known for its fishing and agricultural histories. Most experts generally agree that bird dogs all come from the same common stock, but the actual development of the Brittany is unclear, although it is believed that the Brittany is one of the oldest spaniels in France. Brittanys came to the United States in the 1930s. Over the years, the breed changed from the original French type, as American hunters tended to prefer a lighter-bodied dog with a longer leg and a wider running ability. The differences in body shape and hunting style eventually led many fanciers to separate out the "American-style" from the French.

Easy to handle and train, the Brittany is an extremely companionable dog. He is happy, friendly, alert, even-tempered, and always ready for some fun and frolic. He also an intense and tireless hunter who is best behaved when his working instincts are employed.

Exercise, Training, Grooming, and Health

- The Brittany is a high-energy dog who needs lots of exercise. He's a joy to take for walks in the park because he listens and pays attention to his owner while at the same time actively searching out a scent.

- The intelligent and gentle Brittany will wither under harsh training conditions, but let him learn from someone who's patient and uses praise and he blossoms into a dog who is extremely biddable.

- The fine, medium-length hair of the Brittany is relatively easy to keep clean. It needs regular brushing to look its best and to keep him comfortable, and the fringing on his body should be kept clean.

- Average life span is 10 to 12 years. Breed health concerns may include ear infections; hip dysplasia; and seizures.

Breed Facts

- **Country of Origin**: Belgium

- **Height**: 7–8 in (18–20 cm) [est.]

- **Weight**: 7.5–13 lb (3.5–6 kg)|small dogs and bitches no more than 7 lb (3 kg)/large dogs more than 7 lb (3 kg) to 11 lb (5 kg)/large bitches more than 7 lb (3 kg) to 12 lb (5.5 kg) [CKC]

- **Coat**: Two varieties—*rough* is wiry, hard, dense; beard and mustache/*smooth* is short, straight, tight, glossy

- **Colors**: Black|also reddish brown, black and reddish brown, black with reddish brown markings [CKC][UKC]|also red, black and tan [AKC][KC]|also beige [AKC]|red, reddish [FCI]

- **Other Names**: Griffon Bruxellois

- **Registries (With Group)**: AKC (Toy); ANKC (Toys); CKC (Toys); FCI (Companion and Toy); KC (Toy); UKC (Companion)

History and Personality

The Brussels Griffon is one of three small terriers from Belgium, which also include the Griffon Belge and his smooth-coated brethren the Petit Brabançon. (In Europe, the three breeds are shown separately, but in the US the AKC groups all three together.) These dogs have been around since the 13th century. Back then, he was a peasant's dog and was quite a bit larger than modern specimens (more like the size of a Fox Terrier). In early times, he was known as the *Griffon D'Ecurie* (Stable Griffon), for he earned his keep by killing the rats and mice in the stable.

The Brussels Griffon is a fun, confident, adaptable breed. He is quite intelligent and sensitive and can be moody. Affectionate and alert, he bonds strongly with his owner. He has a tendency to be shy with strangers.

Exercise, Training, Grooming, and Health

- This toy Griffon is content to stroll alongside his devoted companion on their outings. His curiosity keeps him active around the house, which provides him with additional exercise.

- The Brussels Griffon gets bored easily, so keeping training interesting is a must. He can be hard to housetrain.

- The rough-coated Brussels Griffon needs professional grooming to keep his coat from becoming disheveled and coarse. Like the coat of a terrier, it needs to be hand-stripped so that it lays just-so. Special attention should be paid to the face with its pushed-in nose and somewhat bulging eyes.

- Average life span is 12 to 15 years. Breed health concerns may include eye problems; hip dysplasia; patellar luxation; Poodle eye; respiratory problems.

Breed Facts

- **Country of Origin**: Great Britain
- **Height**: 12–16 in (30.5–40.5 cm) [est.]
- **Weight**: Males 50–55 lb (22.5–25 kg)/females 40–50.5 lb (18–23.5 kg)
- **Coat**: Short, straight, flat, close, fine, smooth, glossy
- **Colors**: Brindle (all varieties), piebald, red, fawn, fallow, white|also smut acceptable [ANKC][FCI][KC]
- **Other Names**: English Bulldog
- **Registries (With Group)**: AKC (Non-Sporting); ANKC (Non Sporting); CKC (Non-Sporting); FCI (Molossoid); KC (Utility); UKC (Companion)

History and Personality

Between the 13th and 19th centuries, ancestors of the Bulldog were used for the heinous sport of bullbaiting. The Bulldog's unusual undershot jaw stems from those terrible days, as it enabled him to grab a bull at any point, clamp down, and hang on. Bullbaiting was banned in 1835, after which time the Bulldog evolved into the shorter, squatter dog we are familiar with today. He was also bred to be a kind companion, and many consider him a symbol of courage and tenacity.

The Bulldog is one of the gentlest breeds, though he retains a strong protective instinct and makes a wonderful watchdog. He is extremely affectionate with his family and craves their affection and attention.

Exercise, Training, Grooming, and Health

- His short nose and broad head make breathing somewhat difficult for the Bulldog, who shouldn't be overstressed with exercise. A simple stroll or the workout he gets keeping up with his family will fulfill his needs.

- The Bulldog easily settles into a routine around the house and can learn basic manners. He just needs early training from someone who appreciates that it may take him a little longer to learn than some of the more obedience-oriented breeds.

- His short coat is easy to care for—brushing with a soft brush a few times a week will keep him looking good. The wrinkles around his eyes and nose need regular attention, as they need to be kept clean and dry to ward off infection.

- Average life span is 10 to 12 years. Breed health concerns may include cherry eye; elongated soft palate; entropion; hip dysplasia; hypoplastic trachea; patellar luxation; and stenotic nares.

Breed Facts

- **Country of Origin**: Great Britain
- **Height**: Males 25–27 in (63.5–68.5 cm)/females 24–26 in (61–66 cm)
- **Weight**: Males 110–130 lb (50–59 kg)/females 90–120 lb (41–54.5 kg)
- **Coat**: Short, hard, dense, weather resistant, lying flat to body
- **Colors**: Brindle, fawn, red; may have white marking; black muzzle essential
- **Registries (With Group)**: AKC (Working); ANKC (Utility); CKC (Working); FCI (Molossoid); KC (Working); UKC (Guardian)

History and Personality

During the late 1800s Bullmastiffs were used to bring down poachers on large estates. Poaching carried the death penalty in England, so the dogs used to catch these desperate poachers needed to be tough, fearless, and absolutely silent in order to bring them down. Today the Bullmastiff's guarding abilities have ensured his continued popularity, although he is certainly a more mellow and tractable dog than were his ancestors.

Devoted and alert, he is affectionate and trustworthy with his family, whom he keeps a close eye on. Should he feel that he or someone close to him is in danger, he will respond.

Exercise, Training, Grooming, and Health

- The Bullmastiff does not need a lot of exercise but does need to be walked twice a day. He can be lazy, so it's important to get him out and about.

- Training should start from an early age. Bullmastiffs are independent-minded and quickly grow big and strong; thus, basic manners are essential so they can be easily controlled.

- The Bullmastiff's wrinkly face is the area that needs the most attention in order to keep it clean and infection-free. Otherwise, his short, smooth coat is easy to care for using a firm bristle brush a few times a week.

- Average life span is 8 to 10 years. Breed health concerns may include allergies; bloat; cardiomyopathy; elbow dysplasia; entropion; hemangiosarcoma; hip dysplasia; lymphoma; mast cell tumors; osteosarcoma; progressive retinal atrophy (PRA); and subaortic stenosis (SAS).

Bull Terrier

Breed Facts

- **Country of Origin**: Great Britain

- **Height**: Impression of maximum substance to size of dog|20–24 in (51–61 cm) [est.]

- **Weight**: Impression of maximum substance to size of dog| 45–80 lb (20.5–36.5 kg) [est.]

- **Coat**: Short, flat, harsh, glossy|soft-textured undercoat may be present in winter [ANKC][FCI][KC]

- **Colors**: Two varieties—*white*, may have markings on head/ *colored* can be black brindle, red, fawn, tricolor|*colored* can be any color other than white [CKC][UKC]|only white acceptable (may have markings on head) [AKC]

- **Other Names**: English Bull Terrier

- **Registries (With Group)**: AKC (Terrier); ANKC (Terriers); CKC (Terriers); FCI (Terriers); KC (Terrier); UKC (Terrier)

History and Personality

In the early 1800s, when dog fighting was legal and actually quite popular, breeders were always looking to produce dogs with tenacity, endurance, and agility, and the Bull Terrier's ancestry stems from there. Today, thankfully, dog fighting of any kind is illegal, and they are strictly companions. Their egg-shaped heads quickly distinguish them from all other breeds, and their looks and personality have endeared them to many.

The Bull Terrier is charming, friendly, playful and very attached to his family. He needs a lot of companionship and a good deal of supervision in order to make a good pet. He gets along well with children and tends to be protective of them. From early puppyhood, he needs to be introduced to all sorts of people, other dogs, other animals, and environments so that he does not feel threatened by them.

Exercise, Training, Grooming, and Health

- Bull Terriers need regular exercise, and plenty of it! Because of their tendency to be overly playful, they can sometimes be intimidating to other dogs, which can lead to rough play. If allowed off lead, be sure it is in an enclosed area and that your Bull Terrier is extremely well socialized.

- It may be challenging to train a Bull Terrier, but many have done it with great results.

- His short coat should be gone over with a hound glove and a soft bristle brush.

- Average life span is 10 to 12 years. Breed health concerns may include allergies; deafness; familial nephropathy; mitral dysplasia; patellar luxation; and zinc deficiency.

Cairn Terrier

Breed Facts

- **Country of Origin**: Great Britain

- **Height**: 11–12 in (28–31 cm)|males 10 in (25.5 cm)/females 9.5 in (24 cm) [AKC]

- **Weight**: 13–17 lb (6–7.5 kg)|males 14 lb (6.5 kg)/females 13 lb (6 kg) [AKC]

- **Coat**: Hard, weather-resistant double coat with harsh, profuse outercoat and short, soft, close, furry undercoat

- **Colors**: Cream, wheaten, red, gray, nearly black; brindling in all these colors acceptable|any color except white [AKC]

- **Registries (With Group)**: AKC (Terrier); ANKC (Terriers); CKC (Terriers); FCI (Terriers); KC (Terrier); UKC (Terrier)

History and Personality

The Hebrides Islands to the north of Scotland is the place the Cairn Terrier originally called home. He is named after the rocky cairns that were home to the pests that he was developed to burrow into their lairs and rout out—a job of pest control he's been doing for over 500 years.

Cheerful, alert, and bursting with joy for life, the Cairn endears himself to all he meets. His affectionate nature and kind heart make him a beloved family member, and his sturdy, compact body serves him well as a child's playmate. He gets along well with other people and animals, but socialization from an early age is important.

Exercise, Training, Grooming, and Health

- The curious, active Cairn benefits tremendously from several walks a day—preferably long walks. He likes to investigate the world, which makes him easy to exercise.

- While the Cairn Terrier typically dotes on his owner, asking him to follow basic obedience commands may cause him to change his tune. The best way to work with his seemingly stubborn streak is with positive, motivational training.

- Because it is thick and tends to the scruffy side, the Cairn's coat needs regular brushing, and the hair around his eyes should be trimmed. Professional grooming several times a year to keep his coat plucked and looking its best is advised.

- Average life span is 12 to 15 years. Breed health concerns may include allergies; cataracts; craniomandibular osteopathy; cryptorchidism; globoid cell leukodystrophy; hypothyroidism; Legg-Calve-Perthes disease; ocular melanosis; patellar luxation; portosystemic shunt; progressive retinal atrophy (PRA); and von Willebrand disease.

Canaan Dog

Breed Facts

- **Country of Origin**: Israel

- **Height**: 20–24 in (51–61 cm)|males 20–24 in (51–61 cm)/ females 19–23 in (48–58.5 cm) [AKC]

- **Weight**: 40–55 lb (18–25 kg)|males 45–55 lb (20.5–25 kg)/ females 35–45 lb (16–29.5 kg) [AKC]

- **Coat**: Double coat with straight, harsh, flat-lying outercoat of short to medium length and straight, soft, short, flat-lying undercoat; slight ruff

- **Colors**: Sand to red-brown, white, black, or spotted, with or without mask|two color patterns—predominantly white with mask, with or without patches of color/solid, with color ranging from black through all shades of brown (sandy to red or liver) [AKC]|solid or spotted, colors including any shade between cream and red-brown; no liver [UKC]

- **Other Names**: Kelev K'naani

- **Registries (With Group)**: AKC (Herding); ANKC (Non

Sporting); CKC (Working); FCI (Spitz and Primitive); KC (Utility); UKC (Sighthound & Pariah)

History and Personality

Cave drawings from 2200 BCE show dogs who look remarkably like the Canaan. He was a guard dog and herding dog to the ancient Israelites, and when the Jewish people were dispersed from the land thousands of years ago, these dogs began living in the Negev Desert. When the Jews returned to the land in the 1930s, they discovered these pariah dogs, almost like living fossils, existing in a feral state. The breed's modern history began in the late 1930s to produce a dog to guard the kibbutz. Today's Canaan Dog is a highly intelligent and trainable dog whose versatility has been tapped for mine detection work, sentry and messenger work, guiding the blind, and much more.

With ancestors who survived for thousands of years on their own, he retains a strong flight instinct as well as an innate ability to care for itself, so keeping him on leash in all but securely enclosed areas is a must unless he is highly trained. He is a devoted companion who is intelligent, affectionate with his family, and loves to play. He should be socialized with children and other animals from an early age to help lessen his natural reticence with strange people and animals.

Exercise, Training, Grooming, and Health

- The smart, quick Canaan Dog needs daily activity that will challenge him mentally and physically. Several long walks a day are not enough for this alert and responsive dog. He needs a job or to be involved in a sport.

- Because he is highly trainable and is an eager worker, training him is a joyful experience.

- He sheds seasonally, but otherwise the Canaan Dog is an easy breed to keep clean and neat with regular brushing.

- Average life span is 12 to 15 years. There are no reported breed-specific health concerns.

Cane Corso

Breed Facts

- **Country of Origin**: Italy

- **Height**: Males 24–27.5 in (61–70 cm)/females 23–26 in (58.5–66 cm)

- **Weight**: Males 92.5–110 lb (42–50 kg)/females 84–100 lb (38–45.5 kg)|proportionate to height [AKC]

- **Coat**: Double coat with short, stiff, shiny, dense outercoat and light undercoat

- **Colors**: Black, gray, fawn, red; brindling allowed; may have eye mask; white markings

- **Other Names**: Cane Corso Italiano; Cane Corso Mastiff; Italian Corso Dog; Italian Mastiff; Italian Molosso

- **Registries (With Group)**: AKC (Working); ANKC (Utility); CKC (Working); FCI (Molossoid); UKC (Guardian)

History and Personality

Two mastiff-type dogs descended from legendary Roman war dogs—the Cane Corso and the Neapolitan Mastiff. The lighter of the two, the Cane Corso, was used to hunt game and work as an all-around farm dog, where for centuries he served as the protector of his family, livestock, and property.

He is a favorite playmate of children and the faithful friend of families, a guard dog who is intelligent and ready to please. Great with children and devoted to his family, he is an alert watchdog who is suspicious of strangers but knows when to go into protective mode and when to back down. A well-bred Cane Corso has a stable temperament but can be territorial and dominant toward other dogs, so the more socialization he receives from puppyhood, the better.

Exercise, Training, Grooming, and Health

- The Cane Corso is an athletic, energetic dog who needs plenty of exercise. He also likes to stretch his legs patrolling house and home on a steady basis.

- The eager-to-please Cane Corso is highly trainable and with direction and encouragement is capable of doing just about anything requested of him.

- His short coat is easy to maintain. A wipe-down with a damp cloth and occasional brushing is all he needs. He is a light shedder.

- Average life span is 12 to 15 years. Breed health concerns may include allergies; bloat; ectropion; elbow dysplasia; entropion; epilepsy; heart murmur; and hip dysplasia.

Breed Facts

- **Country of Origin**: Great Britain

- **Height**: 10.5–12.5 in (27–32 cm)|12 in (30 cm) [ANKC] [KC]|as near as possible to 12 in (30 cm) [CKC]

- **Weight**: In proportion to size|males 30–38 lb (13.5–17 kg)/ females 25–34 lb (11–15.5 kg) [AKC][UKC]

- **Coat**: Double short or medium-length coat with dense, slightly harsh, weather-resistant outercoat and short, soft, thick undercoat|only medium length [AKC]|slight ruff [UKC]

- **Colors**: Any color; may have white markings|all shades of red, sable, brindle; black; blue merle; may have white markings [AKC][UKC]

- **Registries (With Group)**: AKC (Herding); ANKC (Working); CKC (Herding); FCI (Sheepdogs); KC (Pastoral); UKC (Herding)

History and Personality

The heritage of the Cardigan Welsh Corgi is a particularly ancient one, as it is believed that a dog resembling the Cardigan came to Wales when the Celts migrated there around 1000 BCE. He was used to work cattle, and because of his size could nip at the livestock's heels while avoiding being kicked. Two closely related Welsh Corgis exist today: the Cardigan (long-tailed) and the Pembroke (tailless).

Cardigan Welsh Corgis are noted for their intelligence and devotion. They are adaptable to many living situations and make excellent watchdogs, as they take caring for their family with the utmost seriousness. Playful and lovable, they need to spend quality time with their owners. Corgis are good with children, especially if raised with and socialized with them.

Exercise, Training, Grooming, and Health

- Able-bodied and athletic, the Cardigan Welsh Corgi enjoys spending time outdoors and is often found competing in the dog sports of agility, obedience, and herding. He is happiest with a purpose, and this kind of exercise and mental stimulation keeps him truly satisfied.

- The Cardigan Welsh Corgi is a joy to train. Responsive and intelligent, this breed learns quickly and retains his lessons, always working with enthusiasm.

- Regular brushing and combing of his plush double coat is all he needs to stay looking his best.

- Average life span is 12 to 15 years. Breed health concerns may include canine intervertebral disc disease; glaucoma; and progressive retinal atrophy (PRA).

Catahoula Leopard Dog

Breed Facts

- **Country of Origin**: United States

- **Height**: Males 24 in (61 cm)/females 22 in (56 cm)

- **Weight**: 50–95 lb (22.5–43 kg)

- **Coat**: Single coat, short to medium in length, smooth to coarse texture; lies flat and close to body

- **Colors**: All coat colors and patterns|black, blue, blue merle, brindle, chocolate, red, red, white merle, yellow, yellow merle; tan markings; white trim [AKC]

- **Other Names**: Catahoula Cur; Catahoula Hog Dog; Catahoula Hound; Louisiana Catahoula Leopard Dog

- **Registries (With Group)**: AKC (FSS); UKC (Herding)

History and Personality

The ancestors of the Catahoula Leopard Dog remain a mystery, his name comes from the swampy Parish of Catahoula in Louisiana, where people eked out a living fishing, trapping, and running a few wild hogs and cattle back in the woods. They used him for these dangerous jobs, and today he still herds cattle and is more suited to bringing semi-wild stock out of the bush than escorting tame cattle into the barn for milking.

He is independent, assertive, protective, and territorial. A hardworking dog who has been called a "walking sledgehammer" because of the way he moves livestock, the Catahoula is also playful and personable when comfortable with his people.

Exercise, Training, Grooming, and Health

- The Catahoula Leopard Dog needs plenty of exercise—at least an hour a day—and daily walks should be vigorous. He is an excellent jogging or hiking partner and excels at high-energy sports like agility and herding.

- Smart and quick, the Catahoula is a capable learner.

- His undercoat will shed fairly continuously and more so when he's anxious or uncomfortable. Otherwise, regular brushing keeps it in check.

- Average life span is 12 to 14 years. Breed health concerns may include deafness; eye problems; and hip dysplasia.

Caucasian Ovcharka

Breed Facts

- **Country of Origin**: Russia/Caucasus Mountains region

- **Height**: Males 25.5 in (65 cm)/females 24.5 in (62 cm)

- **Weight**: 99–154 lb (45–70 kg) [est.]

- **Coat**: Three types—*longhaired* has long outercoat; feathering neck ruff/*shorthaired* has thick, relatively short coat/*intermediate longhaired* but without ruff or feathering|intermediate has less feathering than long-coated type [UKC]

- **Colors**: Black, black and gray, cream, fawn, gray, rust, wine; piebald, brindle and white markings|also agouti gray, white, white with gray patches [UKC]

- **Other Names**: Caucasian Mountain Dog; Caucasian Ovtcharka; Caucasian Sheepdog; Caucasian Shepherd Dog; Kavkazskaïa Ovtcharka

- **Registries (With Group)**: AKC (FSS); FCI (Molossoid); UKC (Guardian)

History and Personality

The Caucasus Mountains fill the long finger of land in southwestern Russia that reaches down between the Black Sea and the Caspian Sea to touch Turkey and Iran. Large flocks of sheep have been kept in this area for more than 600 years, and the ancient Ovcharkas herded and protected the livestock. A favorite of the Soviet army during the Cold War, he was once used to patrol the Berlin Wall.

The proper Ovcharka is confident, strong-willed, and fearless, with a large dose of independence. He can be ferocious and aggressive in defending his territory, but his intensity for his purpose is mirrored in his devotion to his people, whom he guards and protects with his life and otherwise showers with affection.

Exercise, Training, Grooming, and Health

- The large Ovcharka needs regular exercise, preferably long walks in areas where he can stretch his legs.

- He needs a firm and fair leader to bring out the best in him, and socialization from puppyhood is critical. This is not a dog recommended for inexperienced trainers.

- The short-coated Ovcharkas are easier to care for; the longer-coated ones need regular brushing and combing to keep them free of tangles and other obstructions.

- Average life span is 13 to 15 years. There are no reported breed-specific health concerns.

Cavalier King Charles Spaniel

Breed Facts

- **Country of Origin**: Great Britain
- **Height**: 12–13 in (30.5–33 cm)
- **Weight**: 11–18 lb (5–8 kg)
- **Coat**: Long, silky, straight or slight wave; feathering|coat of moderate length [AKC]
- **Colors**: Blenheim (chestnut markings on white background), tricolor (black markings on white background and tan markings), ruby (rich red), black and tan (black with bright tan markings)
- **Registries (With Group)**: AKC (Toy); ANKC (Toys); CKC (Toys); FCI (Companion and Toy); KC (Toy); UKC (Companion)

History and Personality

Toy spaniels were developed in Great Britain circa CE 1016, and their first function was that of a hunter. By the 1500s they were companions to the wealthy, as only the rich could afford a dog who didn't earn his keep by ratting or hunting. In the 1600s, both King Charles I and King Charles II adored the breed, and it was from the latter that they were eventually named the Cavalier King Charles Spaniel. Type changed during the Victorian era to a more domed-head, and those dogs became King Charles Spaniels. In the 1920s there was renewed interest in the older type and breeders worked to revive the breed, and the Cavalier King Charles Spaniel eventually gained notable popularity.

It is the rare Cavalier who does not greet everyone and everything with great joy. Still, he is not a hyper dog at all; rather, he is naturally well-behaved and downright adoring. Because Cavaliers are so people-oriented, they are not content to spend a lot of time alone. They get along well with children and other animals.

Exercise, Training, Grooming, and Health

- The Cavalier King Charles Spaniel needs regular exercise but can adapt to the activity level of his owner.

- He wants to please and is fairly easy to train, though he may need some extra time with housetraining.

- The silky coat of the Cavalier is easy to keep clean and shiny using a firm-bristled brush and wide-toothed comb several times a week.

- Average life span is 12 to 14 years. Breed health concerns may include chiari-like malformation (CM); hip dysplasia; mitral valve disease (MVD); patellar luxation; and syringomyelia (SM).

Central Asian Shepherd Dog

Breed Facts

- **Country of Origin**: Russia

- **Height**: Males 25.5 in (65 cm) or over/females 23.5 in (60 cm) or over

- **Weight**: Males 121–176 lb (55–80 kg)/females 88–143 lb (40–65 kg) [est.]

- **Coat**: Two types—*longhaired* and *shorthaired*, both having a double coat with coarse, straight hair and well-developed undercoat

- **Colors**: Black, brindle, fawn, gray, white; white markings|also russet, gray-brown, parti-colored, flecked [ANKC][FCI][UKC]

- **Other Names**: Central Asia Shepherd Dog; Central Asian Ovtcharka; Central Asian Shepherd; Middle Asian Ovcharka; Sredneasiatskaïa Ovtcharka

- **Registries (With Group)**: AKC (FSS); ANKC (Utility); FCI (Molossoid); UKC (Guardian)

History and Personality

Artifacts in their native lands date Central Asian Shepherd Dogs to nearly 3000 BCE. Their heritage is one of natural selection dictated by the demands of the people they lived with and the territories they inhabited, primarily along the ancient silk route. He was used as for guarding livestock, home protection, and fighting. He was (and still is) capable of surviving day to day in the face of extreme climate changes, formidable predators, and warring peoples.

He is a protective breed who bonds first to his human caretaker(s) and next with his perceived possessions. Bred to solve problems, he is independent-minded, strong, brave, and responsible. He is a large but agile dog, sometimes described as a cat in dog's clothing. With his strong guarding and territorial instincts, he is not a breed for the novice owner.

Exercise, Training, Grooming, and Health

- The large Central Asian Shepherd Dog may spend a considerable amount of time moving around in his native lands, and this kind of slow but steady exercise is what he likes best.

- Sensitive and smart, the Central Asian Shepherd responds best to someone who can inspire while also providing strong leadership.

- Neither the longhaired nor shorthaired coat require a lot of grooming, but the thick undercoat results in steady shedding, which can be helped with regular brushing.

- Average life span is 10 to 15 years. Breed health concerns may include elbow dysplasia; entropion; and hip dysplasia.

Breed Facts

- **Country of Origin**: Czech Republic

- **Height**: 10–13 in (25.5–33 cm)|males 11.5 in (29 cm)/females 10.5 in (27 cm) [UKC]

- **Weight**: 13–22 lb (6–10 kg)|males 16–22 lb (7.5–10 kg)/ females slightly less [AKC]

- **Coat**: Long, fine but firm, slightly wavy with silky gloss; beard

- **Colors**: Gray-blue, light coffee brown; yellow, gray, white markings acceptable|any shade of gray; black, white, brown, yellow markings acceptable [AKC]

- **Other Names**: Bohemian Terrier; Ceský Teriér; Czech Terrier; Czesky Terrier

- **Registries (With Group)**: AKC (Miscellaneous); ANKC (Terriers); CKC (Terriers); FCI (Terriers); KC (Terrier); UKC (Terrier)

History and Personality

A relatively new breed, the Cesky Terrier exists due to the efforts of a Czechoslovakian breeder named Frantisek Horak. Horak wanted a terrier who was a stealthy vermin hunter but who also had a narrower head and chest and a softer coat to make it easier for the dog to enter burrows. He crossed Sealyam Terriers and Scottish Terriers and possibly some other breeds, including the Dandie Dinmont Terrier. Horak also bred for a more easy-going temperament than that of the typical terrier, as he wanted a breed who could hunt in packs. The Cesky Terrier is noted for his abilities as a hunter, tracker, watchdog, and guard dog.

He is a happy dog who is easily trained and content to oblige. Sporty yet calm, playful yet protective, he loves people—especially children. His is a terrier, however, and will show that hot, feisty streak, which serves him well as a watchdog for his family.

Exercise, Training, Grooming, and Health

- The Cesky Terrier is a dog who enjoys exercise and especially loves his walks and romps outdoors with the family, but he doesn't require particularly rigorous exercise.

- Responsive and even solicitous, the Cesky Terrier enjoys learning from and with his trainer. Socialization from an early age will ensure that he reaches his outgoing potential with all kinds of people and other animals.

- His terrier coat requires regular trimming, and for the pet Cesky, that means quarterly visits to a professional groomer. He is clipped rather than stripped, which makes coat care somewhat easier. His longer hair should be brushed and combed several times a week.

- Average life span is 12 to 15 years. Breed health concerns may include Scottie cramp.

Chesapeake Bay Retriever

Breed Facts

- **Country of Origin**: United States
- **Height**: Males 23–26 in (58.5–66 cm)/females 21–24 in (53–61 cm)
- **Weight**: Males 65–80 lb (29.5–36.5 kg)/females 55–70 lb (25–31.5 kg)
- **Coat**: Water-resistant double coat with short, harsh, thick, oily outercoat and woolly, dense, fine undercoat
- **Colors**: Any color of brown, sedge (red-gold), or deadgrass (straw to bracken); white markings acceptable
- **Registries (With Group)**: AKC (Sporting); ANKC (Gundogs); CKC (Sporting); FCI (Retrievers); KC (Gundog); UKC (Gun Dog)

History and Personality

Ducks have always been especially plentiful along the Chesapeake Bay, and sportsmen with able retrievers have enjoyed great success there.

So valued was the right kind of retriever that over time, a special dog was developed—one who could withstand the icy water and rough waves of the saltwater bay. In the later part of the 1800s, the "Chesapeake Bay Ducking Dog" (one of the many names the breed was called) was being promoted and standardized. Records show that some of these dogs could average a thousand ducks each fall, and the tougher the hunting conditions, the more they seemed to like it.

Today the Chesapeake Bay Retriever ("Chessie") is as constitutionally tough as his forebears, able to hunt in harsh conditions. This stick-to-itiveness can be intimidating to inexperienced dog owners. For those who can handle a dog with a mind of his own, the Chessie makes an exceptional sporting companion. He is intelligent and affectionate, good with children, and easy to care for. He excels in sports and makes a formidable watchdog. Socialization from an early age is beneficial.

Exercise, Training, Grooming, and Health

- Relatively inactive indoors, the Chessie loves being outside, and one of his favorite activities is swimming—no matter what the weather. Long jaunts that include visits to his favorite watering holes suit this breed just fine.

- Particularly responsive and adept in hunting and retrieving situations, and certainly capable of much more, the Chessie will excel under the guidance of someone who can handle him.

- His coarse, thick, and almost oily coat is self-maintained and needs only an occasional brushing with a firm bristle brush. He is an average shedder.

- Average life span is 10 to 12 years. Breed health concerns may include allergies; degenerative myelopathy; hip dysplasia; progressive retinal atrophy (PRA); and seizures.

Chihuahua

Breed Facts

- **Country of Origin**: Mexico
- **Height**: 6–9 in (15–23 cm) [est.]
- **Weight**: Up to 6 lb (2.5 kg)|1–6.5 lb (453.5 g–3 kg) [FCI] [UKC]
- **Coat**: Two types, both of which can be single or double coated—*smooth* coat soft, close, glossy; neck ruff/*long* coat soft, silky, flat or slightly curly; neck ruff
- **Colors**: Any color|but never merle [ANKC][KC]|long coats a solid color; solid-colored markings/short coats any color [CKC]
- **Registries (With Group)**: AKC (Toy); ANKC (Toys); CKC (Toys); FCI (Companion and Toy); KC (Toy); UKC (Companion)

History and Personality

While the Chihuahua's history remains shrouded in lore and legend, the breed has two claims to fame: He is the oldest breed on the American continent, and he is also the smallest. Long associated with Mexico and certainly refined there, it is believed that the breed traces back to dogs who came to the country with Spanish travelers who had dwarfed dogs from China; these dogs were bred to the native hairless breeds to form the Chihuahua. Still others believe that he is a miniaturized native pariah dog. Regardless, he gained notoriety and popularity in Mexico City around 1895 and soon found his way into Texas.

The Chihuahua enjoys a top place among the world's most popular dogs due both to his personality and to his size. Lively, alert, large-hearted, playful, and affectionate, he bonds closely with his owners and wants to be with them at all times. Fortunately, he is so portable that this is easily accomplished. It is critical that a Chihuahua be socialized from puppyhood so he is not easily intimidated. Particularly active or noisy children are not the best companions for this tiny breed.

Exercise, Training, Grooming, and Health

- Most of the Chihuahua's exercise needs can be met by following his owner around inside, plus several play sessions a day.

- Chihuahuas are intelligent and become bored easily, so upbeat, fun, positive training is necessary. Patience is required in the housetraining department.

- The longhaired variety needs special attention—brushing, bathing, and trimming—while the shorthaired Chihuahua is kept clean with occasional brushing and wiping with a soft, damp cloth.

- Average life span is 15 years or more. Breed health concerns may include collapsing trachea; eye injuries; hypoglycemia; mitral valve disease (MVD); patellar luxation; pulmonary stenosis; and seizures.

Chinese Crested

Breed Facts

- **Country of Origin**: China/Africa
- **Height**: Males 11–13 in (28–33 cm)/females 9–12 in (23–30 cm)|11–13 in (28–33 cm) [AKC][UKC]
- **Weight**: Varies but no more than 12 lb (5.5 kg)
- **Coat**: Two types—*hairless* has soft, silky, flowing hair on head, tail, feet/*powderpuff* has double coat with straight, soft, silky outercoat and short, silky undercoat
- **Colors**: Any color or combination of colors
- **Other Names**: Chinese Crested Dog
- **Registries (With Group)**: AKC (Toy); ANKC (Toys); CKC (Toys); FCI (Companion and Toy); KC (Toy); UKC (Companion)

History and Personality

Hairless mutations have occurred in pariah-type litters, and from these, the modern hairless breeds evolved. The hairless-type dogs found in China probably trace their roots back to African Hairless Terriers, who were most likely picked up by Chinese traders for use as ratters on their ships. In China, the hairless dogs were cultivated into two types: the "treasure house guardian," or deer type, and the "hunting dog," which was the larger, heavier type. Today, Chinese Cresteds enjoy a loyal following around the world.

Lively, exuberant, playful, and affectionate, the Chinese Crested easily wins over the hearts of everyone he meets. He may be timid with strangers at first, but proper socialization will help make him outgoing and lovable. He has a hare foot (longer than most) and can grasp and hold onto toys, food, or people— owners describe how a Chinese Crested hugs when held. He also likes to dig and climb.

Exercise, Training, Grooming, and Health

- Chinese Cresteds enjoy brisk walks with their people, and they also get exercise in their daily routines of accompanying family members around the house and wherever they go.

- The Chinese Crested is quite receptive to positive training and is eager to comply with basic requests.

- Both varieties are clean, with no doggie odor. The Hairless variety needs regular bathing and applications of oil or cream on his skin to keep it soft and supple. The Powderpuff's long, silky topcoat and woolly undercoat need regular brushing, especially during times of shedding.

- Average life span is 10 to 12 years. Breed health concerns may include allergies (Hairless); dental problems (Hairless); Legg-Calve-Perthes disease; patellar luxation; and skin problems (Hairless).

Breed Facts

- **Country of Origin**: China

- **Height**: 17–20 in (44–51 cm)

- **Weight**: 40–60 lb (18–27 kg)

- **Coat**: Single, straight, harsh coat; length varies from short and bristly ("horse coat") to long and thick ("brush coat")

- **Colors**: Only solid colors and sable|no white [ANKC][FCI] [KC]

- **Other Names**: Chinese Fighting Dog; Shar Pei; Shar-Pei

- **Registries (With Group)**: AKC (Non-Sporting); ANKC (Non Sporting); CKC (Non-Sporting); FCI (Molossoid); KC (Utility); UKC (Northern)

History and Personality

The exact origin of this ancient, unique breed is unknown, although it is believed that the Chow Chow and the Mastiff are among his ancestors.

Pictures of dogs resembling the Chinese Shar-Pei have been found on pottery dating back more than 2,000 years. For many centuries, this willing and versatile worker was used for hunting, herding, and protection. He was also used in dog fights, his loose skin enabling him to turn on his opponent even when he was grasped firmly.

With his hippopotamus-like face, tiny ears, and abundant wrinkles, one look at a Shar-Pei puppy is usually all it takes to fall in love with this breed. Prospective owners must keep in mind the guard-dog component of this dog's heritage, however, and be sure to properly socialize him. Although independent and aloof by nature, he is devoted and loyal to his family members once he has learned to trust and respect them.

Exercise, Training, Grooming, and Health

- A brisk walk at least once daily will provide not only adequate exercise but also important bonding with his owner.

- A firm but gentle hand is necessary when training the Chinese Shar-Pei. He tends to have a stubborn streak, so training must be made fun to keep him interested for any length of time. Early socialization and training are necessary.

- Although the Chinese Shar-Pei is shorthaired, his coat and skin require special vigilance daily care to make sure that the skin folds, especially those on his face, do not stay moist and become irritated. He should be gently brushed regularly, but his coat should never be trimmed. Bathing once a week using a mild shampoo is recommended.

- Average life span is 9 to 10 years. Breed health concerns may include cherry eye; entropion; hip dysplasia; hypothyroidism; patellar luxation; pyoderma; Shar Pei Fever; and skin problems.

Chinook

Breed Facts

- **Country of Origin**: United States
- **Height**: Males 23–27 in (58.5–68.5 cm)/females 21–25 in (53–63.5 cm)
- **Weight**: Males 70 lb (31.5 kg)/females 55 lb (25 kg)
- **Coat**: Double coat with medium-length coarse, close-lying outercoat and thick, soft, downy undercoat; neck ruff
- **Colors**: Tawny; black and buff markings|also fawn, gray-red, palomino, red-gold, silver-fawn, black, black and tan, buff, gray and tan, white; also black mask; also white markings [AKC]
- **Registries (With Group)**: AKC (FSS); UKC (Northern)

History and Personality

The Chinook breed is named after a single dog: Chinook, bred by Arthur Walden at his Wonalancet Farm in New Hampshire in 1917. Walden was an active explorer and wanted a dog with speed, power, endurance, and a good temperament. He started with a direct descendant of Admiral Peary's team and bred the dog to a Mastiff-type female. Chinook was one of three pups in the litter, and his intelligence and abilities quickly distinguished him from his littermates. He became Walden's constant companion and the star of many sled-dog competitions. He even accompanied Admiral Byrd's Antarctic Expedition in the late 1920s. While the all-American Chinook is still a rare breed, this sled dog, with his incredible history, is alive and well today.

Chinook fanciers will tell you that their breed has the fortitude and courage typical of northern breeds combined with a personality that is atypically affectionate. He is calm, nonaggressive, and a willing and eager learner who is people-oriented. He is, however, first and foremost a working dog whose talents include sledding, pulling carts, carrying packs, search and rescue, and other physically and mentally demanding activities.

Exercise, Training, Grooming, and Health

- Consistent but moderate daily exercise, which can include a fast-paced walk, is necessary. His exercise needs should be met through participation in some kind of activity or sport.

- The smart and responsive Chinook is easily trained to do almost anything. Although he can be pushy, with clear direction and positive reinforcement he will easily master whatever his owner wants him to do.

- His double coat requires only regular brushing to keep shedding under control but otherwise takes care of itself.

- Average life span is 12 to 14 years. Breed health concerns may include cryptorchidism; epilepsy; and hip dysplasia.

Chow Chow

Breed Facts

- **Country of Origin**: China

- **Height**: Males 18–22 in (45.5–56 cm)/females 17–20 in (43–51 cm)|17–20 in (43–51 cm) [AKC][UKC]|minimum 18 in (45.5 cm) [ANKC]

- **Weight**: 45–70 lb (20.5–31.5 kg) [est.]

- **Coat**: Two types—*rough* has abundant, dense, straight and offstanding, rather coarse outercoat and soft, thick, woolly undercoat; neck ruff/*smooth* has hard, dense, smooth outercoat with definite undercoat

- **Colors**: Red, black, blue, fawn, cream|any clear, solid color [CKC]

- **Other Names**: Chow

- **Registries (With Group)**: AKC (Non-Sporting); ANKC (Non Sporting); CKC (Non-Sporting); FCI (Spitz and Primitive); KC (Utility); UKC (Northern)

History and Personality

Historians trace the Chow Chow to the 11th century BCE. He was considered a delicacy in China, where the eating of dog flesh was (and still is) common. His meat was eaten and the skin was used as clothing, but he also served gamely as draft, guard, and flock dogs. For centuries, these dogs were never seen outside of China, but today the Chow Chow is a commonly kept companion around the world. One of his most distinguishing features is his blue-black tongue, lips, and gums.

The Chow Chow tends to bond strongly to one person and is typically aloof with strangers. It is said that he will readily die for his master but not willingly obey him—he can be bossy and protective. If pushed to comply, he can become aggressive. He should be heavily socialized from puppyhood to combat his natural aloofness and protective nature.

Exercise, Training, Grooming, and Health

- Daily walks are a must to keep the Chow Chow in good shape, but he does not need much more exercise than that.

- The Chow Chow needs a trainer who can be firm and fair at the same time. He is inclined to do what he wants to do, and the temptation to be heavy-handed with him can be strong. This will lead to only more trouble, however, as the Chow Chow does not like to be pushed.

- Both types of coats have dense fur that needs regular brushing with a steel comb. They also have wrinkles around their face that need to be kept clean and dry to avoid becoming infected.

- Average life span is 13 to 15 years. Breed health concerns may include ectropion; elbow dysplasia; entropion; hip dysplasia; patellar luxation; and thyroid problems.

Breed Facts

- **Country of Origin**: Italy

- **Height**: Males 18–20 in (45.5–50 cm)/females 16.5–18 in (42–45.5 cm)

- **Weight**: Males 22–26.5 lb (10–12 kg)/females 17.5–22 lb (8–10 kg)

- **Coat**: Straight, stiff, smooth; semi-long, close lying

- **Colors**: Fawn, white; may have orange patches; white markings|also light sand, light to dark tan [KC]

- **Other Names**: Sicilian Greyhound; Sicilian Hound

- **Registries (With Group)**: AKC (FSS); FCI (Spitz and Primitive); KC (Hound); UKC (Sighthound & Pariah)

History and Personality

The Cirneco Dell'Etna has been living on Sicily for several thousand years. Dell'Etna is a reference to Mount Etna, the 10,000-foot active volcano on Sicily's eastern side, where he hunts rabbits on the terrain formed by molten lava. He is a uniquely preserved breed who has survived the centuries relatively unchanged, and his devotees are keeping it that way.

He was developed to hunt over arid terrain and to hunt hard all day, and the resilient and adaptable characteristics he needed are still alive in him today. He is said to be one of the most responsive sighthounds, devoted to and eager to please his family. He is an active and competitive participant in lure coursing and agility, both excellent showcases for his athleticism.

Exercise, Training, Grooming, and Health

- The Cirneco is curious and athletic and should be given opportunities for play or sport that allow for short bursts of energy to be used up.

- The Cirneco Dell'Etna does best with encouraging and consistent training, and socialization from an early age is beneficial.

- His short, smooth coat needs only the occasional going-over with a hound glove to keep him looking sleek and shiny.

- Average life span is 12 to 15 years. There are no reported breed-specific health concerns.

Breed Facts

- **Country of Origin**: Great Britain
- **Height**: Males 18–20 in (45.5–51 cm)/females 17–19 in (43–48 cm)
- **Weight**: Males 68.5–85 lb (31–38.5 kg)/females 55–70 lb (25–32 kg)|males 79.5 lb (36 kg)/females 65 lb (29.5 kg) [ANKC] [FCI][KC]
- **Coat**: Silky, dense, straight, flat, weather resistant
- **Colors**: Primarily white with lemon or orange markings
- **Registries (With Group)**: AKC (Sporting); ANKC (Gundogs); CKC (Sporting); FCI (Flushing Dogs); KC (Gundog); UKC (Gun Dog)

History and Personality

The Clumber Spaniel was developed in the late 1700s, most likely by a French duke who, when threatened by the Revolution in his country, moved his dogs to Nottingham, England. His family included the English Duke of Newcastle, who became smitten with this breed, used to flush and retrieve birds. It is this Duke's estate, Clumber Park, that is undoubtedly the source of the breed's name. The Clumber Spaniel has remained popular through the centuries, although not as popular as the lighter-boned, faster-working spaniels. He is an excellent hunter of game fowl, working alone or in packs.

Sweet, affectionate, and mellow as an adult, the Clumber relishes his family time. He loves to retrieve and swim, making him a great companion for children. Deeply attached to his family, he can be wary of strangers, although he is never timid or shy.

Exercise, Training, Grooming, and Health

- The Clumber enjoys being outdoors and working the fields and hedgerows where small game may be hiding. He is also equally happy with several strolls a day that allow him to stretch his legs and take in the scents around him.

- Eager and responsive, the Clumber Spaniel is easily trained.

- A heavy shedder, he needs regular brushing and combing. His abundant feathering needs to be kept neat with trimming, and the wrinkles on his face need to be kept clean to avoid infection. His large lips and cheeks cause him to drip and drool, a situation that's easily tended to with towels.

- Average life span is 10 to 12 years. Breed health concerns may include cardiomyopathy; entropion; hip dysplasia; immune mediated hemolytic anemia (IMHA); intervertebral disk disease; and retinal dysplasia.

Cocker Spaniel (American)

Breed Facts

- **Country of Origin**: United States

- **Height**: Males 15 in (38 cm)/females 14 in (35.5 cm)|males 14.5–15.5 in (37–39 cm)/females 13.5–14.5 in (34–37 cm) [FCI][KC]

- **Weight**: 15–30 lb (7–13.5 kg) [est.]

- **Coat**: Double coat with medium-length, silky, flat or slight wavy outercoat and enough undercoat for protection; ears, chest, abdomen, legs well feathered

- **Colors**: Jet black; any solid color other than black (ASCOB), ranging from lightest cream to darkest red; particolored, which is two or more solid colors, one of which must be white, including black and white, red and white, brown and white, roans|also sable [UKC]

- **Other Names**: American Cocker Spaniel

- **Registries (With Group)**: AKC (Sporting); ANKC (Gundogs); CKC (Sporting); FCI (Flushing Dogs); KC (Gundog); UKC (Gun Dog)

History and Personality

The American version of the Cocker Spaniel evolved from early spaniel imports. By the 1940s, he was much smaller and had changed fairly dramatically from his English ancestors, so the breed was given separate status from English Cocker Spaniels. In the middle of the 20th century, he was the most popular breed of dog in the United States—a position he held for many years. He achieved this because he could serve a dual purpose for many families—companion and playmate during the week, hunting dog on the weekends. With his compact size, range of colors, endearing expression, and sweet temperament, he is still a much-loved dog.

A Cocker Spaniel with a sound temperament is possibly the sweetest dog imaginable. Happy, trusting, intelligent, and gentle, with large, soulful eyes, the Cocker Spaniel is utterly endearing. Large enough to be able to share family activities as rigorous as hiking or swimming, yet small enough to be easily transported anywhere, it is no wonder he was America's top dog for so long.

Exercise, Training, Grooming, and Health

- An active, fairly energetic dog who loves to be out and about, the Cocker Spaniel needs regular exercise. Playful and smart, he loves to engage in games.

- He is easy to train and can easily shine in a full range of fun and competitive activities from obedience to agility, hunting tests, flyball, and much more. The properly trained Cocker Spaniel makes an exceptional therapy dog.

- His profuse coat needs regular attention, and owners often decide to use a professional groomer to care for him. He has large eyes and long, feathered ears—these need special attention so they don't become infected or excessively dirty.

- Average life span is 12 to 15 years. Breed health concerns may include allergies; cataracts; cherry eye; ear infections; ectropion; entropion; glaucoma; hemophilia; hip dysplasia; hypothyroidism; immune mediated hemolytic anemia (IMHA); patellar luxation; progressive retinal atrophy (PRA); and skin problems.

Cocker Spaniel (English)

Breed Facts

- **County of Origin**: England

- **Height**: Males 15.5–17 in (39–43 cm)/females 15–16 in (38–40.5 cm)

- **Weight**: Males 28–34 lb (12.5–15.5 kg)/females 26–32 lb (12–14.5 kg)|28–32 lb (12.5–14.5 kg) [ANKC][FCI][KC]

- **Coat**: Double coat is medium length, flat or slightly wavy, silky; well feathered

- **Colors**: Various—solid colors are black, liver, red shades; parti-colors are clearly marked, ticked, or roaned and include black, liver, red shades, all with white; may have tan markings

- **Other Names**: Cocker Spaniel; English Cocker Spaniel

- **Registries (With Group)**: AKC (Sporting); ANKC (Gundogs); CKC (Sporting); FCI (Flushing Dogs); KC (Gundog); UKC (Gun Dog)

History and Personality

All spaniels can be traced to their original country of Spain, where they were predominantly used to hunt game. Many believe that the breed was introduced to England as early as the time of Caesar's invasion (around 55 BCE). They gained prestige as bird dogs with a discerning talent for hunting in forests, pointing in high brush, and flushing birds out of thickets. They were also known for their impressive retrieving skills. By the early 19th century, Springer Spaniels, Sussex Spaniels, and Cocker Spaniels were all born within the same litters. The largest puppies were classified as Springers, the medium dogs were dubbed Sussex Spaniels, and the smallest puppies were considered Cockers. Size alone set the designations. In the late 1800s, type was set and the breeds were separated and no longer interbred.

The English Cocker is a jolly, agreeable dog whose tail wags almost nonstop. He is happy and even exuberant, approaching everything from bath time to hunting time as events to be excited about—as long as he's with you. This lovable and affectionate breed gets along with just about everyone.

Exercise, Training, Grooming, and Health

- The merry English Cocker is a socialite who loves his walks, and he is also a hunter who will thrive on excursions to places where he can rustle up some bird scent. An adept swimmer and retriever, the English Cocker Spaniel will also gamely retrieve tennis balls along the shore.

- Responsive, intelligent, eager, and with a strong desire to please, the English Cocker is a joy to train and truly thrives with it.

- His fine, silky fur—particularly the feathering—needs regular brushing to keep him looking his best. His long, heavy ears lay close to his head, which makes them prone to infection. They must be tended to almost daily.

- Average life span is 12 to 15 years. Breed health concerns may include ear problems; familial nephropathy; hip dysplasia; and progressive retinal atrophy (PRA).

Breed Facts

- **Country of Origin**: Great Britain

- **Varieties**: Rough and Smooth

- **Height**: Males 22–26 in (56–66 cm)/females 20–24 in (51–61 cm)

- **Weight**: Males 45–75 lb (20.5–34 kg)/females 40–65 lb (18–29.5 kg)

- **Coat**: *Rough*: Double coat with harsh, straight outercoat and soft, furry, close undercoat/*Smooth*: Double coat with short, hard, dense, flat outercoat and dense, soft, furry undercoat

- **Colors**: Sable and white, tricolor (black with rich tan markings), blue merle and white; may have white, tan markings|also white [CKC][UKC]

- **Other Names**: Rough Collie; Scotch Collie; Scottish Collie; Smooth Collie; Smooth-haired Collie

- **Registries (With Group)**: AKC (Herding); ANKC (Working); CKC (Herding); FCI (Sheepdogs); KC (Pastoral); UKC (Herding)

History and Personality

Developed centuries ago as hardworking herding and guarding dogs in Scotland and northern England, it is believed his name "Collie" came from the Scottish black-faced sheep—Colleys—the breed was assigned to watch. Collies come in two varieties: Rough and Smooth, differentiated by their coat type. Smooth Collies are much more popular in the United Kingdom than the Rough variety. In the United States, however, the Rough Collie is more popular due to the success of the long-running television show *Lassie*, which starred a Rough Collie.

Intelligent, kind-hearted, and noble, Collies are renowned for their loyalty and bravery. Often described as being able to read their owner's minds, they provide unwavering love and devotion. Collies are easy to train and sociable with children and other pets. They will bark to alert their owners of anyone (human or animal) approaching the property.

Exercise, Training, Grooming, and Health

- The Collie is a breed who benefits tremendously from plenty of exercise—long walks, romps in the woods, and any opportunity to work as a herding or guardian dog.

- The Collie is a joy to train when approached in the proper way, which is with a positive and respectful manner. He will shut down if treated harshly.

- The Rough Collies has a profuse coat that needs regular brushing and combing. The Smooth Collie's fur is shorter but he also needs regular brushing. Collies are seasonally heavy shedders.

- Average life span is 14 to 16 years. Breed health concerns may include Collie eye anomaly; Collie nose; hip dysplasia; and progressive retinal atrophy (PRA).

Breed Facts

- **Country of Origin**: Madagascar
- **Height**: Males 10–11.5 in (26–28 cm)/females 9–10 in (23–25 cm)|10–12.5 in (25–32 cm) [KC]
- **Weight**: Males 9–13 lb (4–6 kg)/females 8–11 lb (3.5–5 kg)
- **Coat**: Single coat is soft, supple, dense, profuse; texture of cotton; can be slightly wavy
- **Colors**: White ground color|also black; gray, yellow, tricolor, white markings [AKC]
- **Other Names**: Coton de Tuléar
- **Registries (With Group)**: AKC (FSS); CKC (Toys); FCI (Companion and Toy); KC (Toy); UKC (Companion)

History and Personality

Tuléar is a wealthy area on the island of Madagascar off the coast of Africa, where small, white dogs lived as favored companions with the residents for centuries. A Bichon-type dog, it is believed he arrived on Madagascar with Spanish and Portuguese sailors in the 16th century. He was little known outside of Madagascar until the 20th century.

Sociable and cute, his gentle, affectionate nature makes him a real charmer. He gets along well with children and other animals and bonds strongly to his family—he does not like to be left alone. He is adept at dancing on his hind legs and can easily learn to perform this trick.

Exercise, Training, Grooming, and Health

- The Coton will get his exercise accompanying his family members around the house and on whatever walks or outings they care to take.

- Although solicitous and eager to please, the Coton has a stubborn, independent streak and is not a pushover. He will learn almost anything quickly if asked in a positive and encouraging way.

- His human-like hair needs the kind of daily attention that we give ours: regular brushing and combing to keep it knot- and tangle-free. A pin brush without balls on the end is recommended so as not to tear the coat. He sheds only minimally, and like other Bichon-type breeds, is a good choice for many allergy sufferers.

- Average life span is 14 to 18 years. There are no reported breed-specific health concerns.

Curly-Coated Retriever

Breed Facts

- **Country of Origin**: Great Britain

- **Height**: Males 27 in (69 cm)/females 25 in (63.5 cm)|males 25–27 in (63.5–68.5 cm)/females 23–25 in (58.5–63.5 cm) [AKC]

- **Weight**: 65–80 lb (29.5–36.5 kg) [est.]

- **Coat**: Single coat is water resistant and has small, tight, crisp, close-lying curls

- **Colors**: Black or liver

- **Other Names**: Curly Coated Retriever

- **Registries (With Group)**: AKC (Sporting); ANKC (Gundogs); CKC (Sporting); FCI (Retrievers); KC (Gundog); UKC (Gun Dog)

History and Personality

This staunch and steady retriever was developed in Great Britain in the early 1800s as an exceptional retriever with a soft mouth. He is especially popular in Australia and New Zealand, where he is treasured as a fine hunting companion and gun dog with a particular talent for quail and waterfowl. His distinctive coat is waterproof and self-drying—definite pluses in areas where such game reside.

Easy to get along with but also with a playful, sometimes mischievous personality, the Curly-Coated Retriever may not be as tractable as some of his retrieving cousins, but he has a lot of talent. He is in his element in the water; an active, outdoor-oriented family companion who thrives with attention and training.

Exercise, Training, Grooming, and Health

- This breed requires a large amount of exercise. The big, sporty Curly also needs and relishes his outdoor time, especially if it involves swimming.

- The Curly-Coated Retriever is an intelligent dog who wants to work and as such needs to be trained and worked with to keep him mentally sharp.

- His curly coat is fairly easy to care for. Brushing and combing will make it frizz but is necessary to remove dead hairs. After brushing, curls can be tightened by wetting them. His distinctive coat is waterproof and self-drying.

- Average life span is 10 to 12 years. Breed health concerns may include bloat; cardiac problems; Curly Coat Problem; epilepsy; eye problems; glycogen storage disease (GSD); and hip dysplasia.

Czechoslovakian Vlcak

Breed Facts

- **Country of Origin**: Czech Republic

- **Height**: Males at least 25.5 in (65 cm)/females at least 23.5 in (60 cm)|males 25.5 in (65 cm)/females 23.5 in (60 cm) [UKC]

- **Weight**: Males at least 57 lb (26 kg)/females at least 44 lb (20 kg)

- **Coat**: Straight, close; undercoat present in winter

- **Colors**: Yellowish-gray to silver-gray, dark gray; light mask|gray, not dark gray [AKC]

- **Other Names**: Ceskoslovenský Vlcak; Czechoslovakian Wolfdog; Czech Wolfdog

- **Registries (With Group)**: AKC (FSS); FCI (Sheepdogs); UKC (Herding)

History and Personality

As his name states, the Czechoslovakian Vlcak, or Czechoslovakian Wolfdog, is indeed part dog and part wolf. It is the recognized breeding effort of some 30 years of experimentation in the Czech Socialist Republic (CSSR) (now the Czech Republic) that began with the breeding of German Shepherds Dog and Carpathian wolves. He looks like a wolf but is tall and lightly built. He will not gaze back at people the way most dogs will; rather, he keeps an eye on his surroundings, yet he is always 100 percent aware of where his master or family is.

Fearless and courageous, with a highly tuned ability to distinguish between behavior that's dangerous and not, he is a great watchdog and is tremendously loyal. He is reserved around strangers and not trustworthy with other pets. It is important to begin training early, and socialization throughout his life is a must.

Exercise, Training, Grooming, and Health

- Retaining strong instincts for the outdoors, including a propensity for tracking, the Czechoslovakian Vlcak needs his outdoor time.

- It is important to begin training a Czechoslovakian Vlcak as a young puppy. He is intelligent and learns quickly and needs training that both motivates and challenges him, as he is quickly bored with rote instructions or expectations.

- Clean and odorless, he needs little grooming outside of his seasonal periods of heavy shedding.

- Average life span is 13 to 16 years. Breed health concerns may include hip dysplasia.

Dachshund

Breed Facts

- **Country of Origin**: Germany

- **Varieties**: *Size*—Standard, Miniature/*Coat*—Longhaired, Smooth, Wirehaired

- **Height**: *Standard*—14–18 in (35–45.5 cm) [est.]|chest circumference 14 in (35 cm) [FCI]/*miniature*—up to 14 in (35 cm) [est.]|chest circumference 12–14 in (30–35 cm) [FCI]

- **Weight**: Males 18 lb (8 kg)/females 17 lb (7.5 kg) [ANKC]/*standard*—16–32 lb (7.5–14.5 kg)|over 11 lb (5 kg) [CKC]|up to 20 lb (9 kg) [FCI]/*miniature*—up to 11 lb (5 kg)|ideal 10 lb (4.5 kg) [ANKC][CKC]|11 lb (5 kg) [KC]

- **Coat**: *Longhaired*: Double coat with sleek, soft, glistening, straight or slightly wavy outercoat/*Smooth*: Short, dense, shiny, smooth fitting/*Wirehaired*: Double coat with uniform short, thick, harsh outercoat and finer, shorter-haired undercoat; beard

- **Colors**: *Longhaired*: One-colored—red, cream/two-colored—
  black, chocolate, wild boar, gray, fawn, all with tan or cream
  markings/dappled [AKC]|black and tan, dark brown, dark
  red, light red, dappled, tiger-marked, brindle [ANKC]|solid
  red, black with tan points, chocolate [CKC]|one-colored—red,
  red-yellow, yellow/two-colored—deep black, brown, gray (not
  FCI), white (not FCI) with brown or yellow markings/dappled
  [FCI][UKC]|all colors allowed except white [KC]/*Smooth*:
  One-colored—red, cream/two-colored—black, chocolate,
  wild boar, gray, fawn, all with tan or cream markings/dappled
  [AKC]|all colors allowed except white [ANKC][KC]|solid
  red, black with tan points, chocolate [CKC]|one-colored—red,
  red-yellow, yellow/two-colored—deep black, brown, gray
  (not FCI), white (not FCI) with brown or yellow markings/
  dappled [FCI][UKC]/*Wirehaired*: One-colored—red,
  cream/two-colored—black, chocolate, wild boar, gray, fawn,
  all with tan or cream markings/dappled [AKC]|all colors
  allowed [ANKC]|solid red, black with tan points, chocolate
  [CKC]|one-colored—red, red-yellow, yellow/two-colored—
  deep black, brown, gray (not FCI), white (not FCI) with

Continued on next page

brown or yellow markings/dappled/also wild boar and dry leaves (FCI)[FCI][UKC]|all colors allowed except white [KC]

- **Other Names**: Dackel; Normalgrösse (Standard); Normalschlag (Standard); Teckel; Zwerg (Miniature); Zwergteckel (Miniature)

- **Registries (With Group)**: AKC (Hound); ANKC (Hounds); CKC (Hounds); FCI (Dachshunds); KC (Hound); UKC (Scenthound)

History and Personality

The Dachshund was developed in Germany to be a close hunter. They are descended from the German schweisshund, of which they are a shorter-legged version. He is a true hunting hound and has been helping hunters and families since the Middle Ages, doing everything from tracking and going to ground for game to protecting the homestead.

Lively, alert, comic, and kind, the Dachshund is a companion who may be short of leg but is not short of personality. When threatened or suspicious, he is a great protector of his family, whom he loves. Most of all, he is known as a versatile and charming pet, as comfortable in a big-city apartment as he is in a rural environment.

Exercise, Training, Grooming, and Health

- The Dachshund is an active and inquisitive hound who needs several daily walks—preferably long but not strenuous ones.

- Dachshunds are scenthounds and therefore easily distracted by scents all around them, and they can seem unresponsive to training.

- The Longhaired's fine fur can knot and mat if not brushed regularly. The Smooth's coat is the easiest to care for—a quick going-over with a hound glove, soft brush, and damp cloth will leave him sleek and shiny. The Wirehaired needs the most grooming attention, as the coarse hairs must be trimmed and kept neat, ideally by a professional groomer.

- Average life span is 12 to 14 years. Breed health concerns may include Cushing's syndrome; dental disease; epilepsy; hypothyroidism; invertebral disk disease; and patellar luxation.

Dalmatian

Breed Facts

- **Country of Origin**: Croatia (formerly Yugoslavia)

- **Height**: Males 22–24 in (56–61 cm)/females 21–23 in (54–59 cm)|19–23 in (48–58.5 cm) [AKC][UKC]

- **Weight**: Males 59.5–70.5 lb (27–32 kg)/females 53–64 lb (24–29 kg)

- **Coat**: Short, sleek, glossy, hard, dense

- **Colors**: Pure white ground color with black or liver-colored spots

- **Other Names**: Dalmatinac; Dalmatiner

- **Registries (With Group)**: AKC (Non-Sporting); ANKC (Non Sporting); CKC (Non-Sporting); FCI (Scenthounds); KC (Utility); UKC (Companion)

History and Personality

This unique breed's history is full of legend as to his true origin and purpose. Whatever his origin, the spotted dog who works with horses has been known in Europe since the Middle Ages. He also became known especially for his presence in fire stations with horse-drawn water wagons. He would often run ahead barking to clear the streets for the firemen. This working tradition continued in the United States, where for years nearly every firehouse had a Dalmatian as a mascot.

He is a dog with a great deal of energy and enthusiasm, and his almost relentless joie de vivre can be frustrating to those who can't manage it. For those who can, he is a loyal and loving athletic companion. He needs socialization and positive training to feel most comfortable around children and other animals.

Exercise, Training, Grooming, and Health

- Dalmatians are high-energy dogs who need regular exercise several times a day. They are great jogging and hiking companions.

- If motivated properly, Dalmatians are quick and capable learners. Their independent nature, however, makes them selective about where they put their attention, and it's not always on the trainer. Consistency and patience are necessary for best results.

- His short coat sheds regularly, and he needs to be brushed and curry-combed often.

- Average life span is 11 to 13 years. Breed health concerns may include congenital deafness; epilepsy; hip dysplasia; hypothyroidism; skin problems and allergies; and urolithiasis.

Dandie Dinmont Terrier

Breed Facts

- **Country of Origin**: Great Britain

- **Height**: 8–11 in (20–28 cm)

- **Weight**: 18–24 lb (8–11 kg)

- **Coat**: Double coat with approx. 2-inch-long (5-cm-long) crisp, hard outercoat and soft, linty undercoat

- **Colors**: Pepper (ranges from dark bluish black to light silvery gray) and mustard (varies from a reddish brown to pale fawn)

- **Registries (With Group)**: AKC (Terrier); ANKC (Terriers); CKC (Terriers); FCI (Terriers); KC (Terrier); UKC (Terrier)

History and Personality

The Dandie Dinmont Terrier hails from the Scottish-English border country and stems from the same stock as the Border,

Lakeland, Bedlington, and Welsh Terriers. He was developed as far back as the 1600s as a specialist for otters and badgers.

An affectionate and at times silly dog, the Dandie can also be willful and standoffish. He is reserved with strangers and protective of his home. He can be plucky and determined, and he is intelligent. He won't tolerate ill-behaved children, but those who are kind will be accepted and loved. Socialization is important from puppyhood to help the Dandie Dinmont feel comfortable with people and other animals. If he doesn't get it, he can be aggressive or overly shy.

Exercise, Training, Grooming, and Health

- The Dandie has moderate exercise requirements—a few walks a day and some playtime are all he needs.

- The independent-minded Dandie Dinmont responds best to positive, motivational training.

- If you want your Dandie to look like a show dog, he will need professional grooming. The combination of soft and coarse hairs must be balanced and professionally maintained. The distinctive look of his face is best left to a professional to achieve.

- Average life span is 12 to 15 years. Breed health concerns may include back problems; epilepsy; glaucoma; hypothyroidism; and primary lens luxation.

Doberman Pinscher

Breed Facts

- **Country of Origin**: Germany

- **Height**: Males 26–28.5 in (66–72 cm)/females 24–27 in (61–69 cm)

- **Weight**: Males 88–99 lb (40–45 kg)/females 70.5–77 lb (32–35 kg)

- **Coat**: Smooth, short, hard, thick, close lying; imperceptible undercoat on neck acceptable|undercoat not allowed [FCI]

- **Colors**: Black; rust markings|also red, blue, fawn; rust markings [AKC][CKC][UKC]|also brown, blue, fawn; rust markings [ANKC][KC]|black and brown only; rust markings [FCI]

- **Other Names**: Dobermann

- **Registries (With Group)**: AKC (Working); ANKC (Utility); CKC (Working); FCI (Pinscher and Schnauzer); KC (Working); UKC (Guardian)

History and Personality

Karl Friedrich Louis Dobermann was a tax collector who worked in a dangerous area and needed a tough, smart, and reliable protection dog. Herr Dobermann bred a lean, mean, fighting machine—a dog whom others described as requiring a good deal of courage to own. He has excelled in all aspects of service to humankind, including search and rescue, therapy, police dog work, guide work for the blind, and much more, as breeders have moved away from breeding for ferocity.

Today's well-bred Doberman is intelligent and loyal, as playful as the original was intimidating. They are athletic and powerful, light footed and aristocratic. Versatility is still a noble characteristic of this breed. He will live peacefully with small animals and children if socialized to them from an early age.

Exercise, Training, Grooming, and Health

- The Doberman needs a good deal of exercise to expend energy and stay in shape, but he is as happy getting it from playing a game of chase or hide-and-seek as going for training sessions on the end of a leash.

- The responsive, alert, highly trainable Doberman is eager to learn and please. He needs a fair leader—one who will encourage his abilities while setting firm limits.

- His sleek, shiny coat is easy to care for—a soft brush and hound glove are all he needs.

- Average life span is 10 to 12 years. Breed health concerns may include bloat; cancer; chronic hepatitis; color dilution alopecia; dilated cardiomyopathy (DCM); hypothyroidism; von Willebrand disease; and Wobbler's syndrome.

Breed Facts

- **Country of Origin**: France

- **Height**: Males 23.5–27 in (60–68.5 cm)/females 22.5–26 in (57–66 cm)

- **Weight**: Males at least 110 lb (50 kg)/females at least 99 lb (45 kg)

- **Coat**: Fine, short, soft

- **Colors**: Self-colored in all shades of fawn; may have white markings; may have black or brown mask

- **Other Names**: Bordeaux Bulldog; Bordeaux Dog; Bordeaux Mastiff; French Mastiff

- **Registries (With Group)**: AKC (Working); ANKC (Utility); FCI (Molossoid); KC (Working); UKC (Guardian)

History and Personality

The Dogue de Bordeaux is closely related to the Mastiff from Asia and the Molossus who made the trek to Gaul from the Roman arenas. Originally a dual-purpose war dog guarding flocks from wolves and bears when not in battle, soon he was being fighting in pits, where occasionally, a dull match was livened up by tossing a jaguar into the pit with the dogs. Near the end of the Middle Ages he went to work as a cattle drover, and later as a guardian of estates.

This large, slobbery dog certainly has some of the personality of a teddy bear, and this side of him should be nurtured, but he is also a formidable animal with a pronounced jaw and powerful build who is capable of inflicting great harm even inadvertently. He is aggressive toward other dogs. He must be socialized from an early age, and he must be worked with despite his size and seeming disinterest.

Exercise, Training, Grooming, and Health

- The Dogue de Bordeaux needs regular exercise. His rolling gait won't get him places particularly quickly, but as long as he is moving along, he is benefiting from the effort.

- The Dogue de Bordeaux needs firm training from someone he can respect—and that's a tricky combination.

- His coat is easy to care for with simple brushing, but his head can be a bit more difficult. The wrinkles are the sources of potential infection if they're not kept clean. A thorough going-over with a clean cloth several times a week will bring any problems to light.

- Average life span is 8 to 12 years. Breed health concerns may include bloat; elbow and hip dysplasia; heart problems; hypothyroidism; panosteitis; and skin problems.

English Foxhound

Breed Facts

- **Country of Origin**: England
- **Height**: 23–25 in (58–64 cm)
- **Weight**: 65–70 lb (29.5–31.5 kg) [est.]
- **Coat**: Short, hard, glossy, dense, weatherproof
- **Colors**: Any recognized hound color and markings|black, tan, white, any combination of these colors, "pies" comprising white and various colors of the hare and badger (or yellow) and tan [AKC][CKC][UKC]
- **Other Names**: Foxhound
- **Registries (With Group)**: AKC (Hound); ANKC (Hounds); CKC (Hounds); FCI (Scenthounds); KC (Hound); UKC (Scenthound)

History and Personality

When foxhunting became the rage in England in the 13th century, a hound was needed specifically for trailing the fast and wily red fox. The Foxhound is followed by mounted horsemen, and the dog must be fast, with tremendous endurance, good voice, drive, and enthusiasm. For many years, each hunt developed its own style of hound, and type was inconsistent. But by 1800, many large standardized packs existed, and the meticulous records kept by each individual estate's Master of Hounds were incorporated in the Masters of Foxhounds Association (MFHA), to which most English Foxhounds can trace their pedigrees back over 150 years.

He is a noble fellow who epitomizes his purpose as a hunter. Pack hounds are so active, athletic, and scent-driven that they can have a tough time transitioning to home and hearth, but he gets along well with other dogs and is a gentle and affectionate dog.

Exercise, Training, Grooming, and Health

- English Foxhounds who are born into hunting packs demand the exercise that the hunt provides for them. Those bred for show and companionship still need to have their strong desire for hunting in the great outdoors satisfied, along with plenty of exercise.

- Because the English Foxhound is pack-oriented and scent-driven, obedience training is often secondary to his own instincts.

- The always dapper-looking English Foxhound is easy to keep clean with occasional brushing.

- Average life span is 9 to 11 years. There are no reported breed-specific health concerns.

Breed Facts

- **Country of Origin**: England
- **Height**: Males 25–27 in (63.5–69 cm)/females 24–25.5 in (61–65 cm)
- **Weight**: Males 55–70 lb (25–31.5 kg)/females 50–60 lb (22.5–27 kg)
- **Coat**: Long, flat, silky; feathering
- **Colors**: Black and white (blue belton), orange and white (orange belton), lemon and white (lemon belton), liver and white (liver belton), tricolor (blue belton with tan markings)|also solid white [CKC][UKC]
- **Registries (With Group)**: AKC (Sporting); ANKC (Gundogs); CKC (Sporting); FCI (Pointing Dogs); KC (Gundog); UKC (Gun Dog)

History and Personality

Setters derived from early couching and hawking dogs used throughout Great Britain. The name "setter" comes from this breed's style of hunting: They creep up on their prey slow and catlike, then set into the point, even sinking a bit in the shoulders as they do so. The development of what we know as the modern English Setter included two breed lines, one bred mainly for appearance, the other for hunting skills. Today he still shows variation in show and field types, but breeders of the show type are interested in hunting ability and are becoming more and more active in hunting tests and field trials, where this fast and able sporting dog can bring up birds with the best of them.

Placid, mild-mannered, and friendly, the English Setter loves affection and is eager to return it. Children are among his favorite playmates. His enthusiasm comes out when he's playing or hunting or going for a favorite walk, but he quickly settles down once back inside, making him a suitable housedog.

Exercise, Training, Grooming, and Health

- Quiet indoors yet playful and boisterous outdoors, the English Setter loves his time spent on long walks and country— or town—outings.

- The English Setter is eager to please but needs a gentle trainer, as he does not respond well to heavy-handed techniques.

- His long, feathered coat needs regular brushing to keep it tangle- and dirt-free. His ears should be checked regularly to stave off infection.

- Average life span is 10 to 12 years. Breed health concerns may include blindness; ear infections; and hip dysplasia.

Breed Facts

- **Country of Origin**: Great Britain

- **Height**: Males 20 in (51 cm)/females 19 in (48.5 cm)|20 in (51 cm) [ANKC][FCI][KC]

- **Weight**: Males 50 lb (22.5 kg)/females 40 lb (18 kg)|40–50 lb (18–22.5 kg) [UKC]|dependent on other dimensions [CKC]

- **Coat**: Double coat with medium-length, straight, weather-resistant outercoat; moderate feathering and short, soft, dense undercoat|also wavy coat [AKC][CKC][UKC]

- **Colors**: Black and white, liver and white, tricolor (liver and white or black and white with tan markings)|also blue or liver roan [AKC][CKC][UKC]

- **Registries (With Group)**: AKC (Sporting); ANKC (Gundogs); CKC (Sporting); FCI (Flushing Dogs); KC (Gundog); UKC (Gun Dog)

History and Personality

British flushing spaniels were often called "springing" spaniels, since they were used to "spring" the game from the cover. These dogs were separated by size, even those born in the same litter. The smallest were the Cockers, the medium-sized were the Fields, and the largest were the Springers. This variety of spaniel sizes led to much confusion—the same dog could be registered as a "field" one year and a "springer" the next as he grew in size. Eventually, in the late 1800s, the breeds were completely separated and there was a ban on interbreeding. Although they are considered the same breed, there are two types of English Springer today: the field variety and the show variety. The field type is bred to be a higher-energy working dog with more white coloring. The show type is stockier and flashier, with more liver or black coloring.

The typical English Springer Spaniel is merry, affectionate, playful, and an all-around lovable dog. He is intelligent and even-tempered, a quick learner, and a respectful partner. He loves to swim and is attracted to water, whether it's a lake or a mud puddle. Because he bonds so strongly with his family, he sometimes has a hard time being left alone and can develop a nuisance barking problem.

Exercise, Training, Grooming, and Health

- The more exercise the Springer gets, the better. Several brisk walks a day are necessary to keep him physically and mentally satisfied.

- Springers want to do what you ask, and they catch on fast to training.

- His fine coat needs regular brushing and attention. The feathering on his ears and extremities needs to be kept clean and free of knots and tangles.

- Average life span is 12 to 14 years. Breed health concerns may include ear infections; epilepsy; hip dysplasia; phosphofructokinase (PFK) deficiency; and progressive retinal atrophy (PRA).

English Toy Spaniel

Breed Facts

- **Country of Origin**: Great Britain

- **Height**: Approx. 10 in (25.5 cm) [est.]

- **Weight**: 8–14 lb (3.5–6.5 kg)

- **Coat**: Profuse, long, straight or slightly wavy, silky, glossy; heavy fringing and feathering; mane

- **Colors**: Blenheim (red and white), Prince Charles (tricolor: white, black, and tan), King Charles (black and tan), Ruby (rich mahogany red)

- **Other Names**: King Charles Spaniel

- **Registries (With Group)**: AKC (Toy); ANKC (Toys); CKC (Toys); FCI (Companion and Toy); KC (Toy); UKC (Companion)

History and Personality

Ever since there were spaniels, toy versions have curled up in laps and warmed hearts. At first these tiny companions were basically miniaturized gun dogs. It wasn't until the 19th century that the shortened muzzle, domed head, and prominent eyes recognizable as breed characteristics today started to become desirable. Called simply "comforters" for many years, these toy spaniels were not only exceptional companions but foot- and hand warmers, too! King Charles II was very fond of them and lent his name to the little dogs—King Charles Spaniels, and they are still known by that name, except in North America, where they are called English Toy Spaniels.

Nicknamed "Charlie," he shares his bigger namesakes' endearing qualities: an exuberance about life, a truly affectionate nature, and a passion for his people. He is naturally well behaved, quiet, and not too demanding for a toy dog, although it is important for him to be with and around people. He is playful and loves to cavort with people of all ages.

Exercise, Training, Grooming, and Health

- Being a sociable fellow, the English Toy Spaniel appreciates and looks forward to his outings, although scampering about underfoot suits him fine, too.

- Charlies are naturally well behaved and are good listeners, too, so they pose few training problems—except for housetraining, which can be a challenge.

- His fine, silky coat and featherings nearly reach the ground and needs to be brushed frequently. The folds of skin around his nose, mouth, and eyes need careful attention as well, since these warm, moist spots harbor infection.

- Average life span is 10 to 12 years. Breed health concerns may include cataracts; ear infections; glaucoma; mitral valve disease (MVD); patellar luxation; and patent ductus arteriosis (PDA).

Entlebucher Mountain Dog

Breed Facts

- **Country of Origin**: Switzerland

- **Height**: Males 17.5–19.5 in (44–50 cm)/females 16.5–19 in (42–48 cm)/15.5–19 in (40–50 cm) [CKC][UKC]

- **Weight**: 55–65 lb (25–29.5 kg)

- **Coat**: Double coat with short, close-fitting, harsh, shiny outercoat and dense undercoat

- **Colors**: Tricolor (black, white, and tan; black, white, and yellow); brown, white, yellow markings|also solid black [AKC]

- **Other Names**: Entelbuch Mountain Dog; Entelbucher Cattle Dog; Entlebucher; Entlebucher Mountain Dog; Entlebuch Cattle Dog; Entlebuch Mountain Dog; Entlebucher Sennenhund

- **Registries (With Group)**: AKC (FSS); CKC (Working); FCI (Swiss Mountain and Cattle Dogs); KC (Working); UKC (Guardian)

History and Personality

The Entlebucher Mountain Dog is the smallest of the four Swiss Mountain dogs, which also include the Appenzeller Sennenhunde, Bernese Mountain Dog, and Greater Swiss Mountain Dog. Originating from the valley of Entlebuch in Switzerland, he was used to drive cattle to market. The breed developed slowly over the years and retains a modest following in his home country, where he is admired for his utility and companionability.

Entlebuchers are a protective but not aggressive breed. Courageous and alert, they maintain a cheerful disposition and make a good family dog. Although they are independent and self-confident, they are also loyal and highly tuned in to their owners. They love people and are friendly with other dogs and animals.

Exercise, Training, Grooming, and Health

- The sturdy Entlebucher enjoys exercising while doing a job, such as pulling a cart or training for a sport. He thrives in the great outdoors, enjoying anything from long hikes to city strolls.

- The Entlebucher is tuned in to his family and gladly takes on opportunities to learn through training. He is highly intelligent and learns quickly, but his independent streak means that he needs a good leader and consistent training.

- He is an easy keeper with a coat that needs little more than the occasional brushing. He sheds but not profusely.

- Average life span is 10 to 12 years. Breed health concerns may include hip dysplasia and progressive retinal atrophy (PRA).

Estrela Mountain Dog

Breed Facts

- **Country of Origin**: Portugal
- **Height**: Males 23.5–28.5 in (65–72 cm)/females 24.5–27 in (62–68 cm)
- **Weight**: Males 88–110 lb (40–50 kg)/females 66–88 lb (30–40 kg)
- **Coat**: Two varieties—*long coat* has flat or slightly waved, slightly coarse, thick, close-lying outercoat and dense undercoat; feathering; ruff/*short coat* has short, slightly coarse, thick outercoat and shorter, dense undercoat
- **Colors**: Brindle, fawn, wolf gray, yellow; white markings; dark mask
- **Other Names**: Cão da Serra da Estrela; Serra da Estrela Mountain Dog
- **Registries (With Group)**: AKC (FSS); FCI (Molossoid); KC (Pastoral); UKC (Guardian)

History and Personality

The Estrela range in central Portugal is where this ancient breed originated. Shepherds would move flocks of sheep from the high Estrela plains, where they grazed in the summer, to the lower elevations from October to March. These Portuguese sheep herders, like those in Spain, followed the same routes for centuries and were always accompanied by flock-guarding dogs. Occasionally, a wealthy landowner would confiscate some of the dogs to use as estate guard dogs. These dogs tended to be larger, and as the flocks and that way of life diminished, the larger dogs prevailed to sustain the line. In the 1930s, the first official breed standard was written for the Estrela Mountain Dog.

A large, athletic dog, the Estrela Mountain Dog is a formidable opponent for any predator. He is calm but fearless and will not hesitate to react to danger, making him an exceptional watchdog. He is intelligent, loyal, and faithful, affectionate to those he knows but wary of those he doesn't. He is instinctively protective of any children in his family. He needs early and continued socialization to be trustworthy around small pets and other dogs.

Exercise, Training, Grooming, and Health

- The Estrela benefits from having a job he can take seriously—preferably one that involves patrolling the outdoors. Without this, he should be exercised through long walks and training for a sport.

- It's important to begin training and socializing the Estrela from puppyhood to nurture his acceptance of different situations. The Estrela is an independent-minded breed and will need persistent training and consistent leadership.

- Both the smooth and long coats have thick fur and shed quite a bit. They need frequent brushing, at least once a week, to keep it under control.

- Average life span is 10 to 14 years. Breed health concerns may include elbow dysplasia and hip dysplasia.

Eurasier

Breed Facts

- **Country of Origin**: Germany
- **Height**: Males 20.5–23.5 in (52–60 cm)/females 19–22 in (48–56 cm)
- **Weight**: Males 50.5–70.5 lb (23–32 kg)/females 39.5–57.5 lb (18–26 kg)
- **Coat**: Double coat with medium-length, harsh, loosely lying outercoat and thick undercoat
- **Colors**: All colors and color combinations except pure white, white patches, liver color|only black, fawn, red, sable, wolf gray; black markings [AKC]
- **Other Names**: Eurasian
- **Registries (With Group)**: AKC (FSS); ANKC (Non Sporting); CKC (Working); FCI (Spitz and Primitive); KC (Utility); UKC (Northern)

History and Personality

The Eurasier is a modern breed developed in the 1960s. Julius Wipfel of Weinheim, Germany, wanted a large and distinctive spitz-type dog who retained the intelligence, independence, and beautiful colors of a typical spitz but with a mellower and more even-tempered character. He started with German Wolfspitz crossed with Chow Chows and later crossed in the Samoyed for his friendly nature and vigor. He is popular in many parts of Europe although is little known outside it.

He is an intelligent, even-tempered, friendly, and calm dog who is instinctively watchful and alert. He is not timid, nor is he aggressive, but he is aloof with strangers. However, with his own family, he's affectionate, loving, and loyal.

Exercise, Training, Grooming, and Health

- The Eurasier was bred to be a family pet and doesn't need copious amounts of exercise, but he does need daily walks and play time to satisfy his needs.

- The Eurasier does not respond well to harsh training methods. He needs a fair, firm, confident leader. Early socialization is required to help combat his watchdog instincts.

- His thick coat should be brushed weekly to keep it from becoming matted and coarse.

- Average life span is 10 to 13 years. There are no reported breed-specific health concerns.

Field Spaniel

Breed Facts

- **Country of Origin**: Great Britain

- **Height**: 18 in (45.5 cm)|males 18 in (45.5 cm)/females 17 in (43 cm) [AKC]

- **Weight**: 35–55 lb (16–25 kg)

- **Coat**: Single coat is moderately long, flat or slightly wavy, silky, glossy, dense, water repellent; moderate feathering

- **Colors**: Black, liver, roan; may have white or tan markings|also golden liver [AKC][CKC][UKC]

- **Registries (With Group)**: AKC (Sporting); ANKC (Gundogs); CKC (Sporting); FCI (Flushing Dogs); KC (Gundog); UKC (Gun Dog)

History and Personality

Early Field Spaniels were a product of larger-size black Cocker Spaniels and various strains of Sussex Spaniels, among others. Overbreeding in the late 1800s caused structrual and health problems in the breed, and almost as quickly as its star rose, it began to fall. Dedicated breeders returned to moderation on all fronts with the Field Spaniel in the 1920s, and their efforts have carried through and sustained the breed.

He's among the rarest of the spaniels, and those who know him say that he's probably the sweetest as well. Mild-mannered and affectionate, he is an easygoing although ready-for-anything companion who has fine hunting instincts paired with a real love of family.

Exercise, Training, Grooming, and Health

- The Field Spaniel does best with regular and often vigorous exercise.

- Responsive and eager to please, the Field Spaniel is a dog who takes well to positive training. He is sensitive, and a harsh tone can backfire on him. When he's inspired, however, he can do almost anything.

- His coat has some feathering that needs special care and should be brushed and combed to look its best.

- Average life span is 10 to 12 years. Breed health concerns may include ear infections; hip dysplasia; and thyroid problems.

Finnish Lapphund

Breed Facts

- **Country of Origin**: Finland

- **Height**: Males 18–20.5 in (45.5–52 cm)/females 16–18.5 in (40.5–47 cm)

- **Weight**: 33–53 lb (15–24 kg) [est.]

- **Coat**: Double coat with profuse straight, long, coarse outercoat and soft, dense undercoat; males, especially, have abundant mane

- **Colors**: All colors permitted; may have markings|only black, blonde, brown, golden, sable tan, white, all with black, cream, gold, tan, gray, white, white and tan markings; black saddle [AKC]

- **Other Names**: Lapinkoira; Lapponian Shepherd Dog; Suomenlapinkoira

- **Registries (With Group)**: AKC (FSS); ANKC (Working); CKC (Herding); FCI (Spitz and Primitive); KC (Pastoral); UKC (Northern)

History and Personality

The Finnish Lapphund is closely related to the Swedish Lapphund, both spitz-type dogs who originated in Lapland, an area that includes parts of northern Norway, Sweden, Finland, and northwestern Russia. They were used by the semi-nomadic Sami tribe, who lived in the region, to hunt reindeer and for protection. When the tribes began to settle, the function of these dogs changed from hunting to herding reindeer, and they were used that way for centuries, until the need for reindeer herding began to disappear. Today, he can still be found at work, although mostly he is a prized companion. He is one of the most popular breeds in Finland, and his popularity is on the rise around the world.

A herder at heart, the Lapphund likes to keep his family (and anything else he can herd) together. He is versatile, eager to please, and a quick learner. With his courageous, affectionate, intelligent, and amenable nature, it is no wonder he is among the most popular of breeds in Finland. He is sensitive to the needs of his owners and often picks up on what's expected of him without direction.

Exercise, Training, Grooming, and Health

- The Lapphund thrives with regular exercise. Alert and ready, he does best when he's part of the action, whether that's by his owner's side working on a farm or helping to bring the kids home from school.

- The Finnish Lapphund is easily trained and excels at a number of activities.

- His thick, soft undercoat sheds, and he needs regular brushing to keep his coat growing in properly and to keep it free of mats and dead hair.

- Average life span is 12 to 16 years. Breed health concerns may include cataracts and progressive retinal atrophy (PRA).

Finnish Spitz

Breed Facts

- **Country of Origin**: Finland

- **Height**: Males 17–20 in (43–51 cm)/females 15.5–18 in (39.5–45.5 cm)

- **Weight**: Males 26.5–35 lb (12–16 kg)/females 15.5–29 lb (7–13 kg)|31–35 lb (14–16 kg) [KC]

- **Coat**: Double coat with straight, long, harsh outercoat and short, soft, dense undercoat

- **Colors**: Shades of reddish brown, golden red; may have white markings

- **Other Names**: Suomenpystykorva

- **Registries (With Group)**: AKC (Non-Sporting); ANKC (Hounds); CKC (Hounds); FCI (Spitz and Primitive); KC (Hound); UKC (Northern)

History and Personality

As hunting tribes migrated across what is now Russia thousands of years ago, they brought an ancient spitz-type dog with them. Those who settled in Finland developed over the centuries what is now known as the Finnish Spitz. Originally used for tracking bear and elk but now used for hunting Finnish game birds, he is the national dog of Finland.

Loyalty and bravery are two of his trademarks, and when he is bonded with his family, there is little that can come between them. The "barking bird dog" of Finland likes to express himself vocally. He is not especially inclined to do his family's bidding however adoring he is of the people around him.

Exercise, Training, Grooming, and Health

- An athletic dog, the Finnish Spitz enjoys his exercise. In the proper climate, he can make an excellent jogging companion (he does not do well in the heat). Whatever the weather, getting him outside to run, play, and explore is absolutely necessary.

- The Finnish Spitz is an independent thinker, and his training should consist of regular socialization and frequent but short and motivational training sessions.

- He needs to be brushed often when shedding. Otherwise, his plush coat needs little attention to retain its naturally healthy-looking volume and shine.

- Average life span is 12 to 15 years. There are no reported breed-specific health concerns.

Flat-Coated Retriever

Breed Facts

- **Country of Origin**: Great Britain
- **Height**: Males 23–24.5 in (58.5–62 cm)/females 22–23.5 in (56–60 cm)
- **Weight**: Males 60–80 lb (27–36.5 kg)/females 55–70.5 lb (25–32 kg)|60–70 lb (27–31.5 kg) [CKC]
- **Coat**: Moderate length and density, straight or slightly wavy, glossy, flat lying, weather resistant
- **Colors**: Black, liver
- **Other Names**: Flat Coated Retriever
- **Registries (With Group)**: AKC (Sporting); ANKC (Gundogs); CKC (Sporting); FCI (Retrievers); KC (Gundog); UKC (Gun Dog)

History and Personality

The Flat-Coated Retriever was developed in the mid-1800s to serve as a close-working shooting dog. His ancestry includes the Labrador, Newfoundland, spaniel-type water dogs, setter, and sheepdog. Known as a "gamekeeper's dog," he was used widely on British estates. Unlike many other retrieving breeds, who are often split into "field" and "show" strains, he remains consistent in appearance from the field to the show ring and is proficient in both.

The Flat-Coated Retriever is a companionable hunting retriever—outgoing, enthusiastic, and tractable. He is excellent with children, especially older children who can handle his exuberance. A keen, intelligent hunter, he works confidently in the fields and is happy to return home. He forms close bonds with his owners and needs companionship.

Exercise, Training, Grooming, and Health

- The Flat-Coat needs his exercise—and plenty of it. Without enough exercise and mental stimulation, he can become anxious and even destructive.

- Happy and enthusiastic, the Flat-Coat is up for anything his owner wants to teach him, and he learns quickly.

- The Flat-Coat has a naturally lustrous coat that needs only occasional brushing and combing to keep him looking great. The feathering on his ears, chest, forelegs, and tail can be trimmed if necessary but should never be shaved.

- Average life span is 10 to 12 years. Breed health concerns may include cancer; elbow dysplasia; glaucoma; hip dysplasia; and progressive retinal atrophy (PRA).

French Bulldog

Breed Facts

- **Country of Origin**: France

- **Height**: 12 in (30.5 cm) [est.]

- **Weight**: Males 28 lb (12.5 kg)/females 24 lb (11 kg)|18–30 lb (8–13.5 kg) [FCI][UKC]|light class under 22 lb (10 kg)/heavy class 22–28 lb (10–12.5 kg) [CKC]|not to exceed 28 lb (12.5 kg) [AKC]

- **Coat**: Short, fine, smooth, glossy, soft

- **Colors**: Brindle, fawn|also white, brindle and white [AKC] [CKC][UKC]|also pied [ANKC][FCI][KC]|also any color but black, black and white, black and tan, liver, mouse [AKC] [CKC]|also any color but black and tan, liver, mouse [UKC]

- **Other Names**: Bouledogue Français

- **Registries (With Group)**: AKC (Non-Sporting); ANKC (Non Sporting); CKC (Non-Sporting); FCI (Companion and Toy); KC (Utility); UKC (Companion)

History and Personality

To say that the French Bulldog is a purely French breed is a bit of a misnomer. Bulldogs were at the height of their popularity in England the 1860s, and small varieties of that breed were especially popular in the lace-making region of the English midlands. The Industrial Revolution caused a downturn for the lace makers, and the craftsmen moved to France, bringing their toy Bulldogs with them. There they were bred with various French breeds to create what is now the French Bulldog.

Playful—even clownish—inquisitive, and affectionate, the French Bulldog ("Frenchie") is an exceptional companion and playmate. He gets along well with everyone, including other pets and dogs, and he is essentially a happy-go-lucky fellow. Easy to care for and easygoing, if the Frenchie has a fault, it may be that he tends to snore and drool—results of his shortened muzzle.

Exercise, Training, Grooming, and Health

- The French Bulldog doesn't need a lot of exercise, but he is most happy accompanying his owner on walks around the neighborhood or on daily adventures.

- The Frenchie has a stubborn streak, but his good-heartedness will prevail if training is made worthwhile for him.

- The French Bulldog's short, soft coat is easily kept neat and clean with occasional brushing. The wrinkles on his face should be kept clean and dry to discourage infection.

- Average life span is 10 to 12 years. Breed health concerns may include allergies; brachycephalic syndrome; elongated soft palate; hemivertebrae; canine intervertebral disc disease; stenotic nares; and von Willebrand disease.

German Pinscher

Breed Facts

- **Country of Origin**: Germany
- **Height**: 17–20 in (43–51 cm)
- **Weight**: 31–44 lb (14–20 kg)
- **Coat**: Short, dense, smooth, shiny, close lying
- **Colors**: All solid colors from fawn to stag red in various shades, black and blue with reddish-tan markings|only brown in various shades of stag red and black with red or brown markings [CKC]
- **Other Names**: Deutscher Pinscher; Standard Pinscher
- **Registries (With Group)**: AKC (Working); ANKC (Utility); CKC (Non-Sporting); FCI (Pinscher and Schnauzer); KC (Working); UKC (Terrier)

History and Personality

The German Pinscher's history goes back centuries. He was a farmer's terrier, used for home protection and vermin control. Although too large to go to ground, he could hold his own against anything aboveground. This breed certainly factors in the lineage of the Miniature Pinscher and Doberman Pinscher and is closely related to the Standard Schnauzer—they are both believed to be descended from the now-extinct Rat Pinscher. The German Pinscher is noted for his intensity and fearlessness in the pursuits of hunting vermin, guarding the family, and as a companion.

The multitalented and intense German Pinscher has always been valued most for the job that he does, which requires a dog who is highly alert, capable of independent thinking, deliberate, and wary of strangers. Intelligent and assertive, he has highly developed senses and is always "on." If his family is threatened, he proves fearless and tenacious.

Exercise, Training, Grooming, and Health

- With energy to spare, the German Pinscher needs a job to provide him with the physical and mental stimulation to keep him satisfied. If he doesn't get it, he will find ways to express himself, and they will probably be less than desirable.

- The German Pinscher is quite intelligent and can be trained to do almost anything. He needs a firm and fair trainer to handle him, however, because he learns quickly and becomes bored easily. Because he is naturally wary and guarded with strangers, he should be socialized from puppyhood.

- The breed has a dense but short coat that stays neat and clean with occasional brushing.

- Average life span is 12 to 14 years. Breed health concerns may include cataracts; hip dysplasia; and von Willebrand disease.

German Shepherd Dog

Breed Facts

- **Country of Origin**: Germany

- **Height**: Males 23.5–26 in (60–66 cm)/females 21.5–24 in (55–61 cm)

- **Weight**: Males 66–88 lb (30–40 kg)/females 48.5–70.5 lb (22–32 kg)

- **Coat**: Double coat with medium-length, straight, dense, harsh, close-lying outercoat and thick undercoat; may have neck ruff

- **Colors**: Most colors allowed except white [AKC] [CKC]|most colors allowed, including white [UKC]|black with reddish-tan, tan, gold to light gray markings, solid black, solid gray; no white [ANKC][FCI][KC]

- **Other Names**: Alsatian; Deutscher Schäferhund,

- **Registries (With Group)**: AKC (Herding); ANKC (Working); CKC (Herding); FCI (Sheepdogs); KC (Pastoral); UKC (Herding)

History and Personality

The German Shepherd Dog ("GSD") is known and favored in many countries for its intelligence, trainability, adaptability, and fortitude. Its foundation can be traced to the work of Rittmeister Max von Stephanitz who developed the breed based on working dogs who possessed all the qualities essential for a strong, capable herder. Today, the GSD is used in search and rescue, police work, army and sentry work, as guide and assistance dogs, and of course, companions.

The German Shepherd Dog is exceptionally loyal, brave, and intelligent. As a dog who performs a host of tasks, he is by nature poised and unexcitable, with well-controlled nerves. The well-bred German Shepherd Dog is capable of excelling at any number of things, including family companion and protector.

Exercise, Training, Grooming, and Health

- The athletic, intelligent, and sensitive GSD does best with regular and vigorous exercise.

- GSDs thrive with training. They are quick learners who don't bore easily.

- The dense undercoat of the GSD requires regular brushing to keep it under control. He is a seasonally heavy shedder.

- Average life span is 10 to 14 years. Breed health concerns may include allergies; aortic stenosis; bloat; cataracts; Cushing's syndrome; elbow dysplasia; epilepsy; hemangiosarcoma; hip dysplasia; hypothyroidism; and pannus.

Breed Facts

- **Country of Origin**: Germany

- **Height**: Males 23–26 in (58.5–66 cm)/females 21–25 in (53.5–63 cm)

- **Weight**: Males 55–70 lb (25–31.5 kg)/females 45–60 lb (20.5–27 kg)

- **Coat**: Double coat with short, rough, dense, hard outercoat and dense, short undercoat

- **Colors**: Solid liver, liver and white spotted, liver and white spotted and ticked, liver and white ticked, liver roan|also solid black or black and white with same variations as liver [ANKC][FCI][KC][UKC]|may have tan markings [ANKC][[FCI][UKC]

- **Other Names**: Deutsch Kurzhaar; Deutscher Kurzhaariger Vorstehhund

- **Registries (With Group)**: AKC (Sporting); ANKC (Gundogs); CKC (Sporting); FCI (Pointing Dogs); KC (Gundog); UKC (Gun Dog)

History and Personality

In the mid-1800s, Prince Albrecht zu Solms-Braunfels of Germany wanted to create an all-purpose hunting dog and encouraged breeders to follow function over form. His schweisshunds, the German Bird Dog, and English pointers are some of the breeds believed to have formed the basis of the German Shorthaired Pointer ("GSP"). Originally short and heavy bodied with long ears and a slow pace, additions of pointer blood helped create a dog who could excel in water work, retrieving, and tracking. He has maintained his popularity with both serious hunters and with those who admire his good looks and ready disposition.

The German Shorthaired Pointer has an exuberant personality. He is enthusiastic about just about everything, whether it be walks, opportunities to hunt, being with people, going on trips, meals, or organized sports. He is a bright-eyed, happy-go-lucky fellow whose love of family is deep. In fact, he loves all people and is wonderful with children.

Exercise, Training, Grooming, and Health

- Like many of the pointing breeds, the GSP needs exercise—the more, the better. He won't be satisfied with a stroll around the block—he needs to run to help curb his endless energy reserve.

- The German Shorthaired Pointer is an eager, responsive breed. Because he is so people oriented, he aims to please (as long as it's interesting to him).

- The short, sleek coat of the GSP requires only minimal care to keep it looking neat. A good rubbing with a nubbed hound glove removes dead hair and massages the skin—a double treat. The GSP's ears must be kept clean because they tend to become infected.

- Average life span is 12 to 15 years. Breed health concerns may include bloat; epilepsy; eye problems; hip dysplasia; and von Willebrand disease.

German Wirehaired Pointer

Breed Facts

- **Country of Origin**: Germany

- **Height**: Males 23.5–27 in (60–68 cm)/females 22–25 in (56–64 cm)

- **Weight**: Males 55–75 lb (25–34 kg)/females 45–64 lb (20.5–29 kg)

- **Coat**: Double coat with wirehaired, harsh, dense, flat-lying outercoat and dense undercoat; beard

- **Colors**: Solid liver, liver and white [AKC][CKC][UKC]|brown roan with or without patches, black roan with or without patches, brown with or without white chest patch, light roan [ANKC][FCI]|liver and white, solid liver, black and white [KC]

- **Other Names**: Deutsche Drahthaar; Deutscher Drahthaariger Vorstehhund

- **Registries (With Group)**: AKC (Sporting); ANKC (Gundogs); CKC (Sporting); FCI (Pointing Dogs); KC (Gundog); UKC (Gun Dog)

History and Personality

An interest in gundogs with bristly coats always existed in Germany. The German Wirehaired Pointer ("GWP") was created as an all-purpose hunting dog with stamina to spare. Excellent on land and in the water, on all types of terrain, and with a variety of game, GWPs became synonymous with versatility.

The GWP has the same zeal for hunting and the outdoors as his relative, the German Shorthaired Pointer. Overall, though, he is a slightly mellower and more reserved dog, showing his deep affection (and clownish side) only to those he knows well.

Exercise, Training, Grooming, and Health

- The GWP is an athletic hunting dog who needs exercise for physical and mental sanity.

- Smart and willing, the GWP is an especially quick learner in the field and will also excel at other things as long as he is taught with respect.

- The harsh, wiry coat of the GWP is easy to care for with weekly brushings with a stiff bristle brush. His woolly undercoat sheds in the spring, and the outercoat may need to be stripped, especially if his coat is overly long or woolly.

- Average life span is 12 to 4 years. Breed health concerns may include cataracts; elbow dysplasia; hip dysplasia; and skin cancer.

Giant Schnauzer

Breed Facts

- **Country of Origin**: Germany

- **Height**: Males 25.5–27.5 in (65–70 cm)/females 23.5–25.5 in (60–65 cm)|23.5–27.5 in (60–70 cm) [FCI][UKC]

- **Weight**: 75–103.5 lb (34–47 kg)

- **Coat**: Double coat with wiry, harsh, dense, strong outercoat and soft undercoat; beard

- **Colors**: Solid black, salt and pepper; dark mask in salt and pepper coloration

- **Other Names**: Riesenschnauzer

- **Registries (With Group)**: AKC (Working); ANKC (Utility); CKC (Working); FCI (Pinscher and Schnauzer); KC (Working); UKC (Guardian)

History and Personality

The Giant Schnauzer was developed as a cattle-herding dog in southern Germany. His ancestors were most likely smoothhaired droving dogs, a variety of rough-coated shepherd dogs, and possibly black Great Danes and Bouvier des Flandres. Found mostly around the Munich area, he was a farm dog from the 15th century until the arrival of railroads changed the way of life. From the farms he moved to cities, where he guarded beer halls and butcher shops during the 19th century. Today, he is still used in security positions in Germany, and in the United States and other parts of the world he is prized for his courage and loyalty.

Giant Schnauzers are bold, spirited, and protective. They are boisterous and playful and can be intimidating to those who don't understand them. On the other hand, they are loyal and loving almost to a fault. They will protect their loved ones in the face of any danger. Their large size, great intelligence, and guarding/protective instincts make them a challenge for all but the experienced owner, with whom they live in mutual respect and admiration.

Exercise, Training, Grooming, and Health

- The Giant Schnauzer is a breed that needs a lot of exercise. If he can't get it, he will become bored and edgy, taking out his excess energy in potentially harmful and destructive ways.

- The intelligent Giant Schnauzer is a quick learner, and with the proper motivation, can be trained to do just about anything. Training and socialization from puppyhood are absolutely critical.

- Although he has an undercoat, the Giant Schnauzer is practically nonshedding. However, he does need regular brushing and trimming and should be clipped several times a year to maintain his coat. His beard, eyebrows, and ears must be trimmed.

- Average life span is 10 to 12 years. Breed health concerns may include bloat; epilepsy; hip dysplasia; hypothyroidism; and toe cancer.

Glen of Imaal Terrier

Breed Facts

- **Country of Origin**: Ireland

- **Height**: Males maximum 14 in (35.5 cm)/females accordingly less|12.5–14 in (31.5–35.5 cm) [AKC][ANKC][KC]

- **Weight**: Males approx. 35 lb (16 kg)/females slightly less

- **Coat**: Double coat with medium-length, harsh outercoat and soft undercoat

- **Colors**: Wheaten, blue, brindle; may have mask

- **Other Names**: Irish Glen of Imaal Terrier

- **Registries (With Group)**: AKC (Terrier); ANKC (Terriers); FCI (Terriers); KC (Terrier); UKC (Terrier)

History and Personality

This Irish dog is named after the Glen of Imaal in County Wicklow, a scenic but bleak area offering poor soil. The determined, hardworking people from this area had to eke out a living from the rocks and could ill afford a dog who couldn't earn his keep. In these conditions, the Glen of Imaal Terrier flourished, going gamely after the vicious badger, as well as foxes and ever-present rats. These terriers were also put to service in the kitchen as "turn-spits"— they would run in place for hours on a treadmill that would turn meat on a spit as it cooked.

The Glen of Imaal Terrier is a spirited fellow—brave, stubborn, and rambunctious. With his people, though, he is mild mannered, devoted, and gentle with children of all ages. Socialization from an early age helps, but although he will get along with most other pets, he can't be trusted around small animals. Glens are quite playful, and they like to dig and chase.

Exercise, Training, Grooming, and Health

- The Glen gets most of his exercise participating in the activities of the day—he's especially satisfied if they include periods of intense play.

- The Glen can show a stubborn streak in the face of training, which doesn't mean that he's not smart enough to learn, just that he'd rather be doing something else. When engaged through positive methods, the Glen will respond.

- Although he is not a shedder, the Glen needs regular grooming to keep him from becoming overly shaggy. This involves stripping or professional clipping. The hair around his face and between his toes must be trimmed regularly, too.

- Average life span is 12 to 14 years. Breed health concerns may include skin allergies.

Golden Retriever

Breed Facts

- **Country of Origin**: Great Britain

- **Height**: Males 22–24 in (56–61 cm)/females 20–22.5 in (51–57 cm)

- **Weight**: Males 65–75 lb (29.5–34 cm)/females 55–70 lb (25–31.5 kg)

- **Coat**: Double coat with straight or wavy, firm, dense, water-repellant outercoat and good undercoat; neck ruff

- **Colors**: Various shades of golden|also shades of cream [ANKC] [FCI][KC]

- **Registries (With Group)**: AKC (Sporting); ANKC (Gundogs); CKC (Sporting); FCI (Retrievers); KC (Gundog); UKC (Gun Dog)

History and Personality

In the late 1800s, Sir Dudley Majoribanks (Lord Tweedmouth) began a breeding program with a yellow Flat-Coated Retriever. Wanting to strengthen his water-retrieving abilities, he bred him to Tweed Water Spaniels (now extinct), who were light colored and had curly hair. For 20 years he further refined his light-colored hunting dog with crosses to Labradors, red setters, other Wavy Coats, and possibly the Bloodhound. Today, the Golden is one of the best-loved dogs in the world. He is a wonderfully versatile dog who excels in the hunt field and in just about any activity to which he is introduced.

Lovable, easygoing, pleasant companions, it is said that Golden Retrievers are born wanting to please. Always up for an adventure, Goldens are as at home hiking in the wild as they are curled up on the couch with their family. They are smart and sociable, understanding almost intuitively what's desired of them from those around them. They get along fabulously with other pets, children, and people.

Exercise, Training, Grooming, and Health

- The Golden Retriever does best with plenty of exercise. Because he is so good at so many things, one way to give it to him is by participating in sports or other activities.

- The Golden Retriever is truly one of the most easily trained breeds in dogdom.

- Golden Retrievers shed regularly and must be brushed several times a week.

- Average life span is 10 to 12 years. Breed health concerns may include cataracts; elbow dysplasia; hip dysplasia; progressive retinal atrophy (PRA); and subaortic stenosis (SAS).

Gordon Setter

Breed Facts

- **Country of Origin**: Scotland
- **Height**: Males 24–27 in (61–68.5 cm)/females 23–26 in (58.5–66 cm)
- **Weight**: Males 55–80 lb (25–36.5 kg)/females 45–70 lb (20.5–31.5 kg)
- **Coat**: Straight or slightly wavy, soft, shiny
- **Colors**: Black with tan markings
- **Registries (With Group)**: AKC (Sporting); ANKC (Gundogs); CKC (Sporting); FCI (Pointing Dogs); KC (Gundog); UKC (Gun Dog)

History and Personality

In Scotland in the 1600s, setting spaniels were differentiated into "black and fallow" setting dogs who were then crossed with local dogs to create a breed that could persevere in the tough conditions of the Scottish terrain. It was Alexander, the Fourth Duke of Gordon, whose name finally came to be permanently associated with these "black and tan setters," as he had many famous specimens in the 18th century.

Admirers of the Gordon Setter use these words to describe him: loyal, gentle, sensible, polite, obedient, cheerful, and affectionate. The Gordon is a large dog with a profuse coat who has a tendency to drool, but that doesn't stop him from winning hearts wherever he goes. In the hunting field, he is steady and honest. At home, he is great with children and slightly reserved with strangers, which serves him as a guarding dog.

Exercise, Training, Grooming, and Health

- The large, athletic Gordon Setter is in his element when allowed to hunt or otherwise explore the great outdoors. Without a few vigorous outings daily, he will become restless and bored, channeling that energy into potentially destructive and harmful behaviors.

- The Gordon Setter needs a gentle but firm hand when being taught something new. He can be stubborn, and he will not respond to harsh training methods. Socialization is important.

- The Gordon is a relatively easy breed to groom. His fine coat of moderate length requires only a going-over with a brush and comb every so often to look its best.

- Average life span is 10 to 12 years. Breed health concerns may include bloat; hip dysplasia; hypothyroidism; and progressive retinal atrophy (PRA).

Grand Basset Griffon Vendéen

Breed Facts

- **Country of Origin**: France

- **Height**: Males 15.5–17.5 in (40–44 cm)/females 15.5–17 in (39–43 cm)

- **Weight**: 40–45 lb (18–20.5 kg) [est.]

- **Coat**: Moderate length, rough, flat structure

- **Colors**: Black and tan, fawn, white and black, white and gray, white and grizzle, white and lemon, white and orange, white and sable, white black and tan [AKC]|black and white, black and tan, black with light tan markings, white and orange, tricolor, fawn and black, pale fawn and black [FCI]|white with any combination of lemon, orange, sable, grizzle, or black markings; tricolor [KC]

- **Other Names**: Grand Basset Griffon Vendeen

- **Registries (With Group)**: AKC (FSS); FCI (Scenthounds); KC (Hound); UKC (Scenthound)

History and Personality

The hounds from the Vendée region on the western coast of France are among the oldest varieties of French hunting dogs. Grand Basset Griffon Vendéens ("GBGV"), like other small French hounds, were bred to hunt rabbits, hares, and occasionally, foxes. In France and elsewhere, they are hunted primarily in packs.

The Grand Basset Griffon Vendéen has a devil-may-care attitude and happy hunting dog nature. He relishes his time outdoors and with his family. Bred to work in packs, he gets along well with other dogs and isn't overly possessive about anything. He is a fine companion for children of all ages.

Exercise, Training, Grooming, and Health

- Short of hunting opportunities, GBGVs must have plenty of long walks and time outdoors.

- Griffons don't particularly take to being told what to do. They don't mind being cajoled, bribed, or played with, and if these things lead them to do something their owners like, then everyone's happy.

- The tousled appearance of the GBGV comes naturally, and any trimming is highly discouraged. His double coat needs to be brushed and combed.

- Average life span is 12 to 15 years. Breed health concerns may include allergies; elbow dysplasia; eye problems; hip dysplasia; and hypothyroidism.

Breed Facts

- **Country of Origin**: Germany

- **Height**: Males 30 in (76 cm)/females 28 in (71 cm)|males at least 31.5 in (80 cm)/females at least 28.5 in (72 cm) [FCI]

- **Weight**: Males 119 lb (54 kg) minimum/females 101.5 lb (46 kg) minimum

- **Coat**: Short, thick, glossy

- **Colors**: Brindle, fawn, blue, black, harlequin, mantle|also boston [CKC]

- **Other Names**: Deutsche Dogge; German Mastiff

- **Registries (With Group)**: AKC (Working); ANKC (Non Sporting); CKC (Working); FCI (Molossoid); KC (Working); UKC (Guardian)

History and Personality

For hundreds of years, Dane-like "Boar Hounds" served as a boar hunter, bullbaiter, and war dog for both the Germans and the Celts. Hunting savage wild boars required a powerful, agile, tough dog, and these dogs became so renowned that German nobility began to take the best specimens for their estates. The Germans continued to refine the breed, and so loved were they in Germany that they were declared the national dog of that country in 1876. The only Danish part of him is his name, and he's only called the Great Dane in English-speaking countries; in Germany, he's called the Deutsche Dogge.

Today's Great Dane is a lover, not a fighter—although he retains a strong protective instinct toward his family. Mostly, though, he is affectionate, playful, and patient. He enjoys the company of children, although his desire to be close to people can lead to him leaning too closely against or sitting on a small child.

Exercise, Training, Grooming, and Health

- For as large as he is, the Great Dane does not need a tremendous amount of exercise. Of course he needs to stretch his legs, and a few brisk walks a day are a necessity and a pleasure.

- The Great Dane can be a challenge to train. He's not exactly nimble, but he is intelligent and obliging. He was bred to be an independent thinker, and holding his attention requires a creative repertoire of training tricks (with desirable rewards). Because of his protective instincts and large size, socialization is important.

- The short, thick coat of the Great Dane is easy to care for— although there's a lot of it. He's an average shedder, so he needs regular brushing or going-over with a hound glove to loosen dead hair and stimulate the skin.

- Average life span is 7 to 10 years. Breed health concerns may include bloat; cardiomyopathy; cervical vertebral instability (CVI); hip dysplasia; lymphoma; and osteosarcoma.

Greater Swiss Mountain Dog

Breed Facts

- **Country of Origin**: Switzerland

- **Height**: Males 25–28.5 in (63.5–72 cm)/females 23.5–27 in (60–68.5 cm)

- **Weight**: Males 132.5–154.5 lb (60–70 kg)/females 110–132.5 lb (50–60 kg) [est.]

- **Coat**: Double coat with medium-length, thick, dense outercoat and dense, short undercoat

- **Colors**: Black with rich rust and white markings

- **Other Names**: Great Swiss Mountain Dog; Grosser Schweizer Sennenhund

- **Registries (With Group)**: AKC (Working); CKC (Working); FCI (Swiss Mountain and Cattle Dogs); UKC (Guardian)

History and Personality

Descended from mastiff-type dogs used by the Roman armies on their conquests through Europe, the Greater Swiss Mountain Dog is one of four varieties of Swiss Sennenhunds, or "dog of the Alpine herdsmen." He is believed to be the oldest of the four varieties, which also include the Appenzeller Sennenhunde, Bernese Mountain Dog, and Entlebucher Mountain Dog. The Greater Swiss Mountain Dog ("Swissy") served Swiss farmers for centuries as a butcher's dog, draft dog, and guardian.

Even-tempered, intelligent, and generally mellow, the Swissy is a wonderful family dog. He enjoys pulling carts or sleds—especially if children are riding in them—and he is a real people-loving dog. He still retains some guard-dog instincts, too, and is protective of his family (although not aggressive).

Exercise, Training, Grooming, and Health

- The Greater Swiss Mountain Dog is a large dog who enjoys his time outdoors, and his double coat protects him from the elements.

- His calm, obedient nature makes training the Swissy a pleasure. He may not be the most enthusiastic of performers, but he is reliable and steady.

- The short, dense coat of the Swissy is easy to care for. Brushing once a week or so will remove dead hair and reinvigorate the skin and coat.

- Average life span is 10 to 12 years. Breed health concerns may include bloat; epilepsy; and hip dysplasia.

Great Pyrenees

Breed Facts

- **Country of Origin**: France

- **Height**: Males 27–32 in (68.5–81 cm)/25–29.5 in (63.5–75 cm)

- **Weight**: Males 110 lb (50 kg) minimum/females 88 lb (40 kg) minimum|males 100 lb (45.5 kg)/females 85 lb (38.5 kg) [AKC][CKC]

- **Coat**: Weather-resistant double coat with long, flat, thick, coarse outercoat and dense, fine, woolly undercoat; neck ruff

- **Colors**: White, white with gray, badger, reddish-brown, tan markings

- **Other Names**: Chien de Montagne des Pyrénées; Pyrenean Mountain Dog

- **Registries (With Group)**: AKC (Working); ANKC (Utility); CKC (Working); FCI (Molossoid); KC (Pastoral); UKC (Guardian)

History and Personality

Although the exact origin of the Great Pyrenees ("Pyr") isn't known, it is certain that he has been guarding the shepherds' flocks in the Pyrenees Mountains for thousands of years. "Discovered" by the French nobility before the revolution, Great Pyrenees were brought in to guard the large chateaux in southern France. This didn't affect their popularity with the shepherds who needed them most—or lead to any dilution of their talents. They remained sure-footed and completely reliable with the sheep. Today, the Pyr continues to serve French farmers while enjoying a reputation as a gentle giant and magnificent show dog around the world.

The Great Pyrenees would give his life to protect his flock—livestock or otherwise. He can be wary of strangers (as he was bred to be), although with his family, his devotion knows no bounds—to the point of being upset if left alone or abandoned. He is a large, intelligent, imposing dog who, although gentle and trustworthy at home, can appear forbidding to those who aren't dog savvy. He should be socialized from puppyhood.

Exercise, Training, Grooming, and Health

- The Pyr doesn't require excessive exercise, but he needs regular exercise. Several long walks a day will satisfy him.

- The Great Pyrenees is amenable to instruction about household manners and other aspects of life away from the farm but needs a patient and persistent trainer. He can be stubborn, and he will not respond to harsh methods.

- The Great Pyrenees' dense coat must be brushed almost daily to keep it looking its best. It should not be shaved, as it is meant to protect him in all kinds of weather.

- Average life span is 10 to 12 years. Breed health concerns may include bloat; degenerative myelopathy; elbow dysplasia; Factor XI deficiency; hip dysplasia; osteosarcoma; progressive retinal atrophy (PRA); and skin problems.

Greyhound

Breed Facts

- **Country of Origin**: Great Britain

- **Height**: Males 27–30 in (68.5–76 cm)/females 26–28 in (66–71 cm)

- **Weight**: Males 65–75 lb (29.5–34 kg)/females 60–70 lb (27–31.5 kg)

- **Coat**: Short, smooth, firm, close lying

- **Colors**: Black, white, red, blue, fawn, fallow, brindle, or any of these colors broken with white

- **Registries (With Group)**: AKC (Hound); ANKC (Hounds); CKC (Hounds); FCI (Sighthounds); KC (Hound); UKC (Sighthound & Pariah)

History and Personality

Egyptian tombs dating to the 4th century BCE show drawings of dogs similar in overall appearance to what are now known as Greyhounds and Salukis. The breed was developed and refined in

Great Britain, and became a favorite of royalty and the wealthy. These exceptional hunters of swift prey are considered the fastest dog breed, reaching speeds of 45 mph (70 kph).

Gentle, affectionate, playful, and noble, the Greyhound is a marvelous companion on all levels: instinctively compassionate, easy to manage, docile yet with a playful sense of humor. He is reserved with strangers and somewhat cat-like in manner. He should not be trusted off leash because he has a strong prey drive.

Exercise, Training, Grooming, and Health

- The Greyhound actually needs little outright exercise time—although he still needs to get out.

- Although natrually well-mannered, they can be a challenge to train and are extremely sensitive to harsh methods.

- The short, smooth coat of the Greyhound needs only occasional brushing and a nice rub with a hound glove or currycomb.

- Average life span is 10 to 12 years. Breed health concerns may include bloat; osteosarcoma; and thyroid problems.

Breed Facts

- **Country of Origin**: Great Britain

- **Height**: 19–21.5 in (48–55 cm)

- **Weight**: 40–60 lb (18–27 kg) [est.]

- **Coat**: Short, hard, dense, glossy, weatherproof

- **Colors**: Any color|any recognized hound color [ANKC] [UKC]|usually white as base color, with shades of black to orange [FCI]

- **Registries (With Group)**: AKC (Hound); ANKC (Hounds); CKC (Hounds); FCI (Scenthounds); UKC (Scenthound)

History and Personality

The Harrier is a relative of the English Foxhound; in fact, it is most likely that he is a smaller version of the English Foxhound— developed from the same stock that created the larger hound by using crosses of heavy scenthounds with lighter, smaller hounds like the

Beagle. His original purpose was to follow large, slower European hares in front of hunters who went out on foot. Later, like the foxhounds, they were followed by hunters on horseback.

The Harrier is described as more playful and outgoing than a Foxhound but slightly more reserved than a Beagle. This makes him an easygoing, good-natured, and adaptable hound who loves all people. As a pack animal, he is good with other dogs, but he may be less tolerant of other pets unless raised with or socialized to them from puppyhood. Like the Beagle, the Harrier has a sonorous voice that he likes to use.

Exercise, Training, Grooming, and Health

- The Harrier should have access to large, open spaces over which he can hunt and run. Barring that, his needs can be met only by taking him out on long walks several times a day—walks that allow him to freely use his nose.

- The Harrier can be stubborn and single-minded, and his training should be approached with a positive but firm command.

- The short, hard coat of the Harrier is kept clean with occasional brushing or by rubbing with a hound glove to remove dead hair and stimulate new growth.

- Average life span is 10 to 12 years. Breed health concerns may include hip dysplasia.

Havanese

Breed Facts

- **Country of Origin**: Cuba

- **Height**: 8.5–11.5 in (21.5–29 cm)

- **Weight**: 7–14 lb (3–6.5 kg)

- **Coat**: Double coat with long; soft; abundant; flat, wavy, or curly outercoat and woolly, not well-developed undercoat

- **Colors**: All colors|shades of fawn, black, havana brown, tobacco, reddish brown, particolors, rarely pure white [ANKC][FCI]|two varieties—shades of fawn, black, havana brown, tobacco, reddish brown, particolors, rarely pure white; also black

- **Other Names**: Bichon Havanais; Havana Silk Dog

- **Registries (With Group)**: AKC (Toy); ANKC (Toys); CKC (Toys); FCI (Companion and Toy); KC (Toy); UKC (Companion)

History and Personality

Old World Bichon-type dogs were brought to Cuba from Europe in the 17th century. They adapted to the climate and customs of the island and produced a smaller dog with a silkier coat, called the Blanquito de la Habana, or Havanese Silk Dog. This dog was a favorite of the Cuban aristocracy during the 18th and 19th centuries. The Havanese Silk Dogs were eventually crossed with French and German Poodles, which had become increasingly popular, and named Bichon Havanese. They are now popular around the world.

The Havanese is a delightful companion—responsive, alert, mindful, and fond of everyone. He gets along with people of all ages, as well as all kinds of other pets. Outgoing yet intelligent, he is a good watchdog, as he will alert to unusual activity, yet he is not prone to excessive barking or nervousness.

Exercise, Training, Grooming, and Health

- The Havanese is a curious and delightful dog who enjoys getting out and about to exercise and socialize.

- A dog who thrives on the attention of his family, the Havanese is an eager and quick learner.

- Pet owners typically keep their Havanese in a short, clipped coat, as the long hair needs a great deal of attention. Because the dead hair rarely sheds, it needs to be removed by brushing, which should be done several times a week.

- Average life span is 13 to 15 years. Breed health concerns may include deafness; ear infections; hip dysplasia; juvenile cataracts; patellar luxation; and progressive retinal atrophy (PRA).

Ibizan Hound

Breed Facts

- **Country of Origin**: Spain

- **Height**: Males 23.5–28.5 in (59.5–72 cm)/females 22.5–26.5 in (57–67 cm)|22–29 in (56–74 cm) [ANKC][KC]

- **Weight**: Males 45–55 lb (20.5–25 kg)/females 40–50 lb (18–22.5 kg)

- **Coat**: Two varieties—*smooth* is strong, hard, shiny, dense, rough/ *rough* is wiry, hard, dense; may have beard/mustache [AKC] [CKC][FCI][UKC]

- **Colors**: White or red, solid or in any combination|also chestnut [ANKC][KC]|also fawn in rough coat only [FCI]

- **Other Names**: Ca Eivissencs; Ibizan Podenco; Ibizan Warren Hound; Podenco Ibicenco

- **Registries (With Group)**: AKC (Hound); ANKC (Hounds); CKC (Hounds); FCI (Spitz and Primitive); KC (Hound); UKC (Sighthound & Pariah)

History and Personality

The Ibizan Hound, whose name derives from the island of Ibiza, has been known throughout the Balearic islands for more than 5,000 years. He earned his keep by hunting rabbits and other small game, which supplemented the islanders' otherwise meager food supply. Over time, he became known on the European continent, first in Catalonia, Spain, where he was called Ca Eivissencs, and in Provence, France, where he was called Charnique, and was prized by poachers. Today, the Ibizan Hound is a prized hunter, coursing dog, show dog, and companion animal all over the globe.

The Ibizan Hounds (or "Beezer," as they're more familiarly called) are generous with their affection, sensible, polite, and even playful. They are pack animals and so fit in with families just fine. They need to be raised with or seriously socialized to pets like cats and other small animals, as these are considered prey to them unless otherwise instructed. Beezers are clean and quiet indoors.

Exercise, Training, Grooming, and Health

- Beezers thrive with plenty of exercise. It is never a good idea to exercise an Ibizan Hound off lead unless in a safely enclosed area.

- The independent-minded Beezer can be willful and seemingly inattentive, but he wants to be part of the family and will learn household manners. His training is best done through positive, reward-based methods, and patience and persistence are key.

- Shorthaired or roughhaired, the Ibizan Hound is a naturally clean dog whose coat is easy to care for. The shorthaired variety requires only a quick going-over with a hound glove; the roughhaired variety needs just occasional brushing.

- Average life span is 10 to 12 years. Breed heath concerns may include allergies.

Icelandic Sheepdog

Breed Facts

- **Country of Origin**: Iceland

- **Height**: Males 18 in (45.5 cm)/females 16–16.5 in (40.5–42 cm)

- **Weight**: 20–30 lb (9–13.5 kg) [est.]

- **Coat**: Two varieties—*shorthaired* is double coated with medium-length, straight or slightly wavy, fairly coarse or smooth, weatherproof outercoat and thick, soft undercoat; neck ruff/*longer-haired* is double coated with longer-length, straight or slightly wavy, fairly coarse or smooth, weatherproof outercoat and thick, soft undercoat; neck ruff

- **Colors**: Tan shades, chocolate brown, gray, black, all with white markings; tan, gray dogs have black mask

- **Other Names**: Iceland Dog; Iceland Sheepdog; Islenskur Fjárhundur

- **Registries (With Group)**: AKC (Miscellaneous); CKC (Herding); FCI (Spitz and Primitive); UKC (Herding)

History and Personality

Iceland's only native dog, the Icelandic Sheepdog was brought to Iceland by the Vikings when they colonized it in 880 CE. These small herding dogs were used for centuries for rounding up livestock in Iceland's difficult terrain. They were considered essential for driving sheep, and most farms had several working Icelandic Sheepdogs. Their sense of smell is legend, and there are claims that they can find a sheep buried under a foot (0.3 m) of snow.

The Icelandic Sheepdog is alert and active. He is an enthusiastic and friendly dog who gets along well with everyone and adores children. Playful, inquisitive, and courageous, he wants to be involved in all the goings-on around him.

Exercise, Training, Grooming, and Health

- The Icelandic Sheepdog is an athletic and energetic breed that requires vigorous exercise to keep him physically and mentally fit.

- An eager learner and enthusiastic participant, the Icelandic Sheepdog responds well to training—especially if it challenges and exercises him.

- Both the longhaired and shorthaired types need to be brushed and combed frequently to keep their thick fur under control.

- Average life span is 11 to 14 years. Breed health concerns may include cataracts.

Irish Red and White Setter

Breed Facts

- **Country of Origin**: Ireland
- **Height**: Males 24.5–26 in (62–66 cm)/females 22.5–24 in (57–61 cm)
- **Weight**: 50–75 lb (22.5–34 kg) [est.]
- **Coat**: Long, straight, flat, silky, fine, with feathering
- **Colors**: White with solid red patches
- **Registries (With Group)**: AKC (Sporting); ANKC (Gundogs); CKC (Sporting); FCI (Pointing Dogs); KC (Gundog); UKC (Gun Dog)

History and Personality

The presence of "setting dogs" in Ireland has been recorded as far back as the 17th century. These dogs were used to hunt fowl, and they had to "freeze" in place after prey was flushed instead of chasing it, so as not to get in the way of the hunter's gun sights. The Irish Setter was originally a red and white, particolored dog, with an occasional allred dog born in a litter. By the 1850s, however, the rare reds started to become the more desirable of the dogs, and the red and white's popularity began to decline. The particolors held on in certain parts of Ireland, where hunters preferred working with the more easily seen red/white dogs.

Full of life and energy, the Irish Red and White Setter is a wonderful companion for a family who enjoys the outdoor life. This is a high-energy breed that has been described as giddy and boisterous, although these characteristics could also be rephrased as an ever-present *joie de vivre*. His hunting instincts are strong, and being able to use them helps keep the Irish Red and White Setter physically and mentally sound.

Exercise, Training, Grooming, and Health

- The high-spirited Irish Red and White Setter needs lots of exercise, some of which should include being able to extend himself in wide open spaces.

- The exuberant Irish Red and White Setter may find it difficult to focus on his training. It's best to work him in short stints and frequently. He bores easily, and patient repetition is the way to get results.

- The Irish Red and White Setter's long, silky coat demands regular brushing to look its best—especially the feathering on his tail, legs, and underside.

- Average life span is 11 to 13 years. Breed health concerns may include bloat; canine leukocyte adhesion deficiency (CLAD); posterior polar cataract (PPC); and von Willebrand disease.

Irish Setter

Breed Facts

- **Country of Origin**: Ireland

- **Height**: Males 23–27 in (58.5–68.5 cm)/females 21.5–25 in (54.5–63.5 cm)

- **Weight**: Males 70–75 lb (31.5–34 kg)/females 60–65 lb (27–29.5 kg)

- **Coat**: Moderate length, straight, flat, with feathering

- **Colors**: Rich chestnut red with no trace of black; may have white markings|also mahogany [AKC][CKC][UKC]

- **Other Names**: Irish Red Setter

- **Registries (With Group)**: AKC (Sporting); ANKC (Gundogs); CKC (Sporting); FCI (Pointing Dogs); KC (Gundog); UKC (Gun Dog)

History and Personality

Setting dogs have existed in Ireland since the 1700s. They were used to locate birds with their highly developed sense of smell, and once the prey was discovered, had to hold their position instead of chasing it, which ensured that they would not accidentally cross into the line of gunfire. Setters bred in Ireland throughout the 18th century and into the 19th century were both red and red and white. It was in the mid 1800s, when all-reds started to turn heads in the show ring, that they became increasingly popular.

Big, elegant, and athletic, with a flowing red coat and upbeat personality, the Irish Setter turns heads wherever he appears. His devil-may-care personality, paired with a happy-go-lucky air, endear him to all he meets. He is more than good looks and personality, though. The Irish Setter is a delightful companion—friend to all he encounters, enthusiastic, intelligent, and loving.

Exercise, Training, Grooming, and Health

- The Irish Setter needs plenty of exercise.

- The Irish Setter's enthusiasm can make it difficult for him to focus on training for long periods of time. Working him often and for shorter periods is the best way to achieve results.

- The long, flowing coat of the Irish Setter must have regular brushing and combing to look its best, especially where there is profuse feathering. Show dogs require professional grooming.

- Average life span is 11 to 15 years. Breed health concerns may include arthritis; bloat; canine leukocyte adhesion deficiency (CLAD); epilepsy; hip dysplasia; hypertrophic osteodystrophy (HOD); hypothyroidism; osteosarcoma; patent ductus arteriosus (PDA); progressive retinal atrophy (PRA); and von Willebrand disease.

Breed Facts

- **Country of Origin**: Ireland

- **Height**: Males 19 in (48 cm)/females 18 in (45.5 cm)|18 in (45.5 cm) [AKC][CKC][FCI][UKC]

- **Weight**: Males 27 lb (12 kg)/females 25 lb (11.5 kg)

- **Coat**: Double coat with wiry, stiff, dense outercoat and softer undercoat; may have slight beard

- **Colors**: Whole-colored bright red, golden red, red wheaten|also wheaten [AKC]

- **Other Names**: Irish Red Terrier

- **Registries (With Group)**: AKC (Terrier); ANKC (Terriers); CKC (Terriers); FCI (Terriers); KC (Terrier); UKC (Terrier)

History and Personality

The Irish Terrier is believed to be one of the oldest terriers, developed several thousand years ago in Ireland. His origin is County Cork, and his purpose has always been to help rid his family's property of vermin and keep them safe from harm. His prowess as a hunter and guardian is still strong in him today.

Good-tempered, loyal, and affectionate with people, the plucky Irish Terrier also has an animated style that has rightly earned him the nickname "daredevil." He is courageous, fiery, and charming, and has an independent streak. Even so, he is attached to his family and particularly good with children.

Exercise, Training, Grooming, and Health

- The Irish Terrier needs plenty of physical and mental exercise. He is athletic and robust for his size and is game for all kinds of activities.

- The Irish Terrier is a quick study, but his "up" temperament can cause him to be easily distracted. His training is best accomplished in short sessions where the focus is on the positive.

- The Irish Terrier looks his best if his wiry coat is hand-plucked several times a year. The rest of the time he is easily kept neat and clean with regular brushing and combing. His coat is low shedding.

- Average life span is 12 to 14 years. There are no reported breed-specific health concerns.

Irish Water Spaniel

Breed Facts

- **Country of Origin**: Ireland
- **Height**: Males 21–24 in (53–61 cm)/females 20–23 in (51–58.5 cm)
- **Weight**: Males 55–65 lb (25–29.5 kg)/females 45–58 lb (20.5–26.5 kg)
- **Coat**: Double coat with abundant hair falling in dense, tight, crisp ringlets or waves
- **Colors**: Solid liver
- **Registries (With Group)**: AKC (Sporting); ANKC (Gundogs); CKC (Sporting); FCI (Water Dogs); KC (Gundog); UKC (Gun Dog)

History and Personality

Although spaniels used for water work go back centuries in Ireland, it wasn't until the 1830s that Irishman Justin McCarthy began to produce the Irish Water Spaniels we know today. His dog, Boatswain, is the acknowledged father of the breed, but McCarthy never revealed his sources for the gene pool. The Irish Water Spaniel is an excellent hunter of waterfowl, and his unique coat protects him in even the iciest water, as it is thick and water repellent.

Although slightly reserved with strangers, with his family and friends, the Irish Water Spaniel is a high-spirited clown. Intelligent, bold, and eager to please, yet with a stubborn streak, the Irish Water Spaniel has the courage and smarts to work a long, honest day, as well as the playful and affectionate qualities that make him a beloved companion.

Exercise, Training, Grooming, and Health

- The athletic and hardworking Irish Water Spaniel does best with plenty of exercise.

- The Irish Water Spaniel is innately trainable. Intelligent and ready to please, he does best with a firm but understanding trainer.

- Although he sheds little and does not need to be clipped like a Poodle, the Irish Water Spaniel's coat needs regular attention. It tends to mat, so regular brushing and combing is essential, and it also needs to be trimmed.

- Average life span is 10 to 13 years. Breed health concerns may include hip dysplasia and hypothyroidism.

Irish Wolfhound

Breed Facts

- **Country of Origin**: Ireland
- **Height**: Males 31–32 in (79–81 cm) minimum/females 28–30 in (71–76 cm) minimum|32–34 in (81–86.5 cm) [UKC]
- **Weight**: Males 120 lb (54.5 kg) minimum/females 89–105 lb (40.5–47.5 kg) minimum
- **Coat**: Rough and hard on body; beard and hair over eyes especially long and wiry
- **Colors**: Gray, brindle, red, black, pure white, fawn, or any other color that appears in the Deerhound|also wheaten and steel gray [KC]
- **Other Names**: Cú Faoil
- **Registries (With Group)**: AKC (Hound); ANKC (Hounds); CKC (Hounds); FCI (Sighthounds); KC (Hound); UKC (Sighthound & Pariah)

History and Personality

Throughout the Middle Ages, the Irish Wolfhound served as a dog of war, a guardian of property, and a hunter of boars, stags, and the

Irish elk (now extinct). By the 15th and 16th centuries, they gradually turned to the specialized hunting of wolves, and it was during this time that the breed became more fixed in type.

Today's Irish Wolfhound is truly a gentle giant. He is an even-tempered, intelligent, patient, and affectionate hound who is extremely loyal to his family. Although his size is imposing, he is completely trustworthy with children and friendly toward all he meets.

Exercise, Training, Grooming, and Health

- The Irish Wolfhound need regular walks and opportunities to run in a securely fenced area.

- The intelligent Irish Wolfhound is quick to pick up on what his owner wants, and training him is relatively easy. Persistence and praise are key ingredients to successful training.

- The rough, medium-length coat of the Wolfhound needs regular brushing and combing to keep it clean and well kept. He is an average shedder who should be taken to a professional groomer a few times a year to have the coarser, longer hairs plucked.

- Average life span is 6 to 8 years. Breed health concerns may include bloat; bone cancer; heart disease; hypothyroidism; liver shunts; and von Willebrand disease.

Breed Facts

- **Country of Origin**: Italy
- **Height**: 12.5–15 in (32–38 cm)
- **Weight**: 8–10 lb (3.5–4.5 kg)|maximum 11 lb (5 kg) [FCI]
- **Coat**: Short, fine, glossy, soft
- **Colors**: Black, blue, cream, fawn, red, white, or any of these colors broken with white; no brindle, black or blue with tan markings [ANKC][KC]|all colors and markings acceptable except for brindle and tan markings found on black and tan dogs [AKC][UKC]|white, cream, fawn, blue, gray, black, red, chocolate, bronze, blue/fawn, red/fawn; may have white markings; no tan points such as those of Manchester Terrier, brindle [CKC]|black, gray, slate, gray and yellow [FCI]
- **Other Names**: Piccolo Levriero Italiano
- **Registries (With Group)**: AKC (Toy); ANKC (Toys); CKC (Toys); FCI (Sighthounds); KC (Toy); UKC (Companion)

History and Personality

Evidence of miniature Greyhounds was found in the tombs of Egypt and on relics and artifacts of Mediterranean countries 2,000 years ago.

It was the Romans who bred this little sighthound to perfection, and they were most likely bred solely as companions. It was during the 16th century that the breed received the moniker "Italian Greyhound," and its popularity began to spread across Europe.

The tiny Italian Greyhound ("Iggy") is affectionate and bonded to his family. He can be reserved around strangers, and children must be mindful around him. He is a fragile companion and his favorite friends are other Italian Greyhounds. Inquisitive and gentle, fast and mischievous, the Italian Greyhound is a complex and compelling companion.

Exercise, Training, Grooming, and Health

- The dainty Italian Greyhound gets sufficient exercise in his daily routine of playing and accompanying his family on walks. He will often adjust to the activity level of his household.

- Short training sessions that involve energetic praise and sufficient reward will capture the Italian Greyhound's attention. Housetraining may take longer than with other breeds.

- The Iggy's short, fine coat sheds little, and he is an easy dog to groom, requiring a simple wiping-down with a soft cloth every so often.

- Average life span is 12 to 15 years. Breed health concerns may include autoimmune disease; dental problems; epilepsy; hypothyroidism; Legg-Calve-Perthes disease; and patellar luxation.

Japanese Chin

Breed Facts

- **Country of Origin**: Japan

- **Height**: Males 10 in (25.5 cm)/females slightly smaller|8–11 in (20–28 cm) [AKC]

- **Weight**: 4–7 lb (2–3 kg)|two classes—under and over 7 lb (3 kg) [CKC]

- **Coat**: Single coat is long, abundant, straight, silky; neck ruff

- **Colors**: Black and white, red and white|also black and white with tan points [AKC][UKC]

- **Other Names**: Chin; Japanese Spaniel

- **Registries (With Group)**: AKC (Toy); ANKC (Toys); CKC (Toys); FCI (Companion and Toy); KC (Toy); UKC (Companion)

History and Personality
Although it is uncertain if the ancestors of the Japanese Chin originated in Korea or China, the breed was most certainly developed

and refined in Japan. Embroideries from ancient palaces and centuries-old illustrations on pottery show that in his native country, the Chin was revered as a dog for the aristocracy. Dogs were held in high esteem by the nobility and were considered gifts of extremely high honor—and the Chin was a breed at the top of the gift list. Today, the breed is a beloved companion around the world.

Japanese Chin seem to have an innate sense of their royal roots. They are demanding of attention yet solicit it in an utterly charming and noble way. Intelligent, lively, happy, and mild-mannered yet playful, they are true companion animals who will delight their owners all day long. They are small and can be fragile, so although they love everyone, it is best to supervise their interaction with small or rowdy children. Chin get along fairly well with other pets, especially if they've been socialized to them from an early age.

Exercise, Training, Grooming, and Health

- The tiny Chin can get the exercise he needs following his family around the house or with a few play sessions a day.

- Although Chin are eager learners and quick thinkers, they are sensitive souls who need a gentle hand with training. This does not mean that training is unnecessary, however, as they still need to learn basic manners and be well socialized to all types of people and pets. They have long been taught to perform tricks for royalty and others, and they enjoy the interaction and stimulation of learning new things.

- The long, human-like hair on the Chin should be brushed and combed regularly.

- Average life span is 10 to 12 years. Breed health concerns may include cataracts; heart murmurs; and patellar luxation.

Breed Facts

- **Country of Origin**: Korea

- **Height**: Males 19.5–21.5 in (50–55 cm)/females 17.5–19.5 in (45–50 cm)

- **Weight**: Males 40–50 lb (18–22.5 kg)/females 33–42 lb (15–19 kg)

- **Coat**: Double coat with medium-length, stiff, somewhat stand-off outercoat and soft, dense undercoat

- **Colors**: Black and tan, brindle, red fawn, gray, white|also black [FCI][UKC]|only shades of red, white, black and tan [KC]

- **Other Names**: Jindo Dog; Korean Jindo; Korea Jindo Dog

- **Registries (With Group)**: AKC (FSS: Non-Sporting); FCI (Spitz and Primitive); KC (Utility); UKC (Northern)

History and Personality

There is no written history for the Jindo, but it is believed that he has existed on Jindo Island off Korea for ages. The Jindo Dog Research and Testing Center, located in Jindo County, believes that the Jindo is a pure native hunting breed that goes back to the stone ages. Over the centuries, they became stealthy and able hunters of deer and boars and could bring down Siberian Tigers when hunting in groups.

The Jindo is an extremely loyal dog who relishes his time with his family. He is demanding of attention, independent-minded, and energetic. He does not do well if kept indoors for too long, preferring outdoor activities. Intelligent and clever, the Jindo will try to take over if not properly cared for—meaning that he needs to be kept active and trained with focus and determination. He is an exceptional watchdog, has an uncanny ability to discern friend from foe, does not like water, and practically housetrains himself as a young puppy.

Exercise, Training, Grooming, and Health

- The spirited Jindo prefers to be outdoors and needs to be sufficiently exercised to prevent him from getting bored. This should involve the time and space to run and play.

- The Jindo must have a trainer who is as confident and self-assured as his dog but who is also fair and motivating. Getting frustrated with a Jindo accomplishes nothing. He should be worked with as a young puppy so that he is socialized to many situations.

- The Jindo is a seasonal shedder. Other than times of heavy shedding, he can be kept clean with occasional brushing. He is naturally tidy.

- Average life span 12 to 14 years. There are no reported breed-specific health concerns.

Kai Ken

Breed Facts

- **Country of Origin**: Japan
- **Height**: Males 18.5–22 in (47–56 cm)/females 17.5–20 in (44.5–51 cm)
- **Weight**: 25–55 lb (11.5–25 kg)
- **Coat**: Double coat with medium-length, straight, harsh, thick outercoat and soft, dense undercoat
- **Colors**: All brindle colors equally acceptable|only black brindle, red brindle, brindle [AKC][FCI]
- **Other Names**: Kai; Kai-Ken; Tora Dog
- **Registries (With Group)**: AKC (FSS: Working); FCI (Spitz and Primitive); UKC (Northern)

History and Personality

This Nordic hunter is a native of the Japanese province of Kai on the island of Honshu (now called the Yamanashi Prefecture). The isolation of the mountainous area kept the breed protected for centuries; the Kai is believed to be the purest of all Japanese breeds. Originally used to hunt and track deer and wild boars, the Kai is highly regarded as a hunter and guardian by the Japanese people and considered a national treasure.

The Japanese describe the Kai Ken as a trustworthy, intelligent guardian who is extremely devoted to his owner, to the point that he will lay down his life to protect the ones he loves. It is said that he is more willing to please than other spitz-type breeds, and although he may be reserved with strangers, he warms up to those he feels he can trust. He gets along well with children and does not act aggressively toward other dogs. The Kai Ken makes an excellent watchdog.

Exercise, Training, Grooming, and Health

- The sturdy Kai Ken is an athletic dog who needs and enjoys regular outdoor excursions. He should be kept on leash when out for some exercise, unless in a securely fenced area. Daily vigorous exercise will keep him sound in body and mind.

- The Kai Ken is said to be more responsive to his trainer's requests than many of his close spitz-type relatives. He does best with motivational training that is done with patience and persistence, and he needs a firm yet fair leader.

- His thick, double coat sheds, and the Kai Ken requires regular brushing. Otherwise, his coat is weather resistant and naturally lustrous.

- Average life span is 12 to 15 years. There are no reported breed-specific health concerns.

Karelian Bear Dog

Breed Facts

- **Country of Origin**: Finland

- **Height**: Males 21.25–23.5 in (54–59.5 cm)/females 19.25–21.25 in (49–54 cm)

- **Weight**: Males 55–61.5 lb (25–28 kg)/females 37.5–44 lb (17–20 kg)

- **Coat**: Double coat with medium-length, straight, stiff outercoat and soft, dense undercoat

- **Colors**: Black, may be brownish or dull; white markings

- **Other Names**: Carelian Bear Dog; Karjalankarhukoira

- **Registries (With Group)**: AKC (FSS: Working); CKC (Working); FCI (Spitz and Primitive); UKC (Northern)

History and Personality

The Karelian Bear Dog is a spitz-type dog named for the area of Karelia, a territory in northern Europe currently divided between Russia and Finland. He was developed by the Russian and the Finnish for use as a watchdog and hunter of both small game (like squirrels and martens) and larger game (like moose, boars, and the Eurasian brown bear). He had to be strong and fearless on the hunt and hardy and tough for surviving the harsh conditions in that part of the world. Today, he is among the most popular breeds in Finland.

This breed is self-confident, independent, intelligent, and courageous. He needs a fair and firm leader or he will take matters into his own paws. He is, however, a dog who bonds strongly to his family and sometimes especially strongly to one individual, and to that family or person, he is forever affectionate and faithful. He can be territorial and aggressive toward other dogs and pets, although he is rarely so with people, having a great instinct for discriminating between who may be threatening or not.

Exercise, Training, Grooming, and Health

- The Karelian needs plenty of exercise to keep him occupied and in shape. He should be kept in a secure area when playing or allowing him time off lead; if he picks up a scent, he will pursue it.

- A firm yet fair hand is needed to get results with the independent-minded Karelian. Intelligent and alert, he will quickly figure out if his owner is serious. Motivational training that takes into account his energy level and perceptive instincts will get the best results.

- The thick, double coat of the Karelian sheds about twice a year and should be combed with a metal brush at those times to help remove the dead hairs and speed the process along. Otherwise, he is a neat and easy-to-care-for dog who has little doggy odor.

- Average life span is 10 to 12 years. There are no reported breed-specific health concerns.

Keeshond

Breed Facts

- **Country of Origin**: Netherlands

- **Height**: Males 18 in (45.5 cm)/females 17 in (43 cm)

- **Weight**: 55–66 lb (25–30 kg) [est.]

- **Coat**: Double coat with long, straight, harsh outercoat and thick, downy undercoat; neck ruff

- **Colors**: Mixture of gray, black, cream

- **Other Names**: Wolfsspitz

- **Registries (With Group)**: AKC (Non-Sporting); ANKC (Non-Sporting); CKC (Non-Sporting); KC (Utility); UKC (Northern)

History and Personality

Keeshonden are of the same stem stock as the German Spitz, but the Dutch seemed to especially like and adopt the large, wolf-gray type. He was used for centuries as a companion and watchdog on Dutch farms, barges, and riverboats. He acquired his modern name from Cornelius (Kees) de Gyselaer, a Dutch patriot at the time of the French Revolution, whose loyal dog was a symbol of the common and middle-class Dutch Patriot Party.

Outgoing, family-oriented dogs, Keeshonden are sometimes called "the laughing Dutchman." Cuddly, gregarious, and wonderful with children, they enjoy and thrive on affection and want to be part of all activities. They are good watchdogs who like to use their voices.

Exercise, Training, Grooming, and Health

- Keeshonden love going for walks several times a day, which gives them the opportunity to exercise and explore.

- The self-directed Keeshond can prove to be a training challenge. Repetition and patience are essential.

- He needs to be brushed several times a week and he sheds heavily a couple of times a year, but in general, his grooming needs are not extensive.

- Average life span is 12 to 14 years. Breed health concerns may include Cushing's syndrome; epilepsy; hip dysplasia; hypothyroidism; patellar luxation; and primary hyperparathyroidism (PHPT).

Breed Facts

- **Country of Origin**: Ireland

- **Height**: Males 18–19.5 in (45.5–49.5 cm)/females 17.5–19 in (44.5–48.5 cm)|males 18–19 in (46–48 cm)/females less [ANKC] [CKC][KC]

- **Weight**: Males 33–40 lb (15–18 kg)/females less

- **Coat**: Single coat is wavy, soft, silky, dense

- **Colors**: Any shade of blue-gray or gray-blue; may have small white markings; may have black points

- **Other Names**: Irish Blue Terrier

- **Registries (With Group)**: AKC (Terrier); ANKC (Terriers); CKC (Terriers); FCI (Terriers); KC (Terrier); UKC (Terrier)

History and Personality

The origin of the Kerry Blue Terrier is a mystery, but whatever his beginnings, the Kerry Blue Terrier has been seen in Ireland for at least a century, concentrated around the county Kerry near Lake Killarney. Hardy terriers like the Kerry were used by farmers to kill vermin, hunt, tend stock, guard property, and watch over their families. The Kerry Blue is related to the Irish Terrier and Soft Coated Wheaten Terrier, both of whom played a factor in his development. Over the years, the Kerry Blue Terrier has been used as a police dog, military guard dog, retriever, and herder.

The solidly built Kerry Blue Terrier is a rough-and-tumble playmate for people of all ages. Vivacious, charming, and feisty, he can light up a room and command attention. He is an intelligent and confident dog who can be territorial when it comes to how he views outsiders—especially when they interact with his family. Extensive socialization from puppyhood is needed to quell his sometimes aggressive instincts, and he should be monitored in the company of other dogs.

Exercise, Training, Grooming, and Health

- The Kerry Blue Terrier needs plenty of exercise that keeps him physically and mentally challenged. He is an all-purpose dog who is game for any activity.

- The Kerry needs a firm hand in training but not a harsh one. He loses interest easily and needs reminding as you're working with him. Short, focused lessons are best.

- Kerry Blue Terriers who compete in the show ring require professional grooming to achieve the sculpted look that characterizes them in that arena. Even Kerrys kept as pets need the attention of a professional groomer every 6 to 8 weeks to keep the coat from becoming unruly. They are practically nonshedding, making them a suitable choice for many allergy sufferers.

- Average life span is 12 to 15 years. Breed health concerns may include cerebellar abiotrophy (CA); ear infections; eye problems; hypothyroidism; patellar luxation; and skin problems.

Breed Facts

- **Country of Origin**: Japan
- **Height**: Males 20.5 in (52 cm)/females 18 in (46 cm)
- **Weight**: 30–60 lb (13.5–27 kg) [est.]
- **Coat**: Double coat with harsh, straight outercoat and soft, dense undercoat
- **Colors**: White|also red, sesame (red fawn hair with black tips) [FCI][UKC]
- **Other Names**: Kishu; Kishu Inu
- **Registries (With Group)**: AKC (FSS: Working); FCI (Spitz and Primitive); UKC (Northern)

History and Personality

The Japanese have been breeding spitz-type dogs for millennia. The dogs were used to hunt all kinds of game and assisted the *matagi* (professional hunters). The Kishu is the matagi's dog from the mountainous regions of Wakayama and Mie prefectures. Sometimes used to hunt deer, he was best known for hunting wild boars, where he would courageously run interference if a wounded boar charged the hunter. Today, he is still a hunter in his native Japan but is primarily a companion and guardian.

The Kishu is a self-confident and curious dog. Bred to hunt and take on large game, he is courageous and spirited. A highly prized dog in his native Japan, he is also revered as a guardian of the family. The Kishu should be socialized from puppyhood to ensure that he is adaptable to a variety of people, places, and other pets—especially other dogs.

Exercise, Training, Grooming, and Health

- The athletic Kishu appreciates and needs vigorous exercise. He is comfortable in all kinds of weather, especially liking cool weather.

- The strong-willed Kishu needs a firm and fair trainer who understands his nature to best work with him, since he can seem stubborn and uninterested in training.

- His double coat sheds seasonally, but otherwise, all the Kishu needs for looking great is to be brushed a few times a week.

- The average life span of the Kishu Inu is 12 to 14 years. There are no reported breed-specific health concerns.

Breed Facts

- **Country of Origin**: Hungary

- **Height**: Males 27.5 in (70 cm) minimum/females 25.5 in (65 cm) minimum|23.5–31.5 in (59.5–80 cm), with males 25 in (63.5 cm) minimum/females 23.5 in (59.5 cm) minimum [CKC][KC]

- **Weight**: Males 100–134.5 lb (45.5–61 kg)/females 80–110 lb (36.5–50 kg)

- **Coat**: Double coat with long, wavy or curly, coarse outercoat and dense, soft, woolly undercoat; coarser hairs of outercoat trap undercoat, forming strong cords

- **Colors**: White [AKC][CKC][KC]|ivory [ANKC][FCI] [UKC]

- **Other Names**: Hungarian Komondor; Hungarian Sheepdog

- **Registries (With Group)**: AKC (Working); ANKC (Working); CKC (Working); FCI (Sheepdogs); KC (Pastoral); UKC (Guardian)

History and Personality

The Komondor is directly descended from Owtcharkas (ancient flock guardian dogs) brought to Hungary by the nomadic Magyars more than 1,000 years ago. These fearless dogs were used to protect livestock against predators like coyotes and wolves. The purpose of the corded was to allow for the dogs to blend in with a flock of sheep and to protect them. Fully corded, a Komondor was protected against the weather (wet, cold, and heat) and against the teeth and claws of predators. In his native land, the working Komondor is shaggy, heavily matted, and untidy—quite unlike the meticulously tended coats of those in the show ring.

Still retaining his strong guarding instincts, the Komondor is a tough dog who is not to be taken lightly. He is serious and commanding, ready to take on any challenge. In his native land, he protects sheep against wolves and bears, and these protective instincts mean that if threatened, the Komondor will respond. He is an independent thinker, willful and territorial. He needs an experienced owner who understands his ways and is committed to socializing and training him. To an owner who is firm but fair, he is respectful and affectionate.

Exercise, Training, Grooming, and Health

- The Komondor will become bored if not sufficiently exercised. Long walks or participation in flock-guarding events are necessary if the Komondor isn't a working farm dog.

- The serious, intelligent, and tough Komondor needs a trainer who understands and can work with him. He is independent and used to making his own decisions, which can make obedience training quite a challenge.

- The cording on the Komondor's unusual coat happens naturally as the dog grows. But this does not mean that the coat is low maintenance. In fact, cording takes special care, requiring meticulous training during puppyhood and hours of blow-drying the coat after bathing. In addition, owners spend up to two hours per week hand-separating the cords. It should not be brushed or combed.

- Average life span is 10 to 12 years. Breed health concerns may include bloat; cataracts; entropion; and hip dysplasia.

Kooikerhondje

Breed Facts

- **Country of Origin**: Netherlands

- **Height**: 14–16 in (35–40.5 cm)

- **Weight**: 20–24 lb (9–11 kg) [est.]

- **Coat**: Double coat with medium-length, slightly wavy or straight outercoat and well-developed undercoat

- **Colors**: Orange-red color patches on white

- **Other Names**: Dutch Decoy Dog; Kooiker Hound; Small Dutch Waterfowl Dog

- **Registries (With Group)**: AKC (FSS: Sporting); FCI (Flushing Dogs); KC (Gundog); UKC (Gun Dog)

History and Personality

The Kooikerhondje was used as a tolling dog in the Netherlands for centuries, most likely developed from an ancient type of spaniel. These dogs would help hunters draw ducks into a *kooi* (trap), which is how they got their name. Hunters used a curved ditch leading away from a body of water and nets over the ditch, which formed a pipe-like trap. The dogs were taught to run, weave, and cavort along the lakes, ponds, and canals, drawing the ducks' attention by waving their bushy white tails. The ducks would follow the Kooikerhondje and be lured into the trap, where the hunter would be able to catch an entire flock.

The Dutch consider the Kooikerhondje an ideal family companion—loyal and affectionate with those he knows but somewhat suspicious of strangers. He is described as being neither aggressive nor antisocial; he is calm indoors but has boundless energy outdoors. His delight in life is to hunt all day and sleep with the family at night. He is a trustworthy companion for children young and old. He will alert his owner to visitors but does not bark a lot.

Exercise, Training, Grooming, and Health

- It is important to satisfy the physical needs of the Kooikerhondje because if he does not get enough physical exercise and mental stimulation, he can become bored.

- The Kooikerhondje must be trained with positive methods and rewarded for appropriate behaviors. Sensitive and responsive, when his energy is channeled into something he enjoys, he learns quickly and delights in the shared activity.

- The Kooikerhondje's coat is waterproof and easily repels dirt and grime. Weekly brushings are all he needs to keep his coat in shape.

- Average life span is 12 to 14 years. Breed health concerns may include cataracts; epilepsy; hereditary necrotizing myelopathy; patellar luxation; and von Willebrand disease.

Kuvasz

Breed Facts

- **Country of Origin**: Hungary

- **Height**: Males 28–30 in (71–76 cm)/females 26–28 in (66–71 cm)

- **Weight**: Males 88–136.5 lb (40–62 kg)/females 66–110 lb (30–50 kg)

- **Coat**: Double coat with quite wavy to straight, medium-coarse outercoat and fine, woolly undercoat; neck ruff

- **Colors**: White|white but ivory permitted [ANKC][CKC][FCI] [UKC]

- **Other Names**: Hungarian Kuvasz

- **Registries (With Group)**: AKC (Working); ANKC (Working); CKC (Working); FCI (Sheepdogs); KC (Pastoral); UKC (Guardian)

History and Personality

The Kuvasz has been guarding flocks of livestock in Hungary for thousands of years. Although his exact origins are still up for debate, many cynologists believe that Kuvasz-type dogs were brought to Hungary by nomadic Magyar tribes, who moved along travel routes between Asia and Europe. Some settled in the Carpathian Basin in Hungary around 896 CE and shifted to agricultural living, where flock guards were invaluable to their way of life. The Kuvasz was used in the wetter, mountainous areas, and the Komondor (another of Hungary's native flock guards) was used in the drier, flatter areas.

A typical flock guard in temperament, he is wary and suspicious of that which is not familiar. This is correct temperament for the breed, and owners should be responsible, with enough experience and knowledge to control the protective temperament. The Kuvasz is independent minded and will test his owner's dominance. However, once he has given his devotion, he will be a one-family dog and will protect that family from all intruders. The Kuvasz has an intense loyalty to those he loves and needs proper socialization and training to become a dependable companion dog.

Exercise, Training, Grooming, and Health

- The Kuvasz should ideally have a job to do, and one that keeps him occupied physically and mentally. Barring that, he needs plenty of exercise.

- It is said of the Kuvasz that he must truly be taught, not trained in the way most dog owners commonly think. In other words, the Kuvasz learns as much through example, based on what is being asked of him and what his instincts are toward a situation. He will not do what he does not want to do or what he deems unacceptable. Forcing him is exactly the wrong approach.

- Weekly brushing is a necessity for the thick-coated Kuvasz. His coat naturally sheds dirt, and bathing should be avoided as it strips the natural oils from his fur and skin.

- Average life span is 10 to 12 years. Breed health concerns may include cruciate ligament injuries; hip dysplasia; hypertrophic osteodystrophy (HOD); hypothyroidism; osteochondritis dissecans (OCD); and progressive retinal atrophy (PRA).

Labrador Retriever

Breed Facts

- **Country of Origin**: Great Britain
- **Height**: Males 22–24.5 in (56–62 cm)/females 21.5–23.5 in (54.5–59.5 cm)
- **Weight**: Males 60–80 lb (27–36.5 kg)/females 55–70 lb (25–31.5 kg)
- **Coat**: Double coat with short, straight, dense outercoat and soft, weather-resistant undercoat
- **Colors**: Black, yellow, chocolate
- **Registries (With Group)**: AKC (Sporting); ANKC (Gundogs); CKC (Sporting); FCI (Retrievers); KC (Gundog); UKC (Gun Dog)

History and Personality

In the 1800s, ships traveling from Newfoundland to England carried with them tough and intelligent dogs who were used to retrieve nets and fowl in the icy Canadian waters. The English marveled at their retrieving abilities, and the second Earl of Marlesbury used these Canadian imports to found the first actual kennel for Labradors. In both England and the United States, the Labrador Retriever is a universally popular dog. Famed for his excellent retrieving skills and talents in the hunting field, he is also considered a family dog par excellence.

The Labrador Retriever is sensible, even-tempered, affectionate, intelligent, and willing to please. Labradors love to play with people of all ages and seem to understand that children need to handled appropriately. They are enthusiastic retrievers and swimmers and can be kept happy for hours with a tennis ball or flying disk tossed repeatedly.

Exercise, Training, Grooming, and Health

- The high-spirited Labrador Retriever must have plenty of exercise for his body and mind. He loves to swim, and a long walk that takes him to a body of water where he can retrieve and play in the water (seemingly tirelessly) is his ideal outing.

- The Labrador Retriever is one of the most trainable of breeds. He lives to please his people and is attentive and responsive during training.

- Labs are moderate to heavy shedders and should be brushed frequently.

- Average life span is 10 to 14 years. Breed health concerns may include elbow dysplasia; hereditary myopathy; hip dysplasia; progressive retinal atrophy (PRA); and retinal dysplasia.

Breed Facts

- **Country of Origin**: Italy
- **Height**: Males 17–19 in (43–48 cm)/females 16–18 in (41–46 cm)
- **Weight**: Males 28.5–35.5 lb (13–16 kg)/females 24–31 lb (11–14 kg)
- **Coat**: Double coat with tightly curled, woolly, somewhat rough, waterproof outercoat and waterproof undercoat
- **Colors**: Brown, brown roan, off-white, orange, white with brown patches, white with orange patches; brown mask acceptable
- **Other Names**: Romagna Water Dog
- **Registries (With Group)**: AKC (FSS: Sporting); ANKC (Gundogs); FCI (Water Dogs); KC (Gundog); UKC (Gun Dog)

History and Personality

Curly-coated water dogs have been seen in Italy since Etruscan times. Originally descended from water dogs who hunted and worked the marshes of Romagna, the Lagotto Romagnolo got his name from the Romagnan dialect word *lagotto*, meaning "duck dog." As marshes were drained for arable land in the mid- to late 1800s, waterfowl began to disappear, and the Lagotto's job requirements began to change. His exceptional nose began to be put to use primarily by truffle hunters, who used him to sniff out the earthy and valuable delicacy.

The Lagotto Romagnolo is an active and affectionate dog. Sensible, robust, and loyal, he is loving with people of all ages, and his intelligence and easygoing nature make training and socializing him simple. Because of this, although he is eager and enthusiastic, he is also willing to please and is an able listener and learner, making him an excellent family companion.

Exercise, Training, Grooming, and Health

- The Lagotto enjoys and needs plenty of exercise to keep him physically and mentally sound.

- The eager-to-please Lagotto is a quick study and able learner.

- He is a practically nonshedding breed, but his dense, woolly coat has a tendency to mat if it's not brushed or combed regularly, and the hair grows, so it will need occasional clipping.

- Average life span is 14 to 16 years. Breed health concerns may include hip dysplasia.

Lakeland Terrier

Breed Facts

- **Country of Origin**: Great Britain

- **Height**: Males 14.5 in (37 cm)/females 13.5 in (34.5 cm)|14.5 in (37 cm) [ANKC][FCI][UKC]|not exceeding 14.5 in (37 cm) [KC]

- **Weight**: Males 17–17.5 lb (7.5–8 kg)/females 15–15.5 lb (7 kg)

- **Coat**: Double coat with wiry, hard, weather-resistant outercoat and soft, close-lying undercoat

- **Colors**: Blue, black, liver, red, wheaten, black and tan, blue and tan, red grizzle|also tan grizzle [CKC]

- **Registries (With Group)**: AKC (Terrier); ANKC (Terriers); CKC (Terriers); FCI (Terriers); KC (Terrier); UKC (Terrier)

History and Personality

The hardworking Lakeland Terrier emerged from terriers who were abundant in the lake districts of northern England.

Numerous varieties of hardworking, solid-colored, broken-coated terriers worked farms and fields during the 1800s. Their job was to assist in foxhunting, going to ground for a fox when it was driven into its den by the hounds. Today, he is an exceptional eliminator of vermin on the family farm and is equally adept as a steadfastly loyal companion.

Down to earth and levelheaded, the Lakeland Terrier is a confident dog who is always on the alert. He makes a good watchdog but can be barky. He is intelligent and inquisitive and has a zest for life that is sure to keep his family amused. He can be territorial with food and toys. He is courageous, cheerful, and quite affectionate, especially with children.

Exercise, Training, Grooming, and Health

- The Lakeland Terrier doesn't have to be exercised excessively, but he needs to get out and about daily to rid him of any excess energy.

- The Lakeland can be a challenge to train, as he bores easily and needs to be sufficiently challenged.

- Like other terriers, the Lakeland sheds little to no hair, but he still needs grooming to look his best. His coat requires regular hand-plucking, which involves manually pulling the old, dead hairs from his coat to thin and shape it.

- Average life span is 12 to 15 years. Breed health concerns may include eye problems and Legg-Calve-Perthes disease.

Lancashire Heeler

Breed Facts

- **Country of Origin**: Great Britain
- **Height**: Males 12 in (30 cm)/females 10 in (25 cm)
- **Weight**: 6–13 lb (2.5–6 kg) [est.]
- **Coat**: Double coat with short, flat, hard, thick, weather-resistant outercoat and fine undercoat
- **Colors**: Black and tan, liver and tan
- **Other Names**: Ormskirk Heeler; Ormskirk Terrier
- **Registries (With Group)**: AKC (FSS: Herding); KC (Pastoral)

History and Personality

This breed's roots are believed to trace back to black and white Corgi-type dogs who were used to drive cattle in the northwest of England. These heelers became popular farm dogs, especially around the Lancashire area. They were adept at moving cattle by nipping at their heels and were built low to avoid getting kicked by the livestock. In addition, their passion for hunting rabbits, exterminating rats, and alerting to intruders made them an excellent family farm dog.

The Lancashire is an upbeat, active, and intelligent dog. His size belies his energy level and athletic abilities—he likes to be kept busy and is happiest rounding up and keeping an eye on his family. Sturdy and long lived, the Lancashire Heeler makes a wonderful companion for an active family. He prefers the company of older children, but when socialized, gets along with everyone.

Exercise, Training, Grooming, and Health

- The Lancashire Heeler needs exercise, and best of all, exercise with a purpose. Besides several vigorous walks a day, he should have some kind of directed activity to keep his mind sharp.

- His training needs to be focused and positive to hold his attention. When engaged by the training, the Heeler is a quick study.

- The Heeler should be brushed and combed a couple of times a week so that he looks and feels great.

- Average life span is 11 to 14 years. Breed health concerns may include Collie eye anomaly (CEA); persistent pupillary membrane (PPM); and primary lens luxation.

Leonberger

Breed Facts

- **Country of Origin**: Germany

- **Height**: Males 28–31.5 in (71–80 cm)/females 25.5–29.5 in (65–75 cm)

- **Weight**: 80–150 lb (36.5–68 kg) [est.]

- **Coat**: Double coat with long, medium-soft to coarse, close-fitting, water-resistant outercoat and thick, soft undercoat; feathering; mane

- **Colors**: Lion yellow, golden to red-brown, sand, and all combinations in between; black mask

- **Registries (With Group)**: AKC (Miscellaneous); ANKC (Utility); CKC (Working); FCI (Molossoid); KC (Working); UKC (Guardian)

History and Personality

The development of the Leonberger in the 19th century can be credited to one man—Heinrich Essig. An alderman in the town of

Leonberg, Germany, Essig was an animal trader and breeder who wanted to produce a large, noble dog to help promote his business and his hometown. Although he kept no detailed breeding records, Essig claimed to have crossed a Landseer Newfoundland with a St. Bernard, then backcrossed to a Great Pyrenees to develop the Leonberger. It is likely that local dogs were also incorporated into the base stock, as well as German or Austrian scenthounds, Greater Swiss Mountain Dogs, or Kuvaszok. The results were large, strong dogs who quickly gained popularity as working animals and a leonine status symbol for the city of Leonberg and surrounding estates. Today, he is increasingly popular and is familiarly called the "Gentle Lion" or "Leo."

The Leonberger is grand and imposing yet supremely affectionate, intelligent, and noble. He is even-tempered, patient, and loving. The Leonberger is a family-oriented dog, meaning that he needs to be part of the family "herd" and is not happy left by himself. He especially loves children and can do well with other dogs and animals as long as he's properly socialized.

Exercise, Training, Grooming, and Health

- As a puppy, the Leo should not be overexercised. As an adult, the Leonberger loves long walks, playtimes, and opportunities to swim.

- Although the Leonberger might not be the ideal competitive obedience dog, his loyal nature makes him aim to please. Paired with his intelligence, this makes teaching him basic household manners fairly easy. Leos need lots of socialization from puppyhood.

- The Leo's thick fur sheds, and he has two seasonal "molts" that cause profuse shedding. Because of this and the need to keep the long hair free of tangles and debris, he should be brushed several times a week.

- Average life span is 8 to 10 years. Breed health concerns may include Addison's disease; bloat; ectropion; entropion; hip dysplasia; osteochondritis dissecans (OCD); osteosarcoma; and panosteitis.

Lhasa Apso

Breed Facts

- **Country of Origin**: China (Tibet Region)

- **Height**: Males 10–11.5 in (25.5–29 cm)/females slightly smaller

- **Weight**: 13–18 lb (6–8 kg) [est.]

- **Coat**: Double coat with "good length," straight, hard, heavy, dense outercoat and dense undercoat; whiskers and beard

- **Colors**: Golden, sandy, honey, dark grizzle, slate, smoke, particolor, black, white, brown|all colors and combinations acceptable [AKC][CKC][UKC]

- **Other Names**: Abso Seng Kye; Tibetan Apso

- **Registries (With Group)**: AKC (Non-Sporting); ANKC (Non Sporting); CKC (Non-Sporting); FCI (Companion and Toy); KC (Utility); UKC (Companion)

History and Personality

Small, shaggy dogs were known in Tibet as far back as 8000 BCE. When Tibet converted to Buddhism in the 7th century CE, breeders of the small dogs wanted to fix a type to resemble the lion.

Lhasas—"lion dogs"—became fixtures inside the homes of Tibetan nobility and in lamas' monasteries. Lhasas, with their sharp bark and fine hearing, were most likely used as sentinels to alert their owners to a stranger's approach. They were also beloved companions and friends.

Today's Lhasa Apso is true to his long and distinguished past of serving as a spirited and highly regarded companion. In his heart, he believes that he is the special one in the household, the one whom others should respect and even defer to. He is friendly and assertive, with a unique ability to distinguish friend from foe and letting those he loves know when he is bothered by someone. Lhasas can be somewhat territorial with other dogs and pets and aren't always tolerant of children who are too rough around them.

Exercise, Training, Grooming, and Health

- Although the Lhasa Apso is small, he's not delicate or toy-like—this sturdy companion will gladly accompany his family on regular outings or even extended walks.

- Lhasa Apsos are used to being spoiled, and this does incline them to do things when they are ready, not necessarily when their owner is. Fortunately, they are devoted companions and when trained with rewards that motivate them, they are quick and able learners. Socialization is critical for this breed.

- Lhasa Apsos who compete in the show ring need daily attention to their coats to keep them dirt- and mat-free. People who don't show their Lhasas typically keep the coats clipped for ease of grooming. Any Lhasa should be brushed regularly to keep the fur from tangling.

- Average life span is up to 18 years. Breed health concerns may include progressive retinal atrophy (PRA) and renal dysplasia.

Breed Facts

- **Country of Origin**: France

- **Height**: 8–14 in (20–35.5 cm)

- **Weight**: 4.5–13 lb (2–6 kg)

- **Coat**: Single coat is long, moderately soft, wavy, dense

- **Colors**: All colors and combinations acceptable

- **Other Names**: Little Lion Dog; Petit Chien Lion

- **Registries (With Group)**: AKC (Non-Sporting); ANKC (Toys); CKC (Non-Sporting); FCI (Companion and Toy); KC (Toy); UKC (Companion)

History and Personality

The exact origins of the Löwchen are a mystery, but this small breed has been established in Spain, France, and Germany since the 1500s. The breed undoubtedly evolved from the family of bichons as they traveled from the Mediterranean into Europe. He came to be called "the little lion dog" because of the favored clip of his coat—a style similar to that of the Portuguese Water Dog "lion" trim.

Owners should not be fooled by the Löwchen's small size—he is all dog. Full of a sense of purpose, the Löwchen commands attention not with needy entreaties but with his unmistakable presence. He is also sensitive and responsive, playful and intelligent, and happy to comply with the wishes of a respected owner.

Exercise, Training, Grooming, and Health

- A spunky and energetic dog, the Löwchen enjoys getting out for regular walks and brisk exercise.

- Although the Löwchen is no pushover, he is basically agreeable and wants to please his owner. He responds well to reward-based training, and he is a quick learner.

- Löwchens are practically nonshedding, so they can be desirable dogs for some allergy sufferers. The dead hair is removed by regular brushing, and the area around his hindquarters should be clipped short for the traditional lion trim. He can also be kept in a puppy clip for ease of care.

- Average life span is 12 to 14 years. Breed health concerns may include patellar luxation.

Maltese

Breed Facts

- **Country of Origin**: Italy
- **Height**: Males 8.5–10 in (21–25 cm)/females 7.5–9 in (19–23 cm)|not over 10 in (25 cm) [ANKC][KC]
- **Weight**: 6–9 lb (2.5–4 kg)
- **Coat**: Single coat is long, flat, silky, dense
- **Colors**: Pure white; light tan or lemon markings permissible
- **Other Names**: Bichon Maltiase
- **Registries (With Group)**: AKC (Toy); ANKC (Toys); CKC (Toys); FCI (Companion and Toy); KC (Toy); UKC (Companion)

History and Personality

The Maltese is an ancient breed, one of several small "bichon" dogs found around the Mediterranean for thousands of years. His exact place of origin is a mystery, but most historians pinpoint Malta for the development of the breed. On Malta, small dogs were bred entirely as companions and "comforters." The Maltese maintained his demand as a companion through the centuries and today remains a popular show dog and beloved pet.

The Maltese is a small dog with a *big* personality. Spirited, affectionate, loyal, mischievous, adorable—no one with a Maltese in the family will ever be bored or lonely. Maltese are playful dogs who thrive on positive interactions. They are happy to cavort with people of all ages and sizes and are wonderful companions for children who will not be too rough with them.

Exercise, Training, Grooming, and Health

- The Maltese enjoy daily walks and will gladly play catch or fetch with small toys, inside or out.

- Because the Maltese thrives on human interaction, training him to do the basics is not difficult, especially if you use positive, reward-based training methods. One aspect of training that can prove difficult is housetraining.

- A Maltese kept in a long coat for the show ring is high maintenance. Most people who keep Maltese as pets choose to keep them in a "puppy clip," which requires less frequent brushing and combing. His human-like hair is practically nonshedding.

- Average life span is 15 or more years. Breed health concerns may include hypoglycemia; patellar luxation; patent ductus arteriosis (PDA); portosystemic shunts; and white shaker dog syndrome.

Breed Facts

- **Country of Origin**: Great Britain

- **Varieties**: Standard and Toy

- **Height**: *Standard*: Males 15.5–16 in (40–41 cm)/females 15 in (38 cm); *Toy*: 10–12 in (25.5–30.5 cm) [est.]

- **Weight**: Standard: 12–22 lb (5.5–10 kg); *Toy*: No more than 12 lb (5.5 kg)

- **Coat**: Short, smooth, glossy, dense, tight

- **Colors**: Jet black and rich mahogany tan

- **Other Names**: Black and Tan Terrier

- **Registries (With Group)**: AKC (*Standard*: Terrier, *Toy*: Toy); ANKC (Terriers); CKC (*Standard*: Terrier, *Toy*: Toy); FCI (Terriers); KC (Terrier); UKC (*Standard*: Terrier, *Toy*: Toy)

History and Personality

The Manchester Terrier is most certainly descended from the Black and Tan Terrier, England's original ratting terrier. During the mid-1800s, a breeder from Manchester named John Hulme wanted to produce an agile, superb ratter with "true grit," so he crossed the Black and Tan Terrier with the coursing Whippet. This combination created the breed now known as the Manchester Terrier. Backcrossing to fix type was mainly to more terriers, and Hulme's dream of "true grit" was definitely attained. Today he can be found in two sizes: Standard and Toy.

Manchesters are true terriers: spirited, intelligent, crafty, and independent yet extremely loyal and devoted. Although they are independent-minded and not particularly clingy, they need to be with their people to be content. Neat and clean indoors, they are sporty and eye-catching dogs about town. Manchesters retain their ratting instincts in their desire to chase and play—they enjoy many games and pouncing on small toys. They benefit from active socialization from puppyhood, especially with children of all ages.

Exercise, Training, Grooming, and Health

- The able and athletic Manchester Terrier is happy to accompany his family on all outings. He loves games of fetch in the yard and long walks around the neighborhood.

- Manchester Terriers have a stubborn streak and need firm, fair training. Motivational methods get the best results, especially when they are started early and done regularly.

- The Manchester Terrier's short coat is easy to groom— occasional brushing is all that's needed.

- Average life span of the Manchester Terrier is 15 or more years. Breed health concerns may include cardiomyopathy (Toy); Legg-Calve-Perthes disease; and von Willebrand disease.

Mastiff

Breed Facts

- **Country of Origin**: Great Britain
- **Height**: Males 30 in (76 cm) minimum/females 27.5 in (70 cm) minimum
- **Weight**: 175–200 lb (79.5–90.5 kg) [est.]
- **Coat**: Double coat with moderately short, straight, coarse outercoat and short, dense, close-lying undercoat
- **Colors**: Fawn, apricot, brindle
- **Other Names**: English Mastiff; Old English Mastiff
- **Registries (With Group)**: AKC (Working); ANKC (Utility); CKC (Working); FCI (Molossoid); KC (Working); UKC (Guardian)

History and Personality

The Mastiff is an ancient breed type, believed to be the oldest English breed. The dogs' courage and power so impressed the Romans that they took examples of the breed back to Rome to fight in the arenas with gladiators, bulls, bears, and other fierce opponents. The breed served as a war dog and guardian throughout Europe and wherever armies traveled. Mastiffs also served time fighting in the pits facing large, tough opponents during the Elizabethan era.

Despite his giant size and forbidding appearance, the Mastiff is a good family companion. He is an exceptional watchdog and protector—self-confident, patient, steady, and docile. He rarely barks but will certainly let those by whom he feels threatened know that he is not to be pushed. He is great with children although defensive of them, which can lead to an exaggerated sense of protectiveness.

Exercise, Training, Grooming, and Health

- Care should be taken not to overexercise the Mastiff as he is growing, as this can put too much pressure on his bones and joints. Long walks and play sessions are best, and these can certainly be continued into adulthood.

- The Mastiff is generally an easygoing dog who understands what is asked of him and is fairly compliant. His suspicious nature paired with his large size make socializing him an absolute must.

- The short, smooth coat of the Mastiff needs only occasional brushing. The wrinkles all over his head must be kept clean and dry to prevent infection.

- Average life span is 9 to 11 years. Breed health concerns may include bloat; cystinuria; ectropion; elbow dysplasia; hip dysplasia; osteosarcoma; persistent pupillary membrane (PPM); progressive retinal atrophy (PRA); and seizures.

Breed Facts

- **Country of Origin**: Great Britain
- **Height**: No more than 14 in (35.5 cm)|10–14 in (25.5–35.5 cm) [AKC]
- **Weight**: 25–35 lb (11.5–16 kg) [est.]
- **Coat**: Short, flat, glossy, harsh|soft-textured undercoat may be present in winter [ANKC][FCI][KC]
- **Colors**: For white, pure white coat; may have markings/for colored, any color predominating
- **Registries (With Group)**: AKC (Terrier); ANKC (Terriers); CKC (Terriers); FCI (Terriers); KC (Terrier); UKC (Terrier)

History and Personality

Bred from crosses of the bullbaiters and the now-extinct English White Terrier, with a bit of Dalmatian thrown into the mix, the Bull Terrier remains the closest to the original bull-and-terrier breeds. Englishman James Hinks first standardized the breed in the early 1850s, selecting for white color, gameness, and the unique egg-shaped head. After type was fixed, the color variety was added. The Miniature was bred with the same features of the larger-sized "Bully" but in a more manageable size. Bred to aid their larger brothers in ratting duties, they were a great favorite of those who preferred a smaller, more manageable house pet.

"Active" is probably the best word to describe the Miniature Bull Terrier. He is playful and clownish and retains a child-like curiosity for most of his life. He is adoring of his family and can make a good alarm dog, but owners must be careful not to let his protective instincts turn to jealousy or inappropriate guarding behaviors. Mini Bulls enjoy being the center of attention and want to be part of everything going on around them.

Exercise, Training, Grooming, and Health

- The Mini Bull is a playful, energetic fellow who needs lots of exercise. He is a great playmate, enjoying all kinds of fetching and finding games.

- When it comes to training, the Mini Bull can march to the beat of his own drummer. It doesn't mean he isn't interested in pleasing his owner; it's just his nature. He needs a firm but fair leader to get the best out of him. Using positive, motivational training methods from puppyhood and working in short sessions that keep the Mini Bull focused will yield the best results.

- The Miniature Bull Terrier is easy to keep clean. His short, coarse coat should be gone over with a hound glove to loosen and remove dead hairs, then brushed with a soft brush to restore the luster.

- Average life span is 10 to 14 years. Breed health concerns may include allergies; compulsive tail chasing; deafness (in whites); mitral dysplasia; primary lens luxation; and subaortic stenosis (SAS).

Miniature Pinscher

Breed Facts

- **Country of Origin**: Germany

- **Height**: 10–12.5 in (25.5–31.5 cm)

- **Weight**: 9–13 lb (4–6 kg)

- **Coat**: Short, straight, dense, smooth, shiny, close

- **Colors**: Solid red, stag red, black with rust-red markings, chocolate with rust-red markings|also blue with tan markings [ANKC][KC][UKC]|also fawn with rust-red markings [UKC]

- **Other Names**: Zwergpinscher

- **Registries (With Group)**: AKC (Toy); ANKC (Toys); CKC (Toys); FCI (Pinscher and Schnauzer); KC (Toy); UKC (Companion)

History and Personality

The Miniature Pinscher (nicknamed "Min Pin") has been bred for several hundred years and was originally a formidable ratter. He is part of the German Pinscher family, which encompasses dogs of many sizes, including Schnauzers and Affenpinschers. His heritage is not known for sure, but he is most likely a direct descendent of his larger cousin, the German Pinscher. It's possible that terriers, Dachshunds, and Italian Greyhounds were introduced to the smallest pinschers to obtain their diminutive size and hunting abilities.

The Min Pin is a self-assured, gregarious, fun-loving showman who can light up a room—it's no wonder he's been given the title "King of Toys." Curious and fearless, there is not much that the Min Pin misses. He bonds steadfastly to his family and wants to be with them always and everywhere. His guarding instincts and a robust and confident nature are evident, and he is not shy about using his voice freely.

Exercise, Training, Grooming, and Health

- The Min Pin is up for anything, and getting exercise by accompanying his family on their daily rounds is at the top of his list.

- Short, motivational training sessions will help the Min Pin become well mannered.

- The Miniature Pinscher has a low-maintenance coat and is easily groomed with minimal brushing.

- Average life span is 15 or more years. Breed health concerns may include cervical (dry) disk; epilepsy; eye problems; heart problems; hypothyroidism; Legg-Calve-Perthes disease; and patellar luxation.

Miniature Schnauzer

Breed Facts

- **Country of Origin**: Germany
- **Height**: Males 14 in (36 cm)/females 13 in (33 cm)|12–14 in (30.5–35.5 cm) [AKC][CKC][FCI][UKC]
- **Weight**: Approx. 9–17.5 lb (4–8 kg)
- **Coat**: Double coat with hard, wiry outercoat and soft, close, dense undercoat
- **Colors**: Salt and pepper, black and silver, solid black
- **Other Names**: Zwergschnauzer
- **Registries (With Group)**: AKC (Terrier); ANKC (Utility); CKC (Terriers); FCI (Pinscher and Schnauzer); KC (Utility); UKC (Terrier)

History and Personality

Schnauzers have been popular farm dogs in Germany for centuries. Sizes ranged because there was no set type, and the smaller dogs were used as general vermin exterminators. The Miniature Schnauzer was developed by breeding the smallest of the Standards with Affenpinschers and small black Poodles. Miniature Pinschers, Wire Fox Terriers, and Zwergspitz may also have been used in the mix. Although he may not be used for farm work much anymore, he is still a capable and spirited pet.

Lively, alert, charismatic, and ultimately charming, the Miniature Schnauzer has something for everyone. He is rugged and alert and makes an excellent watchdog. The Miniature Schnauzer is intelligent, devoted, and serious about being a member of the family—he needs to be included in everything that goes on. He is fearless without being aggressive, and he gets along well with children and other dogs.

Exercise, Training, Grooming, and Health

- Daily sessions of exercise for the Miniature Schnauzer are necessary or his energy will turn to destructive behaviors.

- The Miniature Schnauzer is a smart dog who learns quickly. With methods that encourage and reward him, the Mini Schnauzer will pick up almost anything.

- The Miniature Schnauzer's tough outer coat and soft undercoat (considered a "broken" coat), requires stripping or clipping to keep it from getting too bushy or unruly.

- Average life span is 15 or more years. Breed health concerns may include allergies; canine neuronal ceroid-lipofuscinosis (NCL); Cushing's syndrome; diabetes; epilepsy; liver shunts; myotonia congenita; pancreatitis; progressive retinal atrophy (PRA); renal dysplasia; retinal dysplasia; and urolithiasis.

Mudi

Breed Facts

- **Country of Origin**: Hungary

- **Height**: Males 16–18.5 in (41–47 cm)/females 15–17.5 in (38–44 cm)

- **Weight**: Males 24–33 lb (11–15 kg)/females 17.5–26 lb (8–12 kg)

- **Coat**: Short, straight, smooth on head and front of limbs and very wavy or slightly curled, dense, shiny on other parts of body

- **Colors**: Fawn, black, blue merle, ash, brown [CKC][FCI]|black, brown, gray, gray-brown, white, yellow; merle markings [AKC]|black, white, fawn shades, brown, gray, gray-brown, blue merle, red merle [UKC]

- **Other Names**: Hungarian Mudi

- **Registries (With Group)**: AKC (FSS: Herding); CKC (Herding); FCI (Sheepdogs); UKC (Herding)

History and Personality

When the Mudi was "discovered" working with shepherds in Hungary in the early 1900s, he had already been doing his job for what is believed to be centuries, although written records of it don't go back that far. He is the product of necessity, not invention—that much is known—and he evolved as a first-rate "driver dog" who assisted shepherds and farmers in their many farm chores. Dr. Dezsö Fényes helped establish him as a separate breed from the other Hungarian herding dogs, the Puli and Pumi. Today, the Mudi continues to work with shepherds in his native Hungary and is enjoying increased popularity around the world.

The Mudi's talents on the farm are many and include his responsiveness, trainability, and character. He is extremely intelligent and learns quickly. Loyal and true to his family, the Mudi is courageous and will protect and defend against any perceived threat without hesitation. Wary around strangers, he is ever-alert to what could impact his family and farm. When socialized to people of all ages, other pets, and different places from puppyhood, the Mudi is much less reserved. He has a playful, fun-loving side, too, and likes to use his voice.

Exercise, Training, Grooming, and Health

- The Mudi is an energetic dog who is happiest with a full-time job. Smart and driven, he must have his body and mind exercised to be happy.

- The intelligent Mudi is responsive and ready to work, which makes training him a joy. His owner must be one step ahead at all times or the Mudi will end up training his owner. Harsh methods will cause this soft-tempered breed to shut down. When positive, reward-based methods are used, however, the Mudi can accomplish just about anything.

- The Mudi's medium-length, tufted coat is easy to care for. He needs only to be brushed and combed to keep dirt and debris from his fur. He is an average shedder.

- Average life span is 11 to 14 years. There are no reported breed-specific health concerns.

Breed Facts

- **Country of Origin**: Italy
- **Height**: Males 25–31 in (63.5–78.5 cm)/females 23.5–29 in (59.5–73.5 cm)|females slightly less [KC]
- **Weight**: Males 132–154 lb (60–70 kg)/females 110–132 lb (50–60 kg)
- **Coat**: Short, hard, stiff, glossy, dense
- **Colors**: Gray, lead, black, brown, fawn, deep fawn; may have white markings
- **Other Names**: Italian Mastiff; Mastino Napoletano
- **Registries (With Group)**: AKC (Working); ANKC (Utility); CKC (Working); FCI (Molossoid); KC (Working); UKC (Guardian)

History and Personality

The Neapolitan Mastiff is most likely descended from the Roman Molossus, an ancient Mastiff who was introduced to the Romans by the Greeks. The Molossus was a renowned fighting dog who accompanied many armies into battle across Europe and was also used as an arena-fighting dog by the Romans. They were also regular fixtures as guardians of castles and estates, especially in Campania in southern Italy, where the Neapolitan Mastiff has existed for more than 2,000 years.

Although the Neapolitan Mastiff is capable of fearless protection, he is also capable of bottomless affection and care. Behind his imposing exterior is a smart and sensitive dog who easily discerns a real threat but who is calm and steady in the face of all but the most pressing need to defend himself or his charges. Regardless of how gentle he can be, he should be socialized extensively from puppyhood to avoid overprotectiveness on his part. Although he doesn't bark much, he drools and snores.

Exercise, Training, Grooming, and Health

- Neapolitan Mastiffs require several long walks a day to stay fit and mentally stable.

- This is an intelligent and responsive breed that must be trained as young as possible and worked with throughout his life.

- The short coat of the Neapolitan Mastiff is easy to take care of. However, the generous folds around his face, neck, and ears all require regular attention to keep them clean and dry.

- Average life span is up to 10 years. Breed health concerns may include bloat; cherry eye; hip dysplasia; hypothyroidism; and panosteitis.

Newfoundland

Breed Facts

- **Country of Origin**: Canada

- **Height**: Males 28 in (71 cm) average/females 26 in (66 cm) average

- **Weight**: Males 130–152 lb (59–69 kg)/females 100–120 lb (45.5–54.5 kg)

- **Coat**: Double coat with moderately long, moderately straight, coarse, oily, water-resistant outercoat and soft, dense undercoat

- **Colors**: Black, brown, white with black markings|also gray [AKC][UKC]|only black; white markings permissible [CKC]

- **Registries (With Group)**: AKC (Working); ANKC (Utility); CKC (Working); FCI (Molossoid); KC (Working); UKC (Guardian)

History and Personality

Records from the 1600s show that European fishing vessels were frequent visitors to the Maritimes. Because these travelers often arrived with dogs, their European breeds most likely crossed with native dogs to contribute to today's Newfoundland. These most likely included the Portuguese Water Dog and Great Pyrenees. Eventually, two distinct types developed: the so-called Lesser St. John's Dog (who developed into the Labrador Retriever) and the Greater St. John's Dog (who became the Newfoundland). Both were invaluable assistants to fishermen. The Newfoundland's duties included hauling in nets, carrying boat lines to shore, rescuing anyone who fell overboard, and whatever else was requested of him. His webbed feet and water-repellent coat enabled him to work in any kind of conditions.

The Newfoundland ("Newfie") has long been considered the gentlest of giants—a big pillow upon which generations of young and old have rested their heads. More than that, he is a noble, honest, and hardworking dog whose purpose is service. He is devoted to his family and is excellent with children and other pets. Although gentle and even-tempered, he is still an active and playful dog.

Exercise, Training, Grooming, and Health

- A growing Newfoundland should not be overly exerted because his bones and muscles could be strained. Once he's an adult, though, the Newfie should be exercised regularly.

- The Newfoundland is responsive and trusting. Reward-based training sessions work wonders on him. He does not tolerate harsh methods.

- The Newfie's thick water-repellent coat should be brushed often to keep it looking its best.

- Average life span is about 10 years. Breed health concerns may include bloat; cystinuria; elbow dysplasia; hip dysplasia; and subaortic stenosis (SAS).

Norrbottenspets

Breed Facts

- **Country of Origin**: Sweden

- **Height**: Males 17.5–18 in (44.5–45.5 cm)/females 16.5–17 in (42–43 cm)

- **Weight**: 26–33 lb (12–15 kg) [est.]

- **Coat**: Double coat with short, straight, hard, close-fitting outercoat and dense undercoat

- **Colors**: All colors permitted, but ideal is white with yellow or red/brown markings|white with fawn markings, orange markings, red patches, sable, tan patches [AKC]

- **Other Names**: Nordic Spitz, Norrbottenspitz; Norbottenspetz

- **Registries (With Group)**: AKC (FSS: Hound); CKC (Hounds); FCI (Spitz and Primitive); UKC (Northern)

History and Personality

For hundreds of years, the Scandinavian countries of Sweden, Finland, and Lapland all had use for this little spitz-type dog as a hunter of small game. Called the Pohjanpystykorva in Finland, it was taken by immigrant farmers to northern Sweden where it was given an even longer name, the *Norrbottensskollandehund*. A common hunting and farm dog for many years, his numbers fell off until a breeding program in mid-1900s reestablished the breed. Today, he is becoming increasingly popular in both countries, prized as a wonderful companion and a crafty hunter of game birds such as grouse and hazel hens.

The Norrbottenspets is an alert, lively, and intelligent breed—he's never shy, nervous, or aggressive. Friendly and fun-loving, he especially loves children. The Norrbottenspets has a plus as a house pet, in that he is not the great barker that most of the other Nordic hunters are.

Exercise, Training, Grooming, and Health

- If he had his way, the Norrbottenspets would go hunting every day Without this, he needs a proper substitute—at least a few long walks daily and preferably the opportunity to run and hunt off lead in a safe area.

- Independent-minded but also with a strong desire to please, the Norrbottenspets is responsive to motivational training— especially when it is done in conjunction with hunting junkets.

- This is a naturally neat and clean breed. The Norrbottenspets's coat requires only brushing and combing to keep it looking great. It is naturally lustrous and shakes clean.

- Average life span is 12 to 14 years. There are no reported breed-specific health concerns.

Breed Facts

- **Country of Origin**: Great Britain

- **Height**: Males 9–10 in (23–25.5 cm)/females slightly smaller|10 in (25.5 cm) [ANKC][CKC][FCI][KC][UKC]

- **Weight**: Males 11–12 lb (5–5.5 kg)/females slightly smaller|11–12 lb (5–5.5 kg)

- **Coat**: Double coat with straight, wiry, hard, close-lying outercoat and definite undercoat; mane; slight whiskers

- **Colors**: All shades of red, wheaten, black and tan, grizzle

- **Registries (With Group)**: AKC (Terrier); ANKC (Terriers); CKC (Terriers); FCI (Terriers); KC (Terrier); UKC (Terrier)

History and Personality

At one time the Norfolk Terrier and Norwich Terrier were interchangeable—both considered a typical farm dog and hunting terrier from the same part of east–central England. In the early 1900s, Frank "Roughrider" Jones bred his Glen of Imaal Terriers and a dark red brindle Cairn-type female to a working terrier from Norwich named Rags, who became the keystone sire of the breed. At first, the name "Norwich Terrier" covered dogs with both prick and drop ears, but eventually, the fold-eared was recognized as a separate breed—the "Norfolk."

These terriers were bred to hunt in packs and are typically more sociable and agreeable than others in the Terrier Group. Still, though, they are feisty and full of themselves as all terriers should be. The Norfolk does not like to be left alone and becomes quite attached and proprietary toward his owner. Although this can be flattering, it can lead to jealousy and aggressiveness, especially with other pets.

Exercise, Training, Grooming, and Health

- The feisty and fun-loving Norfolk does best with several outings a day to keep him exercised and socialized.

- He can be stubborn and distracted, but the Norfolk aims to please. Housetraining can be difficult.

- The Norfolk sports a thick, weather-resistant coat that needs almost daily brushing and combing to keep it maintained and looking its best. A professional groomer can advise on when, if, or how frequently he should be clipped.

- Average life span is 12 to 15 years. Breed health concerns may include mitral valve disease (MVD).

Norwegian Buhund

Breed Facts

- **Country of Origin**: Norway

- **Height**: Males 17–18.5 in (43–47 cm)/females 16–17.5 in (40.5–44.5 cm)|females slightly less [ANKC][KC]

- **Weight**: Males 31–40 lb (14–18 kg)/females 26–35 lb (12–16 kg)

- **Coat**: Double coat with hard, thick, smooth-lying outercoat and soft, dense undercoat

- **Colors**: Wheaten, black; mask acceptable on wheaten|also red, wolf-sable [ANKC][KC]

- **Other Names**: Norsk Buhund

- **Registries (With Group)**: AKC (Miscellaneous); ANKC (Working); CKC (Herding); FCI (Spitz and Primitive); KC (Pastoral); UKC (Northern)

History and Personality

In Norwegian, Bu means "homestead" or "mountain hut," and Buhund was the name given to the spitz-type dogs who took care of the shepherds' flocks and safeguarded their homes. This ancient breed came with people migrating from the north to Scandinavian countries. A Viking grave in Norway dating to CE 900 contained the remains of six dogs who resembled today's Buhund. Because Vikings buried their most treasured possessions with them to help them in the afterlife, these dogs must have been valued indeed. Besides herding sheep, the Buhund was and still is adept at hunting fowl such as turkeys, pheasants, and ducks.

The Buhund has an innate desire to please—a trait that may be stronger in him than in many other spitz dogs. He is an adaptable, intelligent, quick learning, and honest family member. Besides having excellent herding instincts, he is a keen watchdog—vigilant but not excessively noisy. He gets along well with children and doesn't mind other dogs or pets. His independent nature suits him at times when he needs to be left alone for a while.

Exercise, Training, Grooming, and Health

- The Buhund is an active and family-oriented dog who enjoys participating in all activities. He requires both mental and physical stimulation to be at his best.

- The gregarious and quick Buhund is a relatively easy dog to train. He has an independent streak, but his strong desire to please and do what is asked of him so that he can be with people makes him receptive and responsive to requests. He enjoys the mental stimulation that training and working provide.

- A seasonally heavy shedder, the Buhund's thick coat demands regular brushing and combing. He is a naturally clean dog otherwise.

- Average life span is 13 to 15 years. Breed health concerns may include hip dysplasia.

Breed Facts

- **Country of Origin**: Norway

- **Height**: Males 20.5 in (52 cm)/females 19.5 in (49 cm)

- **Weight**: Males 50.5–55 lb (23–25 kg)/females 44–48 lb (20–22 kg)

- **Coat**: Double coat with medium-length, straight, thick, coarse, smooth-lying outercoat and soft, dense, woolly undercoat

- **Colors**: Gray of various shades

- **Other Names**: Gray Norwegian Elkhound; Norsk Elghund Grå

- **Registries (With Group)**: AKC (Hound); ANKC (Hounds); CKC (Hounds); FCI (Spitz and Primitive); KC (Hound); UKC (Northern)

History and Personality

The loyal and courageous Elkhound has been by humankind's side for many thousands of years—skeletal remains nearly identical to today's Elkhound have been dated from 5000 to 4000 BCE. His popularity held steady through time because he was so resourceful. Not only was he invaluable on the hunt, he was also an excellent watchdog, herder, flock guard, sled dog to help haul supplies, and fine family companion.

Even-tempered, intelligent, and alert, the Norwegian Elkhound is an all-around companion. Strong and fearless enough to take the role of watchdog seriously, he is also level-headed and sensible enough not to overdo things, discerning friend from foe with little fanfare. He is naturally reserved with strangers, but with those he knows, he is enthusiastically affectionate.

Exercise, Training, Grooming, and Health

- Norwegian Elkhounds are robust and athletic dogs who thrive on exercise.

- The sensitive, independent-minded Elkhound does best with motivational and reward-based training. Working him for short sessions several times a day is best.

- The thick double coat of the Norwegian Elkhound requires regular brushing and combing to loosen and remove the dead hairs.

- Average life span is 13 to 15 years. Breed health concerns may include Fanconi syndrome; hypothyroidism; infundibular keratinizing acanthoma; and progressive retinal atrophy (PRA).

Breed Facts

- **Country of Origin**: Norway

- **Height**: Males 13–15 in (33–38 cm)/females 12–14 in (30.5–35.5 cm)

- **Weight**: Males 15.5 lb (7 kg)/females 13 lb (6 kg)

- **Coat**: Double coat with harsh, dense outercoat and soft, dense undercoat

- **Colors**: Fallow to reddish brown to tan with white markings, white with red or dark markings|also black, gray [CKC][FCI] [UKC]

- **Other Names**: Lundehund; Norsk Lundehund; Norwegian Puffin Dog

- **Registries (With Group)**: AKC (Miscellaneous); CKC (Hounds); FCI (Spitz and Primitive); UKC (Northern)

History and Personality

Lunde is the Norwegian word for "puffin," and the breed got its name because of its talent at hunting these particular seabirds—a talent due to the breed's drive, tenacity, and unique physiology. He has a small body, and he also has at least six toes on each foot, which gave him increased agility on the cliffs where the puffins built their nests. These toes are double- and triple jointed—making him incredibly sure-footed. In addition, the Lundehund's head can be bent back to the point where it nearly touches his back, and his front legs can turn at 90-degree angles to the sides. These features all allowed him to mold his body to fit into narrow rocky crevices. Today puffins are protected species, so the Lundehund is now prized as a companion, and he is gaining favor worldwide.

The Lundehund's traits include tenacity, perseverance, courage, climbing ability, tracking instincts, and occasional single-mindedness. He needs a safe and secure area in which to run and play and shouldn't be trusted off lead. He can be difficult to housetrain, he can be stubborn, and he is quick to alert to anyone approaching the house. But he is also incredibly loving—especially with his family. He is not at all aggressive, and he gets along fine with children and other dogs, especially when socialized.

Exercise, Training, Grooming, and Health

- The Lundehund is an outdoor activity kind of dog, enjoying any and all occasions to accompany his family on trips and walks. He should get more than a couple of walks a day to keep him happy.

- Lundehunds will not respond to harsh commands or unrealistic expectations. He's usually inclined to do things his own way, so patience is necessary. They can be difficult to housetrain, too.

- Brushing with a bristle brush regularly is the best thing to do for your Lundehund. He is a heavy shedder, and brushing also helps to keep that under control.

- Average life span is about 12 years. Breed health concerns may include Lundehund syndrome.

Beed Facts

- **Country of Origin**: Great Britain
- **Height**: 10 in (25.5 cm)
- **Weight**: 12 lb (5.5 kg)
- **Coat**: Double coat with straight, wiry, hard, close-lying outercoat and thick undercoat; face-framing ruff; slight whiskers
- **Colors**: All shades of red, wheaten, black and tan, grizzle
- **Registries (With Group)**: AKC (Terrier); ANKC (Terriers); CKC (Terriers); FCI (Terriers); KC (Terrier); UKC (Terrier)

History and Personality

At one time the Norfolk Terrier and Norwich Terrier were interchangeable—both considered a typical farm dog and hunting terrier from the same part of east–central England. In the early 1900s, Frank "Roughrider" Jones bred his Glen of Imaal Terriers and a dark red brindle Cairn-type female to a working terrier from Norwich named Rags, who became the keystone sire of the breed. At first, the name "Norwich Terrier" covered dogs with both prick and drop ears, but eventually, the fold-eared was broken out as a separate breed—the "Norfolk."

Because Norwich Terriers were bred to hunt in packs, they are typically more sociable and agreeable than other terriers. Still, though, they are feisty and full of themselves as all terriers should be. One of the smallest of the terriers, the Norwich is a great traveling companion—easy to transport and hardy enough for all kinds of getaways. The Norwich is very attached to his family and can be jealous of other pets, so socialization from puppyhood is essential.

Exercise, Training, Grooming, and Health

- The feisty and fun-loving Norwich does best with several outings a day to keep him exercised and socialized.

- He can be stubborn and distracted, but the Norwich aims to please. Housetraining can be difficult.

- The Norwich sports a thick, weather-resistant coat that requires almost daily brushing and combing to keep it maintained and looking its best. A professional groomer can advise on when, if, or how frequently he should be clipped.

- Average life span is 12 to 15 years. Breed health concerns may include collapsing trachea; elongated soft palate; and epilepsy.

Breed Facts

- **Country of Origin**: Canada

- **Height**: Males 18–21 in (45.5–53.5 cm)/females 17–20 in (43–51 cm)

- **Weight**: Males 44–51 lb (20–23 kg)/females 37–44 lb (17–20 kg)

- **Coat**: Double coat is water repellent, with medium-length, medium-soft outercoat and soft, dense undercoat; whiskers; feathering

- **Colors**: Various shades of red, orange; may have white markings

- **Other Names**: Little River Duck Dog; Yarmouth Toller

- **Registries (With Group)**: AKC (Sporting); ANKC (Gundogs); CKC (Sporting); FCI (Retrievers); KC (Gundog); UKC (Gun Dog)

History and Personality

Canadian hunters developed this tolling retriever to hunt ducks the way they had observed foxes hunting them. What foxes do is work together so that while one plays along the shore swishing his tail to get the ducks' attention and lure them toward shore, the other waits patiently until the ducks are within reach and then pounces to catch them. This hunting style of luring the game in toward shore is called tolling. For more than 100 years, in the Little River district of Yarmouth County in southwestern Nova Scotia, hunters used dogs for tolling.

Although he is the smallest of the retrievers in overall size, the Nova Scotia Duck Tolling Retriever ("Toller") is certainly not short of natural talent, and he is often described as a "retrieving fool." He makes a fine housedog as long as he is sufficiently exercised. He loves his family and is completely devoted to them.

Exercise, Training, Grooming, and Health

- It is critical that the Nova Scotia Duck Tolling Retriever gets enough exercise on a daily basis. He is an athletic and energetic dog who can animatedly retrieve in and out of the water for hours at a time.

- The Toller is responsive and eager when engaged in his favorite pursuit—retrieving. With positive and motivational training methods, he is also a quick learner for other activities.

- He is an average shedder, but the Toller has a dense undercoat that must be brushed regularly to keep it tangle- and dirt-free.

- Average life span is 13 to 16 years. Breed health concerns may include Addison's disease; autoimmune thyroiditis; Collie eye anomaly (CEA); and progressive retinal atrophy (PRA).

Breed Facts

- **Country of Origin**: Great Britain

- **Height**: Males 22–24 in (56–61 cm) and up/females 21–22 in (53.5–56 cm) and up|females slightly less than males [ANKC] [CKC]

- **Weight**: 60–100 lb (27–45.5 kg) [est.]

- **Coat**: Double coat with not straight (but shaggy and free from curl), harsh, profuse outercoat and waterproof pile undercoat

- **Colors**: Any shade of gray, grizzle, blue, blue merle with or without white markings or in reverse

- **Other Names**: Bobtail

- **Registries (With Group)**: AKC (Herding); ANKC (Working); CKC (Herding); FCI (Sheepdogs); KC (Pastoral); UKC (Herding)

History and Personality

Developed in England's West Country, the origin of the Old English Sheepdog ("OES") is not known for sure, but theories suggest the Briard, the Scottish Deerhound, the Russian Owtchar dogs, and the Bergamasco as possible contributors to the breed. This herding dog's profuse coat protected him in damp, raw conditions and was sheared in the summer along with the sheep's coats.

The Old English Sheepdog never misses a beat when it comes to protecting his flock, yet when he's not working, he's a gentle old soul. Today's OES is serious about protecting his charges and keeping them in line, yet he is even-tempered and wise, loving children especially but all who treat him with kindness. He is playful, yet he quickly quiets down in the house.

Exercise, Training, Grooming, and Health

- Although the OES doesn't need intensive exercise, he is a large, athletic dog with a need to explore the great outdoors.

- Bred to be an independent thinker, the OES can be strong willed. However, he wants to please his family, and if trained with respect and patience, he is amazingly responsive.

- The OES needs a lot of attention in the grooming department. He is a heavy seasonal shedder, but all year his thick undercoat needs to be brushed and combed to keep it from forming mats.

- Average life span is 10 to 12 years. Breed health concerns may include bloat; cataracts; cerebellar abiotrophy (CA); deafness; epilepsy; and hip dysplasia.

Breed Facts

- **Country of Origin**: Great Britain
- **Height**: Males 24–27 in (61–68.5 cm)/females 23–26 in (58.5–66 cm)
- **Weight**: Males 75–115 lb (34–52 kg)/females 65–100 lb (29.5–45.5 kg)
- **Coat**: Double coat with long, rough, harsh, dense, waterproof outercoat and evident undercoat; outercoat and undercoat may have slightly oily texture
- **Colors**: All recognized hound colors—whole colored, grizzle, sandy, red, wheaten, blue; may have white markings|any color or color combination acceptable [AKC][UKC]
- **Registries (With Group)**: AKC (Hound); ANKC (Hounds); CKC (Hounds); FCI (Scenthounds); KC (Hound); UKC (Scenthound)

History and Personality

The Otterhound was developed in England to hunt the once-prolific otter, who preyed on the fish in the English rivers. European otters weigh over 20 pounds (9 kg) and cover great distances in the water, mostly underwater. The trail they leave underwater is called a wash; their scent trail is called a drag. Otterhounds had to be able to follow both, which meant that they needed to swim for several hours during a hunt. So good was the Otterhound at his job that the otter population became nearly endangered and the sport was banned.

The Otterhound is rather exuberant despite his shaggy, laid-back appearance. He loves to play—especially in the water—and gets along well with children who enjoy the same activities. He is affectionate and intelligent, with a mind of his own. If a scent captures the Otterhound, even his beloved family will rank a distant second. He has a beautiful voice, which he will use to bay but not to bark incessantly.

Exercise, Training, Grooming, and Health

- The Otterhound needs a fair amount of exercise, which can include jogging or long walks—on leash.

- The Otterhound has a short attention span (except when it comes to his nose), so training must be frequent and focused—and positive.

- The Otterhound's double coat can become matted if not properly cared for, and this involves brushing several times a week.

- Average life span is 10 to 12 years. Breed health concerns may include bloat; elbow dysplasia; Glanzmann's thrombasthenia; and hip dysplasia.

Papillon

Breed Facts

- **Country of Origin**: France

- **Height**: 8–11 in (20–28 cm)

- **Weight**: Two categories—males and females less than 5.5 lb (2.5 kg)/males 5.5–10 lb (2.5–4.5 kg), females 5.5–11 lb (2.5–5 kg)

- **Coat**: Single coat is long, straight, fine, silky, flowing, abundant; chest frill; feathering

- **Colors**: Particolor (white with patches of any color)|particolor with patches of any color except liver [ANKC][KC]|also tricolor (black and white with tan spots) [ANKC][CKC]

- **Other Names**: Continental Toy Spaniel; Epagneul Nain Continental; Phalene

- **Registries (With Group)**: AKC (Toy); ANKC (Toys); CKC (Toys); FCI (Companion and Toy); KC (Toy); UKC (Companion)

History and Personality

Papillons are descended from toy-sized spaniels, called Continental Toy Spaniels, who were popular among European royalty since the beginning of the last millennium. King Henry III of France, Madame Pompadour, and Marie Antoinette were royal masters to these little dogs. Today he is a titled performer in obedience and agility, a standout in the show ring, and a dog who is easy to train as a hearing ear dog or therapy dog.

Happy dogs at heart, Papillons need plenty of socialization from puppyhood to help them feel confident in as many situations as possible. Papillons are full of energy and fun, and they are not generally yappy. They love to learn tricks so that they can further please their people. Extremely intelligent and hardier than they may appear, the versatile Papillon can be trained to do all sorts of things.

Exercise, Training, Grooming, and Health

- Although he won't mind being coddled now and then, the sturdy Papillon needs to use his own four feet to get enough exercise.

- The Papillon is easy to train—with a keen desire to please, positive rewards and motivational training will have him doing most anything his owner asks.

- The Papillon doesn't have an undercoat, so he sheds little to no hair. He should be brushed regularly to prevent matting.

- Average life span is 13 to 16 years. Breed health concerns may include patellar luxation.

Breed Facts

- **Country of Origin**: Great Britain

- **Height**: Males 14 in (35.5)/females 13 in (33 cm)|10–15 in (25.5–38 cm) [UKC]

- **Weight**: 13–17 lb (6–7.5 kg)

- **Coat**: Two types—*smooth* and *broken*, both featuring double coat with harsh, close, dense outercoat|also *rough* type with wiry, dense outercoat and short, dense undercoat [UKC]

- **Colors**: White, white with black or tan markings, combination of these (tricolor)|also predominately white with lemon markings [ANKC][CKC][FCI][KC]

- **Other Names**: Parson Jack Russell Terrier

- **Registries (With Group)**: AKC (Terrier); ANKC (Terriers); CKC (Terriers); FCI (Terriers); KC (Terrier); UKC (Terrier)

History and Personality

The Parson Russell Terrier was developed in southern England in the 1800s to assist in foxhunting. He is named after Parson John "Jack" Russell, an avid foxhunter who used his terriers to both help pursue the fox and bring it out from its den so that the hunt could be continued. What Parson Jack most desired was a terrier who could keep up with foxhounds (his legs needed to be long enough), who had a compact chest so that he could get into the fox's den, who was strong enough to keep a fox at bay, and whose temperament was fiery and intelligent. When his terriers began proving themselves, they became increasingly popular.

The bold and athletic Parson Russell Terrier is up for any challenge and any game. If he's busy on the hunt, he is fearless and single-minded; at home, he is an enthusiastic companion, ready to explore and engage in any family activity. He isn't shy about requesting attention, and he will practically insist on being in the center of things—but he should not be quarrelsome or ill tempered with other people or animals. Intelligent, fun loving, and frisky, the Parson is a great companion for someone who shares his enthusiasm for the outdoors and adventure.

Exercise, Training, Grooming, and Health

- The Parson is active and alert, and the occasional stroll will not satisfy his physical or mental needs for stimulation.

- This intelligent breed is also independent minded. For training to work, it needs to be highly focused and interesting to keep him motivated. Short, frequent sessions with well-timed rewards are best.

- The smooth Parson has a dense coat that feels hard to the touch and sheds quite a bit. It can be kept clean and shiny by regular brushing with a slicker brush. The broken- or rough-coated Parson needs to be hand-stripped (if showing) or clipped, although clipping will soften his coat.

- Average life span is 13 to 16 years. Breed health concerns may include cerebellar ataxia; deafness; and Legg-Calve-Perthes disease.

Pekingese

Breed Facts

- **Country of Origin**: China

- **Height**: 6–9 in (15–23 cm) [est.]

- **Weight**: Males no more than 11 lb (5 kg)/females no more than 12 lb (5.5 kg)|limit of 14 lb (6.5 kg) [AKC][CKC][UKC]

- **Coat**: Double coat with long, straight, coarse, stand-off outercoat and thick, soft undercoat; mane; some feathering

- **Colors**: All colors and markings; may have black mask|but no albino, liver [ANKC][FCI][KC]

- **Registries (With Group)**: AKC (Toy); ANKC (Toys); CKC (Toys); FCI (Companion and Toy); KC (Toy); UKC (Companion)

History and Personality

Miniature dogs have been known in China since the T'ang Dynasty of the 8th century. In ancient superstitious times, the "terrifying" lion-like appearance of these dogs, as well as the "Fo Dog" idols that represented them, were supposed to frighten away evil spirits. Their popularity hit a high in China between 1821 and 1851, during the Tao Kuang period and there were thousands of them around the various imperial palaces. No one outside of the nobility was allowed to own one—stealing one was punishable by death—and the dogs knew nothing but pampering and gentle care.

Exhibiting confidence, charm, and a bit of stubborn independence, Pekingese are fearless but never aggressive. Their sole purpose in life is to give comfort and companionship to their owners. They tend to bond strongly to one person. Pekingese are charmers but should be socialized from puppyhood so that they gain the confidence that is so suiting to them. They can be jealous of other pets and children and shouldn't be played or fussed with to excess.

Exercise, Training, Grooming, and Health

- With his shortened muzzle, which causes him to snore and wheeze, strenuous exercise many not be healthy for the Pekingese—but that shouldn't be used as an excuse not to take him out for short daily walks, which he needs.

- A Peke needs to have basic manners and be taught household rules. He can be quite opinionated when it comes to what he will and will not do, but patience and reward-based training will benefit everyone.

- The Peke's long double coat requires daily attention. It should be brushed and combed, with extra care taken to keep the hindquarters clean.

- Average life span is 10 to 12 years. Breed health concerns may include breathing problems; corneal ulcers; degenerative heart valve disease; patellar luxation; and trichiasis.

Breed Facts

- **Country of Origin**: Wales

- **Height**: 10–12 in (25.5–30.5 cm)

- **Weight**: Males 22–30 lb (10–13.5 kg)/females 20–28 lb (9–12.5 kg)

- **Coat**: Double coat with short, thick, weather-resistant undercoat and longer, coarser outercoat

- **Colors**: Red, sable, fawn, black and tan; may have white markings

- **Registries (With Group)**: AKC (Herding); ANKC (Working); CKC (Herding); FCI (Sheepdogs); KC (Pastoral); UKC (Herding)

History and Personality

The Pembroke Welsh Corgi (tail-less) shares the same heritage as the Cardigan Welsh Corgi (long-tailed)—in fact, they were considered the same breed until 1934. Their heritage is a particularly ancient one—the Pembroke came to Wales around the 10th century and was named after the area of Pembrokeshire. These dogs were used to work cattle, and because of their size, could nip at the livestock's heels while avoiding being kicked. Since the 1930s, fanciers have emphasized each breed's individualities—the Pembroke has a foxier look and straighter legs, as well as a lack of a tail. The Pembroke is the favored dog of Queen Elizabeth II, who owns five of them.

The Pembroke Welsh Corgi is an intelligent and devoted dog. An excellent watchdog, he takes caring for his family seriously. This playful and lovable breed wants nothing more than to accompany the family wherever it goes and be included in the action. Corgis are good with children, especially if raised with and socialized with them. Pembrokes like to bark and can be a bit more excitable than their Cardigan cousins. They are initially wary of strangers and can be territorial. Socialization from puppyhood helps them gain confidence in different situations.

Exercise, Training, Grooming, and Health

- Able bodied and athletic, the Pembroke Welsh Corgi is happiest with a purpose, and needs focused exercise and mental stimulation to be truly satisfied.

- Pembroke Welsh Corgis are a joy to train. They are responsive and intelligent, learning quickly, retaining their lessons, and working with enthusiasm. They are sensitive and should never be trained with harsh methods.

- Regular brushing and combing of his plush double coat are all the Pembroke Welsh Corgi needs to stay looking his best.

- Average life span is 12 to 15 years. Breed health concerns may include degenerative myelopathy; glaucoma; hip dysplasia; intervertebral disk disease; and progressive retinal atrophy (PRA).

Breed Facts

- **Country of Origin**: Spain
- **Height**: Males 23–26 in (58.5–66 cm)/females 21.5–25 in (55–63.5 cm)
- **Weight**: Males 92.5–110 lb (42–50 kg) minimum/females 84–99 lb (38–45 kg) minimum
- **Coat**: Single coat is short, flat, coarse
- **Colors**: All shades of fawn, black, brindle; black mask; may have white markings|black, brown, fawn, gold, gray, orange, silver, tiger; brindle markings, white markings [AKC]
- **Other Names**: Canary Dog; Canary Islands Mastiff; Dogo Canario
- **Registries (With Group)**: AKC (FSS: Working); FCI (Provisional Acceptance: Molossoid); UKC (Guardian)

History and Personality

The Perro de Presa Canario, or "Canary Dog of Prey," is named after the place where he was developed: the Canary Islands off the coast of Spain. He is believed to have been fashioned from large dogs who were brought to the islands by Spanish conquistadors. Their large size was put to use to protect estates and the livestock that was raised on them. The breed was used in dog fighting until the 1940s, when dog fighting became outlawed in the Canary Islands.

The Perro de Presa Canario is a large, powerful, and intimidating dog, but he can also be gentle, loyal, and sweet. The proper temperament is created with careful breeding and equally careful socialization and training from puppyhood—these things are absolutely critical because his imposing size can be frightening. It is the Canario dog owner's responsibility to ensure that this companion will greet people and other animals with nonaggressive manners. He is extremely protective of his family and territory and naturally wary of strangers. Confident, athletic, and intelligent, he needs an experienced owner to bring out the best in him.

Exercise, Training, Grooming, and Health

- The Perro de Presa Canario needs several long walks daily to stay physically and mentally sound. He must be properly socialized from puppyhood during these outings so that as he grows and continues to be exercised outside, he is not a threat to others around him.

- This intelligent dog needs an owner who can understand and handle him. Bred to stand up to almost any challenge, using harsh methods will only incite the Canario and could prove dangerous. Instead, owners should work with their Canarios from puppyhood to teach obedience and manners in as positive a way as possible. Working with knowledgeable trainers is critical.

- The Perro de Presa Canario's short, fine coat is easy to keep clean with regular brushing.

- Life span is 9 to 12 years. Breed health concerns may include bloat; elbow dysplasia; epilepsy; hip dysplasia; hypothyroidism; and Wobbler's syndrome.

Peruvian Inca Orchid

Breed Facts

- **Country of Origin**: Peru

- **Height**: Three sizes—*small*: 9.75–15.75 in (25–40 cm)/*medium*: 15.5–19.75 in (39.5–50 cm)/*large*: 19.5–25.75 in (49.5–65.5 cm)

- **Weight**: Three sizes—*small*: 9–17.5 lb (4–8 kg)/*medium*: 17.5–26.5 lb (8–12 kg)/*large*: 26.5–55 lb (12–25 kg)

- **Coat**: Coat is nonexistent, skin is smooth and elastic; vestiges of hair on head and leg and tail extremities permitted|also coated variety is single, short to medium length, moderately coarse [UKC]

- **Colors**: Black, slate black, elephant black, bluish black, scale of grays from dark brown to light blond|black, brown, gray, pink, tan, white; black, blue, chocolate, gold, gray, mahogany, rose, tan, white markings [AKC]

- **Other Names**: Inca Hairless Dog; Perro sin Pelo del Perú; Peruvian Hairless Dog

- **Registries (With Group)**: AKC (FSS: Hound); ANKC (Non Sporting); FCI (Spitz and Primitive); UKC (Sighthound & Pariah)

History and Personality

The Inca civilization is one of the oldest known to man, and the Peruvian Inca Orchid ("PIO") has apparently been a part of it from the beginning. Pottery from the Moche people of Peru dating to 2,000 years old shows these little dogs dressed in ceremonial clothing—indicating the high regard in which they were held. They were valued for companionship and also for their usefulness as bed warmers. Two coat varieties—hairless and coated—have always existed and can appear in the same litter.

The Peruvian Inca Orchid is a trim, elegant-looking dog who is affectionate with his family. Sweet and gentle with those he loves, he is usually aloof with strangers, and early socialization is necessary to ensure that he is comfortable in different situations. He is extremely sensitive and wilts under any kind of heavy-handedness. The PIO is curious and kind, and he enjoys being part of the family's daily activities.

Exercise, Training, Grooming, and Health

- The Peruvian Inca Orchid does not need a lot of exercise, but like all dogs, does best with regular activity that keeps his body and mind in shape. He should be protected from the sun and elements when outside.

- PIOs are sensitive to their families and quickly learn the rules for household manners. They are intelligent and even-tempered, and they don't bark often.

- The hairless variety's sensitivity to the elements means that it has special grooming requirements—he should never go outside without sunscreen applied to his body; to keep the skin from drying out, lotion or oil should be applied regularly; and he should be washed with a very gentle shampoo during baths. The coated variety's silky fur is practically nonshedding but must be brushed daily to keep it from tangling. Their low production of doggy dander makes them ideal companions for some allergy sufferers.

- Average life span is 11 to 13 years. Breed health concerns may include dental problems and skin problems.

Breed Facts

- **Country of Origin**: France

- **Height**: 13–15 in (33–38 cm)

- **Weight**: Approx. no more than 45 lb (20.5 kg)

- **Coat**: Double coat with long, rough outercoat and thick undercoat; beard and mustache

- **Colors**: White with any combination of lemon, orange, tricolor, grizzle markings|also black, sable markings [AKC][FCI]

- **Other Names**: Petit Basset Griffon Vendeen

- **Registries (With Group)**: AKC (Hound); ANKC (Hounds); CKC (Hounds); FCI (Scenthounds); KC (Hound); UKC (Scenthound)

History and Personality

The hounds from the Vendée region on the western coast of France are among the oldest varieties. French hounds are differentiated by height, and there are four breeds of Vendéens: Grand Griffon (largest), Briquette Griffon (mid-sized), Grand Basset Griffon (low to the ground), and Petit Basset Griffon (small and low). The Basset Griffon Vendéen, like other small French hounds, was bred to hunt rabbits, hares, and occasionally, foxes.

The Petit Basset Griffon Vendéen ("PBGV") is lively, alert, and vivacious. He is a hunter at heart, and this is his driving passion. The PBGV relishes his time outdoors and with his family. He is enthusiastic but not high-strung. He is a fine companion for children of all ages.

Exercise, Training, Grooming, and Health

- The PBGV thrives on being able to follow his nose at least once a day. He must have time outdoors, and if he's not working, he'll need daily long walks.

- PBGVs are intelligent and quite capable of learning, but they don't particularly take to being told what to do. They require reward-based training that keeps them interested and engaged.

- The tousled appearance of the PBGV comes naturally, and any trimming is highly discouraged. He does have a double coat that needs to be brushed and combed.

- Average life span is 12 to 15 years. Breed health concerns may include aseptic meningitis; ear infections; glaucoma; hip dysplasia; and patellar luxation.

Pharaoh Hound

Breed Facts

- **Country of Origin**: Malta
- **Height**: Males 22–25 in (56–63.5 cm)/females 21–24 in (53.5–61 cm)
- **Weight**: 45–55 lb (20.5–25 kg) [est.]
- **Coat**: Short, glossy, ranging from fine and close to slightly harsh
- **Colors**: Tan, rich tan; white markings permitted
- **Other Names**: Kelb tal-Fenek
- **Registries (With Group)**: AKC (Hound); ANKC (Hounds); CKC (Hounds); FCI (Spitz and Primitive); KC (Hound); UKC (Sighthound & Pariah)

History and Personality

The Pharaoh Hound may trace his history to ancient Egypt; records indicate that dogs resembling the Pharaoh Hound were living with this civilization in roughly 3000 BCE. It is speculated that Phoenician traders brought him to the island of Malta, where the people of the poor-soiled, rocky island learned to value the breed as rabbit hunters. This is where they acquired the name "Kelb tal-Fenek," or "rabbit dog." For more than 2,000 years, the original dogs bred true on the island, without the introduction of any other type. A sighthound of striking elegance and exceptional speed and ability, the Pharaoh Hound has a large and loyal following around the world today.

Although he may appear standoffish, the Pharaoh Hound is a genuinely friendly and affectionate dog who is completely devoted to his family. Large and cat-like, he is an alert and stealthy hunter who relishes the chase. When not actively hunting, however, he is a calm and even-tempered companion. He has a sense of humor and loves to play, especially with children.

Exercise, Training, Grooming, and Health

- The Pharaoh Hound has great speed, but he doesn't have to gallop every day. However, he does require daily exercise—preferably romps in a safely enclosed area.

- Eager to please and highly intelligent, the Pharaoh Hound is fairly easy to train—especially if positive, motivational methods are used.

- The breed's short, close coat is kept lustrous and clean with occasional brushing.

- Average life span is 11 to 13 years. There are no reported breed-specific health concerns.

Breed Facts

- **Country of Origin**: United States

- **Height**: Males 20–27 in (51–68.5 cm)/females 20–25 in (51–63.5 cm)

- **Weight**: Males 50–75 lb (22.5–34 kg)/females 40–65 lb (18–29.5 kg)

- **Coat**: Single coat is smooth, fine, glossy; rare specimens are double coated with short, soft, thick undercoat and longer, smoother, stiffer outercoat

- **Colors**: Any shade of brindle, including yellow, buckskin, tan, brown, chocolate, liver, orange, red, light or dark gray, blue or Maltese (slate gray), dilute black, black; may have white markings

- **Other Names**: Plott Hound

- **Registries (With Group)**: AKC (Hound); UKC (Scenthound)

History and Personality

In the 1700s Johannes Plott and his brother emigrated from Germany to the US with their Hanoverian-type *schweisshunds*, who would bocame the foundation for the breed. Plott Hounds have been bred and hunted by seven generations of Plotts in the Great Smoky Mountains between North Carolina and Tennessee. Used on a variety of game, they were especially efficient at hunting bears. They became known as coonhounds because there were many more people participating in this type of hunt than in bear or large game hunting, but the breed has retained its original—and exceptional—abilities to cold trail, bay, and tree bear and other large game (as well as coons). They are used to hunt all of these kinds of game today.

For as tough and agile a hunter as the Plott Hound is, he is an equally talented companion animal, gentle and kind with people of all ages and a true friend. He is intelligent and curious, as well as extremely tenacious and courageous—traits that keep him focused on the trail and able to hold even large game at bay until the hunter arrives. The Plott also has a sense of humor, relishing games and play on the trail and at home. He is a large dog with a tendency to drool, but for those wanting a fine hunting dog and home companion, this doesn't seem to matter.

Exercise, Training, Grooming, and Health

- The large, athletic Plott Hound needs plenty of exercise, without which he will become bored and restless. If allowed to work trails at least a couple of times a day, he will get the physical and mental stimulation he requires.

- Plotts are eager and responsive—especially when it comes to figuring out what's desired on the trail—and are fairly easy to train. They can be single-minded about hunting, but if worked in a positive and rewarding way, will quickly and gladly master their lessons.

- The Plott Hound's short coat is easy to keep clean with an occasional brushing and going-over with a hound glove. Attention should be paid to their ears, which must be kept clean and dry to prevent infection.

- Average life span is 12 to 14 years. Breed health concerns may include bloat.

Pointer

Breed Facts

- **Country of Origin**: United Kingdom

- **Height**: Males 25–28 in (63.5–71 cm)/females 23–26 in (58.5–66 cm)

- **Weight**: Males 55–75 lb (25–34 kg)/females 44–65 lb (20–29.5 kg)

- **Coat**: Short, smooth, dense, with a sheen

- **Colors**: Liver, lemon, black, orange, either self-colored, tricolored, or with white

- **Other Names**: English Pointer

- **Registries (With Group)**: AKC (Sporting); ANKC (Gundogs); CKC (Sporting); FCI (Pointing Dogs); KC (Gundog); UKC (Gun Dog)

History and Personality

The Pointer was developed in the United Kingdom to search for game and then stand on point to alert the hunter to his prey's location. Although it's not known for certain, his lineage may include the Foxhound, Greyhound, and Bloodhound, with some Spanish Pointer and certainly some setting spaniel blood.

The Pointer is a devoted and loyal family dog. He has energy to spare for play and activities with young ones, as well as a love of hunting that pleases the more serious and the weekend sportsman. He is a hardworking dog with plenty of courage and stamina in the field, and this hard-driving nature can result in a dog who can be more than some can handle.

Exercise, Training, Grooming, and Health

- An active and energetic dog, the Pointer does best with lots of exercise.

- The Pointer is a joy to train in the hunt field but is easily distracted when training for other activities. Persistent, patient, and frequent training using reward-based lessons and working for short periods can produce great results.

- The Pointer's short, fine coat is easily managed with an occasional brushing and going-over with a soft cloth.

- Average life span is 12 to 14 years. Breed health concerns may include hip dysplasia; skin problems; and thyroid problems.

Breed Facts

- **Country of Origin**: Poland
- **Height**: Males 17–20 in (43–51 cm)/females 16–19 in (40.5–48.5 cm)
- **Weight**: 35–50 lb (16–22.5 kg) [est.]
- **Coat**: Double coat with long, straight or slightly wavy, shaggy, thick outercoat and soft, dense undercoat; long hair covers eyes
- **Colors**: All colors and patches acceptable
- **Other Names**: Polish Owczarek Nizinny; Polski Owczarek Nizinny
- **Registries (With Group)**: AKC (Herding); ANKC (Working); CKC (Herding); FCI (Sheepdogs); KC (Pastoral); UKC (Herding)

History and Personality

Evidence of the existence of the Polish Lowland Sheepdog (or Polish Owczarek Nizinny—"PON" for short) in his native land dates back to at least the 16th century. He is partly descended from the Hungarian Puli and is believed to be the link between the corded and long-coated herding dogs in Eastern Europe. Besides being an excellent herding dog, the Polish Lowland Sheepdog is also a fine guardian and watchdog, so he was of value for many reasons. Despite his small size and cuddly appearance, he is fearless and unrelenting when it comes to any perceived threat of his "pack."

PONs are playful, energetic, intelligent, and loyal. Clever and persistent, they need a fair leader or they will start calling the shots. Their strong herding instinct, paired with a watchdog mentality, means that they don't miss a trick. PONs are loyal and devoted to their family, and they are excellent with children.

Exercise, Training, Grooming, and Health

- The Polish Lowland Sheepdog needs plenty of exercise. Bred to work all day, he is hardy enough to participate in any outdoor activities and also enjoys several long walks a day.

- Although an independent thinker, the responsive and devoted PON will eagerly respond to lessons taught in a positive and rewarding way.

- The Polish Lowland Sheepdog's long coat needs weekly brushing and combing to keep it free from mats and tangles.

- Average life span is 12 to 15 years. There are no reported breed-specific health concerns.

Pomeranian

Breed Facts

- **Country of Origin**: Germany

- **Height**: 7–12 in (18–30.5 cm) [est.]

- **Weight**: Males 4–4.5 lb (2 lb)/females 4.5–5.5 lb (2–2.5 lb)|3–7 lb (1.5–3 kg) [AKC][CKC][UKC]

- **Coat**: Double coat with long, straight, harsh, glistening outercoat and soft, fluffy, thick undercoat; neck ruff

- **Colors**: All colors, patterns, variations [AKC][UKC]|all colors but no black or white shadings [ANKC][KC]|black, brown, chocolate, beaver, red, orange, cream, orange-sable, wolf sable, blue, white, particolor, black and tan, and all combinations of these [CKC]

- **Other Names**: Dwarf Spitz; Toy German Spitz; Zwergspitz

- **Registries (With Group)**: AKC (Toy); ANKC (Toys); CKC (Toys); KC (Toy); UKC (Companion)

History and Personality

This breed received its name from the German province from which it hailed: Pomerania. A descendant of the European herding spitz dogs, early specimens of the Pomeranian weighed up to 30 pounds (13.5 kg) and were less profusely coated than the dogs of today. It was Queen Victoria's preference for smaller dogs that steered the breed in the direction of a toy dog. By the time the Pomeranian made his way to North America, his small size and abundant coat were trademarks of the breed.

The spunky Pomeranian is alert, active, intelligent, wary, and full of himself. He wants to be not just part of the family but part of all activities. He makes an excellent watchdog and will bark whenever he's suspicious. Although the erratic behavior of young children can be upsetting to some Poms, they get along well with older children.

Exercise, Training, Grooming, and Health

- The active Pomeranian thrives on regular exercise. He loves to get out and see the world and should be taken on several walks daily.

- The Pomeranian is a fun dog to train because he is an eager learner.

- The Pom's abundant coat needs regular attention to keep it looking its best. He is a constant shedder with a cottony undercoat, so brushing several times a week is recommended.

- Average life span is 13 to 15 years. Breed health concerns may include collapsing trachea; hypothyroidism; patellar luxation; and patent ductus arteriosus (PDA).

Poodle, Miniature and Toy

Breed Facts

- **Country of Origin**: France

- **Height**: *Mini*: Over 10–15 in (25.5–38 cm)|11–15 in (28–38 cm) [ANKC]|11 in (28 cm) up to 14 in (35 cm) [FCI]; *Toy*: 10 in (25.5 cm) and under|under 11 in (28 cm) [ANKC][KC]|over 9.5–11 in (24–28 cm) [FCI]

- **Weight**: *Mini*: 15–20 lb (7–9 kg) [est.]; *Toy*: 4–8 lb (2–3.5 kg) [est.]

- **Coat**: Two types—*curly* has naturally harsh texture, dense throughout/*corded* hangs in tight, even cords of varying length

- **Colors**: White, cream, brown, apricot, black|also red, silver beige, multicolored [UKC]| also blue, silver [AKC][ANKC][KC] [UKC]|also café-au-lait [AKC][UKC]|also gray [AKC][FCI] [UKC]|also red fawn [FCI]|

- **Other Names**: Caniche

- **Registries (With Group)**: AKC (*Mini*: Non-Sporting/*Toy*: Toy); ANKC (Non Sporting); CKC (*Mini*: Non-Sporting/*Toy*: Toys); FCI (Companion and Toy); KC (Utility); UKC (Companion)

History and Personality

The Poodle as he is recognized today was developed in France. The French admired the Poodle's versatility—he could go from being a tried-and-true retriever by day to a stylish and dignified companion by night. Miniature and Toy Poodles were bred down from the Standard Poodle to their current height limitations and are considered the same breed, judged by the same standard.

Miniature and Toy Poodles are lively, clever dogs who are also very in tune with and devoted to their family. Active and intelligent, they are good natured if not somewhat shy and reserved around strangers. Best with older children, socialization brings out their confidence and cheerfulness. Miniature and Toy Poodles tend to bark a lot.

Exercise, Training, Grooming, and Health

- Miniature and Toy Poodles enjoy the outdoors and the physical and social benefits of going for walks.

- All of the Poodles are highly trainable. Intelligent and sensitive, they are eager to please and do what is asked of them.

- Their naturally curly and dense hair is practically nonshedding but grows out fairly quickly, and they are typically clipped every six to eight weeks by a professional groomer. The coat should also be brushed regularly.

- Average life span is 10 to 15 years. Breed health concerns may include epilepsy; hip dysplasia; Legg-Calve-Perthes disease; patellar luxation; progressive retinal atrophy (PRA); sebaceous adenitis; skin problems; and von Willebrand disease.

Poodle, Standard

Breed Facts

- **Country of Origin**: France

- **Height**: Over 15 in (38 cm)|15 in (38 cm) and over [ANKC]|over 17.5–23.5 in (45–60 cm) [FCI]

- **Weight**: 45–70 lb (20.5–31.5 kg) [est.]

- **Coat**: Two types—*curly* has naturally harsh texture, dense throughout/*corded* hangs in tight, even cords of varying length

- **Colors**: White, cream, brown, apricot, black|also red, silver beige, multicolored [UKC]| also blue, silver [AKC][ANKC][KC] [UKC]|also café-au-lait [AKC][UKC]|also gray [AKC][FCI] [UKC]|also red fawn [FCI]|

- **Other Names**: Caniche

- **Registries (With Group)**: AKC (Non-Sporting); ANKC (Non Sporting); CKC (Non-Sporting); FCI (Companion and Toy); KC (Utility); UKC (Gun Dog)

History and Personality

The Poodle as he is recognized today was developed in France. The French admired the Poodle's versatility—he could go from being a tried-and-true retriever by day to a stylish and dignified companion by night. For a time he was also used to sniff out truffles—a culinary delicacy. Miniature, Toy, and Standard Poodles are considered the same breed, judged by the same standard.

The Standard Poodle is a proud, intelligent, and elegant companion. He is a stable, affectionate, and sensitive dog, very much in tune with his family. He is good with children and other dogs and is generally the calmest of the sizes.

Exercise, Training, Grooming, and Health

- Standard Poodles are great outdoor dogs and enjoy the physical and social benefits of going for walks. They excel at dog sports and activities.

- Poodles are highly trainable. Intelligent and sensitive, they are eager to please and do what is asked of them.

- Their naturally curly and dense hair is practically nonshedding but grows out fairly quickly, and they are typically clipped every six to eight weeks. The coat should also be brushed regularly.

- Average life span is 10 to 15 years. Breed health concerns may include bloat; epilepsy; hip dysplasia; patellar luxation; progressive retinal atrophy (PRA); sebaceous adenitis; skin problems; and von Willebrand disease.

Portuguese Podengo

Breed Facts

- **Country of Origin**: Portugal

- **Height**: Three sizes—*large*: 22–28 in (56–71 cm)/*medium*: 16–22 in (40.5–56 cm)/*small*: 8–12 in (20–30.5 cm)

- **Weight**: Three sizes—*large*: 44–66 lb (20–30 kg)/*medium*: 35.5–44 lb (16–20 kg)/*small*: 9–13 lb (4–6 kg)

- **Coat**: Two types—*smooth* is short, very dense/*wire* is medium length, rough, harsh; beard

- **Colors**: Self-colored yellow, fawn (all shades), black (diluted or faded) with or without white markings or white with markings in listed colors

- **Other Names**: Podengo Português; Podengo Portugueso; Portuguese Warren Hound

- **Registries (With Group)**: AKC (FSS: Hound); FCI (Spitz and Primitive); KC (Hound); UKC (Sighthound & Pariah)

History and Personality

The three sizes of this Portuguese hunting dog developed acording to the type of terrain they hunted. The Grande, with his longer legs, was used to hunt wild boars. The Medio was not as fast on the flat but had greater maneuverability and dexterity to bring down rabbits. The Pequeño is probably the world's smallest hunting dog. He was used to enter the rabbit's warrens and flush the prey and to bring down vermin.

Lively, affectionate companions, the Podengos are also quiet and well mannered. Bred to assist in the elimination of unwanted small animals, Podengos are naturally alert and watchful, making them great watchdogs. They are playful and charming, enjoying time spent with their families in whatever form they desire.

Exercise, Training, Grooming, and Health

- Active, curious, and fun loving, Podengos of all sizes love to be outdoors.

- Responsive and receptive to learning, the Podengos are fun and easy to train.

- Both the wire-coated and smooth-coated varieties are easy to keep clean with weekly brushing.

- Average life span is 12 to 14 years. There are no reported breed-specific health concerns.

Breed Facts

- **Country of Origin**: Portugal
- **Height**: Males 22 in (56 cm)/females 20.5 in (52 cm)
- **Weight**: Males 44–59.5 lb (20–27 kg)/females 35–48.5 lb (16–22 kg)
- **Coat**: Single coat is short, strong, close lying
- **Colors**: Self-colored yellow, brown or with white markings
- **Other Names**: Perdigueiro Portugués; Perdiguero Portugués
- **Registries (With Group)**: AKC (FSS: Sporting); FCI (Pointing Dogs); UKC (Gun Dog)

History and Personality

The Portuguese Pointer is an ancient Iberian hunting dog who dates back to the 12th century, when he was bred by royal kennels to serve as an all-purpose bird dog. He eventually became a dog for everyone, including the English families who settled in the Oporto region of Portugal in the 18th century. Portuguese navigators took the Portuguese Pointer along in their ships during the time of the discovery of the Americas, and he was used in the formation of popular breeds such as the Labrador Retriever and the English Pointer. Taken with the dog's abilities, they sent them to England as well, where their blood contributed to the development of the English Pointer.

The Portuguese Pointer is a tenacious hunter with strong pointing and retrieving instincts. He is also affectionate, loyal, and intensely attached to his owner—sometimes inconveniently so for those more accustomed to an independent hunter. Still, his devotion to his family and to the hunt makes him a wonderful family pet and a fine sporting companion. Portuguese Pointers are gentle and loving with children and will happily sleep at the foot of their owner's bed if allowed.

Exercise, Training, Grooming, and Health

- The hunting Portuguese Pointer enjoys nothing more than doing his job in the field. Lacking this, he should be exercised vigorously several times a day to keep him physically and mentally sound.

- This Pointer loves to hunt and is easily trained for field work. Responsive and kindhearted, he also learns quickly when taught with motivational methods. Early training and consistent socialization bring out the best in him.

- The short, dense coat of the Portuguese Pointer is weather resistant and wash and wear, easy to keep clean and neat with just an occasional wiping down with a soft cloth or bristle brush.

- Average life span is 10 to 14 years. There are no reported breed-specific health concerns.

Portuguese Water Dog

Breed Facts

- **Country of Origin**: Portugal
- **Height**: 19.5–23 in (50–58.5 cm)/females 16.5–21 in (42–53.5 cm)
- **Weight**: Males 42–60 lb (19–27 kg)/females 35–50 lb (16–22.5 kg)
- **Coat**: Two varieties, both single coats—*curly* has compact, cylindrical curls, somewhat lusterless/*wavy* falls gently in waves, has slight sheen
- **Colors**: Black, white, brown tones, combinations of black or brown with white
- **Other Names**: Cão de Agua; Cão de Agua Português
- **Registries (With Group)**: AKC (Working); ANKC (Utility); CKC (Working); FCI (Water Dogs); KC (Working); UKC (Gun Dog)

History and Personality

The Portuguese Water Dog's job through the ages was to herd fish into the fishermen's nets. He also retrieved objects from the water and carried messages and equipment between boats and from boats to the shore. Size and coat type were critical to his effectiveness—he was sturdy and strong enough to navigate even rough waters, and his nonshedding, dense, and waterproof coat, along with his webbed feet, kept him warm and steadied him.

Bred to be of service, the Portuguese Water Dog (PWD) is an extremely intelligent and robust dog. He is an independent thinker, capable of handling himself in tough situations, but is tuned in to what's required of him. The PWD is levelheaded yet lively, sensible yet fun loving. He is great with children and other dogs.

Exercise, Training, Grooming, and Health

- He needs regular and preferably vigorous exercise.

- The happy-to-help, no-nonsense Portuguese Water Dog eagerly takes to training. He needs guidance and direction, and training should begin as early as possible.

- While they are practically nonshedding, both coat types still need plenty of maintenance. The longer wavy coat must be brushed and combed as well as trimmed to keep it free from tangles; the curly coat requires regular brushing and combing and also needs to be clipped every six to eight weeks.

- Average life span is 11 to 14 years. Breed health concerns may include Addison's disease; follicular dysplasia; hip dysplasia; dilated cardiomyopathy (DCM); progressive retinal atrophy (PRA); and glycogen storage disease (GSD).

Breed Facts

- **Country of Origin**: China
- **Height**: 10–14 in (25.5–35.5 cm) [est.]
- **Weight**: 14–18 lb (6.5–8 kg)
- **Coat**: Short, smooth, fine, soft, glossy
- **Colors**: Fawn, black; mask|also silver, apricot [ANKC][FCI] [KC][UKC]
- **Registries (With Group)**: AKC (Toy); ANKC (Toys); CKC (Toys); FCI (Companion and Toy); KC (Toy); UKC (Companion)

History and Personality

The Pug has a relatively ancient heritage going back to the Chinese, who have always loved flat-faced dogs. They originated the Shih Tzu and the Pekingese, both with whom the Pug may share bloodlines. He was highly prized by Chinese emperors, and it was against the law for anyone but royalty to own the dogs. As traders from the

Dutch East India Company made their way around the world in the 16th century, they fell in love with the breed, and brought specimens back to Holland, where they eventually became popular with royals throughout Europe.

The Pug's motto is *multum in parvo*, "a lot in a small package," which captures his essence. He is an even-tempered, happy, affectionate, and jovial companion. Clever and mischievous, he is curious and curious looking, attracting attention and returning affection. The Pug is friend to all types and ages of people and gets along well with other animals, too.

Exercise, Training, Grooming, and Health

- Several walks a day will satisfy his exercise requirements and his curiosity.

- The Pug is an intelligent and curious fellow who appreciates direction and training.

- The Pug's wrinkles must be kept dry and free from dirt, as do the areas around his eyes. His coat needs only occasional brushing.

- Average life span is 12 to 15 years. Breed health concerns may include elongated soft palate; patellar luxation; progressive retinal atrophy (PRA); Pug Dog Encephalitis (PDE); and stenotic nares.

Puli

Breed Facts

- **Country of Origin**: Hungary

- **Height**: Males 15.5–18 in (40–45.5 cm)/females 14–16.5 in (37–41 cm)

- **Weight**: Males 28–33 lb (12.5–15 kg)/females 22–28.5 lb (10–13 kg)

- **Coat**: Double coat is weather resistant, with long, wavy or curly, coarse outercoat and fine, soft, dense undercoat; adult coat forms natural cords

- **Colors**: Solid black, rusty black, all gray shades, white|also shades of apricot [ANKC][KC]

- **Other Names**: Hungarian Puli

- **Registries (With Group)**: AKC (Herding); ANKC (Working); CKC (Herding); FCI (Sheepdogs); KC (Pastoral); UKC (Herding)

History and Personality

When the Magyars invaded Hungary several thousand years ago, they brought their flock-guarding and herding dogs with them. In Hungary, sheepherding dogs developed into three breeds: the Puli, the Komondor, and the Kuvasz—the Pulik (smaller, more agile dogs) were used for herding and droving. His coat is certainly distinctive and can be brushed out to a wavy mass or allowed to form into tight cords. It protects him from livestock, predators, and the elements.

The Puli is a tough dog who is focused on getting the job done. He is naturally suspicious and ever watchful, making him an exceptional watchdog and protector of home and family. Because one cannot see his eyes, it's difficult to see that there's an extremely affectionate and devoted companion underneath that corded coat.

Exercise, Training, Grooming, and Health

- The hardworking Puli is happy to work all day and prefers to have a job to do. Long walks and occasions to run off lead in a safely enclosed area will keep him in shape.

- Pulik are responsive and eager to please. They enjoy the interaction of positive training and are quick learners.

- Once a Puli is fully corded, he is easier to care for because the cords need only occasional separation and trimming.

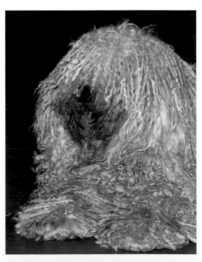

- Average life span is 12 to 14 years. Breed health concerns may include elbow dysplasia; hip dysplasia; patellar luxation; progressive retinal atrophy (PRA); and von Willebrand disease.

Pumi

Breed Facts

- **Country of Origin**: Hungary
- **Height**: Males 16–18.5 in (41–47 cm)/females 15–17.5 in (38–44 cm)
- **Weight**: Males 22–33 lb (10–15 kg)/females 17–28.5 lb (7.5–12.5 kg)
- **Coat**: Double coat with strong, wavy and curly outercoat that forms tufts and soft undercoat
- **Colors**: Gray in various shades, black, fawn with mask, white|also grizzle, rusty brown [AKC]
- **Other Names**: Hungarian Pumi
- **Registries (With Group)**: AKC (FSS: Herding); ANKC (Working); FCI (Sheepdogs); UKC (Herding)

History and Personality

The Pumi shares the same history as the Puli, up until the infiltration of Western sheepherding breeds and terriers into Hungary in the 17th and 18th centuries. The breeding of these terriers to the Puli created a small, quick dog of superior intelligence and drive known for his high energy level and ability to drive livestock. He works well with pigs, sheep, and cattle, and he hunts small rodents, making him a valuable dog for a farmer or shepherd.

The Pumi is certainly cute, but he is no lapdog. Curious, alert, keen, intelligent, and quick, he watches over everything and uses his voice liberally. He is always on the go, keeping an eye on his surroundings and ready at a moment's notice to take action. He is reserved around strangers, but is a devoted companion who is affectionate and playful with his family.

Exercise, Training, Grooming, and Health

- The little Pumi has a lot of spunk and needs an appropriate amount of exercise.

- The Pumi is easy to train and fun to work with. He is intelligent and eager to please.

- The Pumi should have a naturally fluffy appearance, and needs occasional brushing and combing to prevent tangles from forming.

- Average life span is 12 to 14 years. Breed health concerns may include hip dysplasia and patellar luxation.

Pyrenean Shepherd

Breed Facts

- **Country of Origin**: France
- **Varieties**: Rough Faced; Smooth Faced
- **Height**: Males 15.5–21.5 in (39.5–54 cm)/females 15–20.5 in (38–52 cm)
- **Weight**: 15–32 lb (7–14.5 kg) [est.]
- **Coat**: *Rough*: Double coat with long or demi-long, almost flat or slightly wavy, harsh outercoat and minimal undercoat; *Smooth*: Double coat with semi-long or less than semi-long, fine, soft outercoat; muzzle covered with short, fine hair; modest ruff
- **Colors**: Shades of fawn, gray, black, black with white markings, merles of diverse tones, brindle
- **Other Names**: Berger des Pyrenees; Berger des Pyrénées à Poil Long;
- **Registries (With Group)**: AKC (Miscellaneous); CKC (Herding); FCI (Sheepdogs); KC (Pastoral); UKC (Herding)

History and Personality

The Pyrenean Shepherd was developed for his working abilities: to be quick and agile in pursuing sheep and well covered with hair to protect against the elements and predators. Due to the isolation created by the rugged Pyrenees Mountains, each valley individualized the sheepdogs, with small variations in coat length and texture, color, and so on. The breed is still used high in the Pyrenees Mountains as he ever was—herding sheep every day and remaining a constant companion to his shepherd.

He is an intent worker who is courageous to the point of being fearless. Loyal and devoted to his family, he is alert and makes a good watchdog, barking at any unfamiliar noises. The Pyrenean Shepherd is naturally wary of strangers and needs plenty of socialization to be comfortable with strange pets, children, and adults.

Exercise, Training, Grooming, and Health

- The driven Pyrenean Shepherd lives to work. Vigorous exercise—and plenty of it—is a must. It's almost impossible to tire him out, but with enough mental and physical stimulation, he can have his needs met.

- His work comes naturally to the Pyrenean Shepherd, so training is seldom an issue. Sensitive, responsive, and alert, this dog is a quick study.

- The Rough needs brushing about twice a month to prevent matting; the Smooth needs brushing only once a month.

- Average life span is 10 to 14 years. Breed health concerns may include epilepsy; hip dysplasia; and patellar luxation.

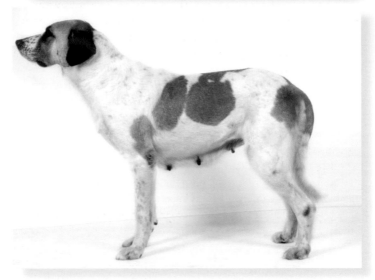

Breed Facts

- **Country of Origin**: Portugal
- **Height**: Males 26–29 in (66–73.5 cm)
- **Weight**: Males 88–110 lb (40–50 kg)/females 77–100 lb (35–45.5 kg)
- **Coat**: Medium length, straight, dense
- **Colors**: Black, wolf gray, fawn, yellow, all with white markings or white with markings of these colors, either dappled, streaked, or brindled
- **Other Names**: Alentejo Mastiff; Portuguese Mastiff
- **Registries (With Group)**: AKC (FSS: Working); FCI (Molossoid); UKC (Guardian)

History and Personality

The Alentejo is a lowland area in southern Portugal, and it is here that the Rafeiro developed into the breed as it is known today. He is believed to be descended from huge dogs who worked the Tibetan highlands thousands of years ago. These dogs made their way across Europe and developed into powerful mastiff types that helped move and protect vast herds of cattle. As the populations he served came to settle in the Alentejo region, his work as a drover gave way to that of a guardian for large estates.

The Rafeiro was developed to be an alert and responsive guardian, and those characteristics make him suspicious of strangers and naturally aloof. This strong, athletic, and domineering dog needs thorough socialization from an early age to encourage his compatibility with other people and animals. He takes his job seriously, and if unable to be true to his nature, may end up finding less desirable ways to pass the time. The noble Rafeiro is good with children; he is not an attack dog. However, he does best with an owner who understands and can support his true purpose, which is to protect and safeguard the family.

Exercise, Training, Grooming, and Health

- Although not a high-energy dog, the Rafeiro does need a lot of time outdoors where he can keep an eye on things. He enjoys long walks and any outings that involve outdoor activity.

- The Rafeiro will respond to training that is respectful and motivational. He does best with a fair and self-assured leader for whom he will gladly work. He can be a dominant dog, although sensitive, which can manifest as stubbornness. Socialization from puppyhood is essential for this normally wary breed.

- His thick coat must be brushed and combed every once in a while to keep shedding under control and to stimulate new growth.

- Average life span is 10 to 13 years. There are no reported breed-specific health concerns.

Rat Terrier

Breed Facts

- **Country of Origin**: United States

- **Varieties**: Miniature; Standard

- **Height**: *Miniature*: not exceeding 13 in (33 cm)/*Standard*: over 13 in (33 cm) but not exceeding 18 in (45.5 cm)

- **Weight**: *Miniature*: 10–18 lb (4.5–8 kg) [est.]/*Standard*: 12–35 lb (5.5–16 kg) [est.]

- **Coat**: Short, smooth, dense, with a sheen

- **Colors**: White, black, shades of tan, chocolate, blue, blue fawn, apricot, lemon; may be bicolor or tricolor but always must have some white; may have mask

- **Other Names**: American Rat Terrier

- **Registries (With Group)**: AKC (FSS: Terrier); UKC (Terrier)

History and Personality

Believed to be a cross between the Smooth Fox Terrier and the Manchester Terrier, the Rat Terrier emerged in England around 1820.

He was named because of his superiority at exterminating vermin—something that was very necessary during the early 1800s. The breed was brought to the United States by British migrant workers in the 1890s, where these tough little working dogs quickly became desirable and were mostly bred for controlling vermin and hunting small game.

Rat Terriers are friendly and lovable dogs. They are excellent workers to have on a farm where control of vermin is an issue, but they are also suitable as companions. Devoted to their families, they are great with children, especially if raised with them. Lively, inquisitive, and playful but not yappy, Rat Terriers are ever ready to participate in any activity.

Exercise, Training, Grooming, and Health

- Like most active breeds, Rat Terriers tend to be happiest when they receive a lot of exercise and mental stimulation.

- Although the Rat Terrier is more amenable to training than some other terriers, he is independent minded and must be trained and consistently handled from an early age.

- The coat can be kept looking its best with regular brushing or a going-over with a grooming mitt.

- Average life span is 12 to 15 years. Breed health concerns include allergies; elbow and hip dysplasia; malocclusion; and patellar luxation.

Redbone Coonhound

Breed Facts

- **Country of Origin**: United States
- **Height**: Males 22–27 in (56–68.5 cm)/females 21–26 in (53.5–66 cm)
- **Weight**: 45–70 lb (20.5–31.5 kg) [est.]
- **Coat**: Short, smooth, coarse enough to protect
- **Colors**: Solid red preferred
- **Other Names**: Redbone Hound
- **Registries (With Group)**: AKC (Miscellaneous); UKC (Scenthound)

History and Personality

Red foxhounds were brought to the Americas in the late 1700s by Scottish immigrants. These dogs, along with Irish Foxhounds, who are also red, came to the United States just before the Civil War and are the two breeds that most certainly contributed to the development of the Redbone Coonhound. Breeders in Georgia and Tennessee fine-tuned the breed by producing hotter-nosed, faster dogs than some of the other coonhounds found in the region. A keen scenthound and treeing dog, he continues to excel on the hunt and is known for his speed and agility.

The Redbone Coonhound is an eye-catching and elegant hound, as well as an exceptional hunting dog. Because he loves to hunt, he is happiest when this activity is a regular part of his life. When it is, his talents really shine. Good natured, easygoing, and kindhearted, he gets along wonderfully with children and other animals.

Exercise, Training, Grooming, and Health

- The Redbone Coonhound is a dedicated hunting dog who needs to be in the great outdoors, preferably trailing and tracking game. He loves to swim, so outings to areas where he can use his nose and also enjoy the water are great ones for him.

- Because the Redbone matures more slowly, both physically and mentally, he may take a longer time to train than some other breeds. True to his instincts, he will eagerly and quickly learn his craft: trailing and treeing game. Other kinds of training may require more creative methods. He aims to please, and with repetition and rewards, will figure out what is expected and comply.

- Their short, shiny coats are kept in great shape with regular brushing with a firm bristle brush.

- Average life span is 12 to 14 years. Breed health concerns may include eye problems; hip dysplasia; and obesity.

Breed Facts

- **Country of Origin**: Zimbabwe (formerly Rhodesia)

- **Height**: Males 25–27 in (63.5–68.5 cm)/females 24–26 in (61–66 cm)

- **Weight**: Males 75–85 lb (34–38.5 kg)/females 65–70.5 lb (29.5–32 kg)

- **Coat**: Short, sleek, glossy, dense

- **Colors**: Light wheaten to red wheaten

- **Other Names**: African Lion Dog; African Lion Hound

- **Registries (With Group)**: AKC (Hound); ANKC (Hounds); CKC (Hounds); FCI (Scenthounds); KC (Hound); UKC (Sighthound & Pariah)

History and Personality

The Rhodesian Ridgeback gets his name from the symmetrical ridge that runs along his spine created by fur growing in the opposite direction from the rest of the coat. The Khoikhoi dog, a sighthound who lived with the Khoikhoi (Hottentot) tribe in South Africa for several hundred years, gave the Ridgeback this distinctive characteristic. Other breeds that contributed to his current makeup include the Mastiff, Bloodhound, Pointer, and Greyhound, which were brought to Africa by European immigrants. These settlers, known as the Boers, were mostly farmers who needed large, brave dogs who could protect their families and were adept at both tracking and retrieving game.

The Ridgeback is a strong and independent-minded dog who needs a firm and fair leader. He is known to be a ferocious hunter and possesses great stamina and strength. Although he is good with children when socialized to them, he isn't particularly tolerant of pestering or rough play. Intelligent and loyal to the extreme, Ridgebacks are loving and protective of their owners.

Exercise, Training, Grooming, and Health

- The athletic and powerful Ridgeback needs lots of exercise.

- This independent and intelligent breed bores easily. He requires motivational and reward-based training. Socialization is critical.

- His short, glossy coat requires only the occasional brushing or going-over with a hound glove.

- Average life span is 10 to 12 years. Breed health concerns may include cataracts; cysts; deafness; dermoid sinus; elbow and hip dysplasia; and hypothyroidism.

Rottweiler

Breed Facts

- **Country of Origin**: Germany
- **Height**: Males 24–27 in (61–68.5 cm)/females 22–25 in (56–63.5 cm)
- **Weight**: Males 110 lb (50 kg)/females 92.5 lb (42 kg)
- **Coat**: Double coat with medium-length, straight, coarse, dense, flat-lying outercoat and an undercoat
- **Colors**: Black with rust to mahogany markings
- **Other Names**: Rottweil Metzgerhund
- **Registries (With Group)**: AKC (Working); ANKC (Utility); CKC (Working); FCI (Molossoid); KC (Working); UKC (Guardian)

History and Personality

The town of Rottweil, Germany was a major European center for livestock commerce for many centuries. The mastiff-type dogs that came to populate Rottweil were used to drive cattle and cart the meat and other wares to market. As railroads and other means of transportation put the Rottweiler out of a job, he lost favor for some time, until the police and military began using him for protection and other work.

A well-bred Rottweiler is a calm, confident, and courageous dog, although he tends to show an aloofness toward strangers and a cautious attitude in new and unfamiliar situations. He is a fierce guardian of family and home, but once convinced that his charges are safe he is a mellow and loving animal who can be extremely playful and even silly. He needs companionship and lots of socialization to bring out his finest qualities.

Exercise, Training, Grooming, and Health

- The Rottweiler thrives on plenty of exercise, and because he is a robust and energetic working dog, he can never have too much to do.

- The Rottweiler must receive obedience training beginning in puppyhood. Positive, firm, careful, and consistent training is essential to handle this powerful breed.

- Average shedders, Rottweilers should be brushed and combed regularly to keep their coats in shape.

- Average life span is 10 to 12 years. Breed health concerns may include allergies; anterior cruciate ligament injury; bloat; cancer; elbow and hip dysplasia; epilepsy; eye diseases; heart problems; hypothyroidism; osteochondrosis dissecans (OCD); paneosteitis; and von Willebrand disease.

Breed Facts

- **Country of Origin**: England
- **Height**: 10–12 in (25.5–30.5 cm)
- **Weight**: 11–13 lb (5–6 kg)
- **Coat**: Three types—rough has double coat with wiry, dense outercoat and short, dense undercoat; beard/broken has closer-lying coat than rough coat and longer guard hairs than smooth coat; may have face furnishings/smooth has short, flat coat
- **Colors**: Solid white or predominantly white with any combination of black, tan, or brown markings
- **Other Names**: FCI Jack Russell Terrier
- **Registries (With Group)**: AKC (FSS: Terrier)

History and Personality

The Russell Terrier shares his heritage with the Jack Russell Terrier and the Parson Russell Terrier. The breed was first developed for use in the sport of foxhunting using breeding strains from Reverend John Russell's original fox-working terriers in early 19th-century England. Although the Russell Terrier originated in England, it was never officially recognized there. Australia was later designated as the country of development for the breed because it was there that the dog, who was smaller than the Jack and Parson, was first standardized.

The Russell Terrier is described as a good working terrier first and foremost. To this end, he is a lively, inquisitive, eager, and alert terrier who is driven to find and eliminate prey. Intelligent, bold, and fearless, he loves to play as much as he loves to hunt and makes a wonderful playmate for older children. The Russell Terrier tends to be aggressive toward other dogs, and because of his strong instincts to chase and seize prey, may not be safe around small family pets if left unsupervised.

Exercise, Training, Grooming, and Health

- The Russell Terrier is an active go-getter who is happiest when he can vent his high energy and occupy his mind with interesting activities. He must be kept busy or he will become bored, rambunctious, and possibly a destructive chewer.

- The Russell will be happy to work with his owner on training, although he can be rather independent minded and stubborn. Although the Russell can become easily distracted, he is reward oriented and eager to please. Keep him focused by setting the rules and sticking to them.

- The smooth-coated Russell's coat can be kept clean and shiny with regular brushing using a firm bristle brush. The broken- and rough-coated needs regular combing and brushing with a slicker brush will remove loose hairs and dirt.

- Average life span is 12 to 16 years. Breed health concerns may include allergies; cataracts; cerebellar ataxia; congenital deafness; Legg-Calve-Perthes disease; myasthenia gravis; patellar luxation; primary lens luxation; and von Willebrand disease.

Breed Facts

- **Country of Origin**: Switzerland

- **Height**: Males 27.5–35.5 in (70–90 cm)/females 25.5–31.5 in (65–80 cm)

- **Weight**: 120–200 lb (54.5–90.5 kg) [est.]

- **Coat**: Two varieties—*shorthaired* has coarse, smooth, dense, close-lying outercoat and profuse undercoat/*longhaired* has medium-length, plain to slightly wavy outercoat and profuse undercoat; neck ruff

- **Colors**: White with red of various shades, red of various shades with white, brindle and white; white markings

- **Other Names**: Alpine Mastiff; Bernhardiner; St. Bernard; Saint Bernard Dog; St. Bernhardshund

- **Registries (With Group)**: AKC (Working); ANKC (Utility); CKC (Working); FCI (Molossoid); KC (Working); UKC (Guardian)

History and Personality

In the late 1600s, monks at a monastery near Great St. Bernard Pass in the Western Alps began to keep large dogs as draft animals and guard dogs. By the year 1700, the dogs had evolved into a role as rescuers. A team of dogs would use their keen sense of smell to find a lost traveler, sometimes under multiple feet (m) of snow. One dog would run back to the monastery for help, while the others crowded around the traveler to keep him warm. There have been more than 2,000 documented rescues by these noble dogs.

Saint Bernards are friendly, patient, loyal, eager to please, tolerant, and intelligent. Some may be aloof with strangers, but most are warm and outgoing. They are especially noted for their tolerance of children.

Exercise, Training, Grooming, and Health

- The Saint Bernard will benefit from a long daily walk.

- Although he can be stubborn on occasion, the Saint is loyal, biddable, and intelligent, and he takes to training amiably.

- A good brushing-out once a week or so with a good, stiff brush will suffice for both coat types.

- Average life span is 8 to 10 years. Breed health concerns may include dilated cardiomyopathy (DCM); ectropion; elbow dysplasia; entropion; epilepsy; hip dysplasia; osteochondritis dissecans (OCD); and osteosarcoma.

Saluki

Breed Facts

- **Country of Origin**: Iran

- **Height**: Males 23–28 in (58.5–71 cm)/females smaller

- **Weight**: 29–66 lb (13–30 kg) [est.]

- **Coat**: Two varieties—*feathered* has smooth, soft, silky texture with slight feathering on legs and feathering at back of thighs/*smooth* has same coat but without feathering

- **Colors**: White, cream, fawn, golden, red, grizzle and tan, tricolor (white, black, tan), black and tan, or variations of these colors|any color or combination of colors [FCI][KC][UKC]

- **Other Names**: Arabian Hound; Gazelle Hound; Persian Greyhound; Saluqi; Tazi

- **Registries (With Group)**: AKC (Hound); ANKC (Hounds); CKC (Hounds); FCI (Sighthounds); KC (Hound); UKC (Sighthound & Pariah)

History and Personality

The graceful, elegant Saluki dates back to ancient Egypt, one of the earliest human civilizations, and represents what is possibly the oldest type of domestic dog. The name *Saluki* comes from a long-gone Arab city in the Middle East, Saluq, and the breed is closely associated with the Middle East and the Arab world. His keen eyesight and amazing speed (capable of bursts up to 40 miles per hour [64.5 kph]) make the Saluki a brilliant sighthunter. Ancient desert tribesmen used him to hunt deer, foxes, hares, and even the swift gazelle.

The Saluki is dignified, intelligent, and independent. This gentle and even-tempered dog has a deep affection for his humans, although he is not demonstrative about it. Generally aloof toward strangers, he may be somewhat shy. Because he is quite sensitive, younger children will probably be too rambunctious for him, but the Saluki does well with older children and adults.

Exercise, Training, Grooming, and Health

- The Saluki should have the opportunity for a fast walk or jog every day—or even better, a daily run in a safe, enclosed area. This breed will chase anything that moves and so cannot be trusted off lead.

- The Saluki's sensitive nature does not take well to harsh discipline, so training must be reward based and gentle.

- The feathered Saluki should be gently groomed a few times a week with a bristle brush to prevent mats from forming. The smoothhaired type requires only occasional brushing to loosen and remove dead hair.

- Average life span is 12 to 14 years. Breed health concerns may include cancer; eye problems; heart problems; and thyroid problems.

Samoyed

Breed Facts

- **Country of Origin**: Russia, Siberia
- **Height**: Males 20–23.5 in (51–59.5 cm)/females 18–21.5 in (46–54.5 cm)
- **Weight**: 35–65 lb (16–29.5 kg) [est.]
- **Coat**: Double coat with short, soft, thick, close, woolly undercoat and longer, harsh, standoff, weather-resistant outercoat; neck ruff
- **Colors**: Pure white, white and biscuit, cream|also all biscuit [AKC][UKC]
- **Other Names**: Bjelkier; Samoiedskaïa Sabaka; Samoyedskaya
- **Registries (With Group)**: AKC (Working); ANKC (Utility); CKC (Working); FCI (Spitz and Primitive); KC (Pastoral); UKC (Northern)

History and Personality
The Samoyed dates back to 1000 BCE, and he hasn't changed much in appearance or temperament in all that time. The breed is named

for the Samoyede people, a nomadic tribe that lived on the tundra of northern Russia and Siberia, near the Arctic Circle. The tribe used the dogs they called bjelkiers to herd reindeer, pull sledges, and occasionally hunt bears. These friendly and useful dogs were much cherished and were treated as members of the family, living with them in their primitive dwellings.

The "Sammy" is exceptionally friendly, easygoing, and affectionate. In fact, his trademark "smile"—the corners of his mouth naturally turn upward—emphasizes his affable temperament. He is also gentle and trusting. Although too friendly to specialize as a guard dog, the Samoyed's bark offers some deterrence. He was bred to work in a team, so he is social; he thrives in a family situation and loves having children to take care of, although he may try to herd them. He is quite playful and sometimes even mischievous.

Exercise, Training, Grooming, and Health

- The Samoyed should have a long walk, jog, or play session every day.

- The Sammy is intelligent and responsive, but he can also have a bit of a stubborn streak.

- His abundant coat should be brushed or combed two to three times a week.

- Average life span is 12 to 15 years. Breed health concerns may include diabetes; hip dysplasia; hypothyroidism; progressive retinal atrophy (PRA); and Samoyed hereditary glomerulopathy.

Breed Facts

- **Country of Origin**: Netherlands
- **Height**: Males 17–20 in (43–51 cm)/females 15.5–18.5 in (40–47 cm)
- **Weight**: 33 lb (15 kg) [est.]
- **Coat**: Double coat with long, slightly wavy outercoat and sufficient undercoat; topknot; beard and mustache
- **Colors**: All colors permitted
- **Other Names**: Dutch Schapendoes; Dutch Sheepdog; Dutch Sheep Poodle; Nederlandse Schapendoes
- **Registries (With Group)**: AKC (FSS: Herding); CKC (Herding); FCI (Sheepdogs); UKC (Herding)

History and Personality

The Schapendoes is believed to share common ancestry with several other shaggy-coated sheepherders: the Briard, Bearded Collie, and Bergamasco. His type has existed for hundreds of years in the Netherlands, where he has served as a skilled and hardworking farm dog.

For centuries, Dutch shepherds have valued the breed's loyalty, intelligence, and willingness to work. These attributes are just as evident in today's Schapendoes, making him an excellent family companion with high-spirited friendliness and an outgoing personality. He especially excels at sports that include running and jumping over obstacles; with his light build and extreme mobility and speed, he is a top contender in canine events such as agility. He gets along well with almost any well-behaved animal or human, giving everyone the benefit of the doubt at first meeting—he approaches one and all with a wagging tail and a smiling face.

Exercise, Training, Grooming, and Health

- Like many herding breeds, the Schapendoes needs quite a bit of exercise to work off his abundant energy. A daily long walk or run on lead supplemented by activities such as vigorous playing, swimming, or retrieving will be necessary to provide sufficient exercise.

- This intelligent breed has a positive response to training and learns quickly, although he can be stubborn. He is happiest when he is given instructions and has a job to do.

- This breed's long, dense, wavy coat requires almost daily brushing to keep it free from tangles and mats. Because the dead hair does not shed out naturally, care must be taken to remove it without disrupting the natural balance of the weather-resistant double coat. He should be bathed only when necessary. No trimming is required, although it seems to be a common misconception that the Schapendoes cannot see through the shaggy hair on his face. Breed aficionados are quick to advise not to use hair bands or bows on the hair around the eyes. For the Schapendoes, the "natural look" is definitely the one of choice.

- Average life span is 12 to 14 years. Breed health concerns may include hip dysplasia and progressive retinal atrophy (PRA).

Breed Facts

- **Country of Origin**: Belgium
- **Height**: Males 11–13 in (28–33 cm)/females 10–12 in (25.5–30.5 cm)
- **Weight**: 12–19 lb (5.5–8.5 kg)
- **Coat**: Double coat with straight, harsh, dense, abundant outercoat and soft, thick undercoat; neck ruff
- **Colors**: Black|usually black but other whole colors permissible [KC]
- **Registries (With Group)**: AKC (Non-Sporting); ANKC (Non Sporting); CKC (Non-Sporting); FCI (Sheepdogs); KC (Utility); UKC (Companion)

History and Personality

The Schipperke hails from the Flemish provinces of Belgium, where he has existed for at least several hundred years. At first called the Spits or Spitske ("little Spits"), the breed garnered acclaim as a ratter, ridding farms, workshops, and homes of vermin. He was also an excellent watchdog. By the late 1800s, he was eliminating vermin on barges and canal boats throughout Belgium, and his name was subsequently changed to Schipperke, Flemish for "little skipper" or "little captain."

The Schipperke is quick, energetic, alert, curious, and protective. He seems to think that he is much bigger than he actually is. A tireless little watchdog, he challenges intruders, is wary of strangers, and backs down from nothing. He is devoted and loyal to family members and especially protective of children. The Schipperke notices and is constantly interested in everything that is going on around him, and he can be quite vocal about it.

Exercise, Training, Grooming, and Health

- This energetic dog requires a daily long walk or jog. He will also enjoy running in a confined area, as well as frequent indoor play sessions.

- The Schipperke can be willful, but he is also intelligent and eager to please, so he trains well. Some are difficult to housetrain.

- His thick, medium-length hair requires regular weekly brushing. Two or three times a year, he will shed his entire undercoat in about a week, so he will need to be brushed more frequently then. He is a moderate shedder the rest of the time.

- Average life span is 13 to 18 years. Breed health concerns may include epilepsy; hip dysplasia; hypothyroidism; MPS-IIIB; and patellar luxation.

Breed Facts

- **Country of Origin**: Scotland
- **Height**: Males 30–32 in (76–81 cm)/females 28 in (71 cm) and over
- **Weight**: Males 85–110 lb (38.5–50 kg)/females 75–95 lb (34–43 kg)
- **Coat**: Harsh, shaggy, thick, close lying; beard and mustache
- **Colors**: Dark blue-gray, darker and lighter gray shades, brindles and yellows, sandy red or red fawn with black points
- **Other Names**: Deerhound
- **Registries (With Group)**: AKC (Hound); ANKC (Hounds); CKC (Hounds); FCI (Sighthounds); KC (Hound); UKC (Sighthound & Pariah)

History and Personality

The dignified, aristocratic Deerhound is of such antiquity that his exact origin is probably lost in the mists of time. The earliest description of the breed suggests that the Scottish Deerhound was originally a type of Greyhound, bred larger and stronger to hunt larger animals and with a heavy coat to withstand the harsh weather of his homeland. The breed was definitively identified as the Deerhound as early as the 16th century. He was highly valued for his speed, strength, and hunting skills, and no one below the rank of earl was allowed to own one.

The Scottish Deerhound is the embodiment of calm gentleness, elegance, dignity, and quiet devotion. Although courageous in the hunt, he is not a watchdog, for he is far too polite and kindhearted to challenge an intruder. As a puppy, he is active, but the adult Deerhound is quite sedentary indoors and enjoys napping (although he needs ample daily outdoor exercise). This loyal dog loves his family and makes an excellent companion for children.

Exercise, Training, Grooming, and Health

- The Scottish Deerhound needs ample daily exercise, such as a long walk or jog. As with all sighthounds, care must be taken to not set him loose in an unconfined area.

- The laid-back Deerhound is often slow to obey commands and can become bored with long training sessions or extensive practice periods.

- The Scottish Deerhound requires only minimal grooming; a thorough going-over with a comb or brush once or twice a week is adequate.

- Average life span is 8 to 11 years. Breed health concerns may include allergies; bloat; cystinuria; fractures; heart problems; hereditary factor VII deficiency; hypothyroidism; osteosarcoma; and pyometra.

Scottish Terrier

Breed Facts

- **Country of Origin**: Scotland
- **Height**: 10–11 in (25.5–28 cm)
- **Weight**: Males 19–22 lb (8.5–10 kg)/females 18–21 lb (8–9.5 kg)|18.5–23 lb (8.5–10.5 kg) [ANKC][FCI][KC]
- **Coat**: Double coat is weather resistant, with intensely hard, wiry, close-lying outercoat and short, dense, soft undercoat
- **Colors**: Black, wheaten, brindle of any color|also steel or iron gray, sandy [CKC]
- **Other Names**: Aberdeen Terrier
- **Registries (With Group)**: AKC (Terrier); ANKC (Terriers); CKC (Terriers); FCI (Terriers); KC (Terrier); UKC (Terrier)

History and Personality

For centuries, hunters in the Scottish Highlands kept sturdy dogs who were compact and fearless enough to go to ground after quarry.

Today, no one is sure which of several terrier types found in the region was the ancestor of what is now known as the Scottish Terrier, or "Scottie," although it is likely that the Scottie, Cairn Terrier, and West Highland White Terrier are closely related. These terriers excelled at killing vermin on farms, as well as badgers.

Full of character, the Scottie is intelligent, courageous, dignified, and loyal. As a puppy, he is playful, but as he grows up, he takes on a more purposeful air. His feisty nature may manifest as aggression toward other dogs, and his strong instinct to go after quarry may extend to regarding the neighbor's cat or a small pet as prey. Otherwise, though, he is even-tempered and deeply devoted to his family. He is aloof toward strangers and so makes an alert watchdog.

Exercise, Training, Grooming, and Health

- Daily exercise is essential in the form of a brisk walk or lively game.

- The Scottie is clever and has an independent spirit, and he will dominate the household unless taught to mind his manners from an early age.

- The Scottish Terrier should be brushed or combed a few times a week. His "jacket" is best maintained if kept fairly short by stripping or clipping every several months.

- Average life span is 12 to 14 years. Breed health concerns may include bladder cancer; cerebellar abiotrophy (CA); crandiomandibular osteopathy; Cushing's syndrome; epilepsy; hypothyroidism; juvenile cataracts; liver shunts; Scottie cramp; and von Willebrand disease.

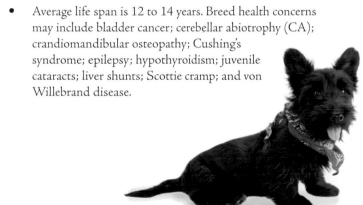

Sealyham Terrier

Breed Facts

- **Country of Origin**: Great Britain
- **Height**: 10.5–12 in (25.5–30.5 cm)
- **Weight**: Males 20–25 lb (9–11.5 kg)/females 17.5 lb (8 kg)
- **Coat**: Double coat with long, hard, wiry outercoat and soft, dense, weather-resistant undercoat
- **Colors**: All white or with lemon, brown, or badger pied markings on head and ears|also blue markings [ANKC][CKC] [FCI][KC][UKC]
- **Registries (With Group)**: AKC (Terrier); ANKC (Terriers); CKC (Terriers); FCI (Terriers); KC (Terrier); UKC (Terrier)

History and Personality

In the mid-1800s, a Welsh sportsman by the name of Captain John Edwardes, whose estate was called Sealyham, decided to build the perfect terrier. He had to be fast enough to keep up with the hounds and horses on a hunt, small enough to go to ground after badgers, and brave enough to face any prey. He also had to be light in color so that the hounds would not at any point mistake him for the object of the hunt. Edwardes spent four decades putting together his terrier, combining a number of breeds that may have included the Bull Terrier, the Cheshire Terrier (extinct), the Corgi, the Dandie Dinmont Terrier, the Old English White Terrier (extinct), the West Highland White Terrier, and the Wire Fox Terrier. The breed soon gained attention for its exceptional courage as a hunter, facing down badgers and otters several times its size.

The Sealyham is proud and inquisitive, and he regards the world around him with a supreme self-confidence. This charming, responsive dog is also a delightful clown. He may be reserved with strangers but is a loyal and devoted companion to those he loves. The Sealyham is relatively low-key for a terrier.

Exercise, Training, Grooming, and Health

- A brisk daily walk or a play session of moderate length should meet his exercise needs.

- The Sealyham can be stubborn and independent, but his friendly nature makes him a bit more trainable. Firm but fair discipline is likely to get the best results.

- The Sealyham's dense, wiry coat should be combed or brushed at least twice weekly, and every two to three months, it should be smoothed and shaped by clipping or stripping. Stripping preserves the hard texture of the outercoat.

- Average life span is 12 to 14 years. Breed health concerns may include back problems; congenital deafness; and eye problems.

Shetland Sheepdog

Breed Facts

- **Country of Origin**: Scotland
- **Height**: Males 14.5 in (37 cm)/females 14 in (36 cm)|13–16 in (33–40.5 cm) [AKC][CKC][UKC]
- **Weight**: 14–27 lb (6.5–12 kg) [est.]
- **Coat**: Double coat with long, straight, harsh outercoat and short, furry, dense undercoat; mane
- **Colors**: Black, blue merle, shades of sable, all marked with varying amounts of white and/or tan|also predominately white [UKC]
- **Registries (With Group)**: AKC (Herding); ANKC (Working); CKC (Herding); FCI (Sheepdogs); KC (Pastoral); UKC (Herding)

History and Personality

During the 1700s, fishing boats arrived regularly on the Shetland Islands, bringing black-and-tan King Charles Spaniels, Yakki dogs from

Greenland, spitz-type herding dogs from the Scandinavian countries, and working sheepdogs from Scotland. These likely ancestors of the Shetland Sheepdog, or "Sheltie," interbred with native island dogs to create alert, eager working dogs. The Shetland Islands are bare and rugged, so the indigenous peoples developed animals that didn't need lush flora to survive. The miniature cattle, dwarf sheep, and tiny Shetland ponies of the islands were herded by correspondingly small sheepdogs. Their gait carried them lightly over rough terrain, and their easygoing manner made them gentle with stock.

The Sheltie's lively but gentle and responsive temperament makes him an outstanding companion. Because he is bright and willing, he is a top performer in obedience, agility, and other canine sports. He was bred to use his voice in herding, so he is likely to bark a lot. His owner should take special care to socialize him as a puppy in order to offset a predisposition to shyness. He is attached to his family and is excellent with children, although he can be reserved with strangers.

Exercise, Training, Grooming, and Health

- Bred to work a full day, the Shetland Sheepdog will benefit from a good walk, jog, or vigorous play or training session daily.

- With his extreme intelligence, desire to please, and natural focus on his owner, the Sheltie is one of the most trainable of all breeds. Harsh methods should never be used on this sensitive fellow; many Shelties work for praise and encouragement even more than for food rewards.

- Brushing every few days will help keep the Sheltie's profuse coat healthy, attractive, and free from mats.

- Average life span is 12 to 14 years. Breed health concerns may include Collie eye anomaly (CEA); dermatomyositis; hemophilia; hip dysplasia; hypothyroidism; Legg-Calve-Perthes disease; MDR-1 gene mutation; progressive retinal atrophy (PRA); and seizures.

Shiba Inu

Breed Facts

- **Country of Origin**: Japan

- **Height**: Males 14.5–16.5 in (37–42 cm)/females 13.5–15.5 in (34.5–39.5 cm)

- **Weight**: Males 23 lb (10.5 kg)/females 17 lb (7.5 kg)

- **Coat**: Double coat with straight, stiff outercoat and soft, thick undercoat

- **Colors**: Red, black and tan, sesame [AKC][CKC]|red, black and tan, sesame, black sesame, red sesame [ANKC][FCI]|red, red sesame, black and tan, white [KC]|red, red sesame, black and tan [UKC]

- **Other Names**: Japanese Shiba Inu, Japanese Small-Size Dog, Shiba, Shiba Ken

- **Registries (With Group)**: AKC (Non-Sporting); ANKC (Utility); CKC (Non-Sporting); FCI (Spitz and Primitive); KC (Utility); UKC (Northern)

History and Personality

The Shiba Inu originated in the mountainous areas of Japan, where his type has been known for nearly 3,000 years. He is the smallest of a group of several Japanese spitz-type breeds of ancient heritage that includes the Akita and is a result of interbreeding ancient types, including the Sanin, Mino, and Shinshu. The Shiba was used to hunt mostly birds and small game, although with his great courage and agility, he occasionally assisted the hunter in bringing down boars, bears, and deer.

Some owners describe the Shiba as cat-like in his independence and fastidiousness. He is exuberant, agile, and quick, and he loves a good romp. Always self-assured, he can be headstrong. He is affectionate and playful with his family but tends toward aloofness with strangers. His natural guarding tendencies make him an excellent watchdog. He can be scrappy with other dogs, and he has a strong instinct to prey upon small animals. Some Shibas can be quite vocal, and when upset or joyful will emit a high-pitched sound that has been described as the "Shiba scream."

Exercise, Training, Grooming, and Health

- The Shiba benefits from a vigorous daily workout to expend some of his boundless energy. A long walk or lively play session each day will keep him fit and happy.

- Early training and socialization are especially recommended for this independent spirit. He is highly intelligent but, like many spitz breeds, may prefer to look the other way rather than heed a command. With patience and persistence he can become quite biddable, though. Owners should think twice before allowing their Shiba to run free, as his acute hunting instinct may send him off on a run at any opportunity.

- His thick double coat requires regular grooming with a stiff slicker brush at least once a week and more frequently during periods of heavy shedding.

- Average life span is 13 to 16 years. Breed health concerns may include allergies; dental problems; eye problems; hip dysplasia; hypothyroidism; and patellar luxation.

Shih Tzu

Breed Facts

- **Country of Origin**: China (Tibet Region)

- **Height**: 8–11 in (20–28 cm)

- **Weight**: Males 9–16 lb (4–7.5 kg)/females less|10–17.5 lb (4.5–8 kg) [ANKC][FCI][KC]

- **Coat**: Double coat with long, flowing, luxurious, dense outercoat and good undercoat

- **Colors**: All colors permissible

- **Other Names**: Chinese Lion Dog, Chrysanthemum Dog

- **Registries (With Group)**: AKC (Toy); ANKC (Non Sporting); CKC (Non-Sporting); FCI (Companion and Toy); KC (Utility); UKC (Companion)

History and Personality
The Shih Tzu probably has ancient roots in Tibet as the smaller cousin of the Lhasa Apso, but the breed was developed and perfected

in China. The elegant and docile little "lion dog" was highly prized by the Chinese court for centuries, living a life of luxury in the royal palace. The breed was further refined during the reign of the Dowager Empress Cixi (T'zu Hsi, 1861–1908). After her death, the palace kennel was dispersed, and the breed became scarce in subsequent years. After China became a republic in 1912, occasional specimens made their way into England and later to Norway and North America, where breeding programs were begun.

This spunky little fellow is both a gentle lapdog and a playful companion. He's surprisingly sturdy and is tolerant and affectionate with children. He can be stubborn one moment, then disarm the next with his charming clownishness.

Exercise, Training, Grooming, and Health

- Because of his small size, a short walk every day supplemented with some indoor playtime is sufficient to meet the Shih Tzu's exercise needs.

- The Shih Tzu can be obstinate, but patience in training will eventually pay off. As with some toy breeds, housetraining can be a challenge.

- When his luxurious coat is kept long, in the traditional style, it should be brushed daily to prevent tangling and matting. The topknot must be maintained (tied up neatly with a rubber band) to hold the hair away from his eyes. Many owners and breeders keep their pets and older animals trimmed shorter for greater ease of coat care.

- Average life span is 11 to 15 years. Breed health concerns may include cleft palate; dental problems; eye problems; hypothyroidism; invertebral disk disease; patellar luxation; renal dysplasia; respiratory problems; and von Willebrand disease.

Siberian Husky

Breed Facts

- **Country of Origin**: Siberia

- **Height**: Males 21–23.5 in (53.5–59.5 cm)/females 20–22 in (51–56 cm)

- **Weight**: Males 45–60 lb (20.5–27 kg)/females 35–50 lb (16–22.5 kg)

- **Coat**: Double coat with medium-length, straight, soft, somewhat smooth-lying outercoat and soft, dense undercoat

- **Colors**: All colors from black to pure white; variety of markings on head are common

- **Other Names**: Arctic Husky

- **Registries (With Group)**: AKC (Working); ANKC (Utility); CKC (Working); FCI (Spitz and Primitive); KC (Working); UKC (Northern)

History and Personality

The nomadic Chukchi tribe of extreme Northeast Asia bred dogs of this type since ancient times to pull sledges and hunt reindeer. For centuries, continuing through the 19th century, the Chukchi people were famous for their excellent long-distance sled dogs. The tribe lived in permanent inland settlements and had to travel long distances to hunt the sea mammals that fed both people and dogs. A small sled dog was ideal—one who could exist on little food. Neither sprinters nor freighters, these dogs were endurance animals who could pull light loads of killed game at moderate speeds over long distances. Then known as the Siberian Chukchi, the breed first arrived in the United States in 1909, brought across the Bering Strait from Siberia to Alaska.

The Siberian is fun loving, friendly, gentle, alert, and outgoing. As a puppy, he is playful and mischievous; as he matures, he becomes more dignified and reserved. Still, he is not possessive, territorial, or suspicious of strangers. He was bred to live and work as part of a team, so he does not like to be alone. The Siberian gets along well with children and other dogs, but he is predatory toward smaller animals. He has a tendency to howl rather than bark.

Exercise, Training, Grooming, and Health

- The Siberian was bred to run tirelessly for long distances in front of a sled. Understandably, his need for ample exercise is inborn. He should have a large, escape-proof yard in which to run around, as well as a daily run or jog on a leash.

- This dog was bred to make his own decisions, and because of his strong prey drive no amount of training will make it safe for him to be off lead outside of a fenced area. He is intelligent and friendly, but he can be stubborn and may obey a command only if he sees a point to it. Positive reinforcement, consistency, patience, and an understanding of sled-dog character are all required.

- The Siberian's coat requires only minimal attention, except during shedding season, when he loses his entire undercoat. He should be combed daily during those periods.

- Average life span is 10 to 14 years. Breed health concerns may include crystalline corneal opacity; epilepsy; hip dysplasia; hypothyroidism; juvenile cataracts; osteochondritis dissecans (OCD); progressive retinal atrophy (PRA); and von Willebrand disease.

Silky Terrier

Breed Facts

- **Country of Origin**: Australia

- **Height**: Males 9–10 in (23–23.5 cm)/females slightly smaller|9–10 in (23–23.5 cm) [AKC][CKC][UKC]

- **Weight**: 8–10 lb (3.5–4.5 kg)

- **Coat**: Single coat is flat, fine, glossy, silky; topknot

- **Colors**: Blue and tan

- **Other Names**: Australian Silky Terrier; Silky Toy Terrier; Sydney Silky

- **Registries (With Group)**: AKC (Toy); ANKC (Toys); CKC (Toys); FCI (Terriers); KC (Toy); UKC (Terrier)

History and Personality

The Silky was developed in Australia in the early 1800s—his history intermixed with that of the Australian Terrier, that country's other blue and tan native terrier breed. The Yorkshire Terrier is known to figure in the Silky's ancestry, although other breeds, such as the Dandie Dinmont Terrier, Skye Terrier, and Cairn Terrier probably also play a part. Although the feisty Silky is adept at killing rats and other vermin, he was developed primarily as a companion and house pet.

The Silky is lively, smart, and friendly. He is affectionate but not demonstrative. He wants to stay near his human companions but isn't a lapdog. This playful imp is not above making a little mischief—if left alone for too long, he may find creative ways to entertain himself. He is docile, although he may not tolerate roughhousing or teasing. Ever alert, he may bark a lot.

Exercise, Training, Grooming, and Health

- The Silky is quite energetic, requiring a little more exercise than most toy breeds. He needs at least a moderate walk daily and will also enjoy play sessions in a confined area.

- Although he can be willful, the Silky is intelligent and eager to please, and he is a quick learner.

- The Silky's luxurious coat needs to be brushed or combed out every day and bathed regularly.

- Average life span is 12 to 15 years. Breed health concerns may include allergies; collapsing trachea; diabetes; elbow dysplasia; epilepsy; invertebral disk disease; Legg-Calve-Perthes disease; and patellar luxation.

Skye Terrier

Breed Facts

- **Country of Origin**: Scotland
- **Height**: Males 10 in (25.5 cm)/females 9.5 in (24 cm)
- **Weight**: 18–40 lb (8–18 kg) [est.]
- **Coat**: Double coat with long, straight, flat, hard outercoat and short, soft, woolly, close-lying undercoat; feathering
- **Colors**: Black, blue, dark or light gray, silver platinum, fawn, cream [AKC][UKC]|black, dark or light gray, fawn, cream [ANKC][FCI][KC]|any color [CKC]
- **Registries (With Group)**: AKC (Terrier); ANKC (Terriers); CKC (Terriers); FCI (Terriers); KC (Terrier); UKC (Terrier)

History and Personality

Hailing from the rugged Isle of Skye, off the west coast of Scotland, the Skye Terrier's history goes back at least 400 years. The Skye was originally used by farmers to locate and kill badgers, foxes, and otters. He gained status during the long reign of breed devotee Queen Victoria, an avid dog fancier who forwarded the cause of many breeds. Skyes competed at the first dog shows in Birmingham, England, in the 1860s. The drop-ear variety was originally favored, but today the prick-eared Skyes predominate for both pet and show.

The Skye is affectionate, friendly, and happy with people he knows, but he distrusts strangers, although he will never be vicious. He is better with older children, and he may not mingle well with strange dogs. The Skye is loyal and an excellent protector. Calm and mild mannered, he has a pluckiness and toughness that hail back to his heritage as a courageous hunter.

Exercise, Training, Grooming, and Health

- For adult Skyes, a good daily walk of at least moderate length, supplemented by runs or play sessions in an enclosed area, will keep them fit.

- The Skye can be sensitive yet stubborn, so patience and consistency in his training are vital. He needs a good deal of early socialization with people and other pets to help overcome his natural reserve.

- Although the Skye has a long, profuse coat, it can be brushed just once a week to prevent mats. Skyes require special attention paid to keeping the hair around their eyes and mouth clean. Many owners tie up the long hair above the eyes with a rubber band.

- Average life span is 12 to 14 years. Breed health concerns may include back problems; renal dysplasia; and Skye limp.

Sloughi

Breed Facts

- **Country of Origin**: Morocco

- **Height**: Males 26–29 in (66–73.5 cm)/females 24–27 in (61–68 cm)

- **Weight**: Males 55–65 lb (25–29.5 kg)/females 45–50 lb (20.5–22.5 kg)

- **Coat**: Short, fine, smooth, dense; undercoat may grow during winter

- **Colors**: Ranges from light sand to red sand (fawn); may have black mask

- **Other Names**: Arabian Greyhound; Arabian Sighthound; Sloughi Moghrebi; Sloughui; Slughi

- **Registries (With Group)**: AKC (FSS: Hound); ANKC (Hounds); FCI (Sighthounds); KC (Hound); UKC (Sighthound & Pariah)

History and Personality

Undoubtedly of ancient descent, this hunting hound is closely related to the Saluki and Azawakh, and his birthplace is in the deserts covering what are now Morocco, Algeria, Tunisia, and Libya. The Sloughi's main role was as a dog of the desert tribes. They have lived for literally thousands of years with their nomadic masters, chasing down desert game and guarding the encampments.

Dignified and proud, Sloughis are loyal and affectionate with their human companions and will defend them when necessary. Otherwise, they are quiet, sensitive, and gentle dogs. Extremely devoted, they develop a deep bond with their owners and can be one-person dogs.

Exercise, Training, Grooming, and Health

- The Sloughi needs to run every day. That is the extent of his activity, though—he is calm and quiet indoors.

- A fair, gentle training program is most appropriate for the sensitive Sloughi.

- A rubdown with a grooming glove, rubber mitt, or soft brush every now and then will suffice to keep his coat in shape.

- Average life span is 12 to 15 years. Breed health concerns may include heart murmur and progressive retinal atrophy (PRA).

Small Münsterländer

Breed Facts

- **Country of Origin**: Germany
- **Height**: Males 21.5 in (54 cm)/females 20.5 in (52 cm)
- **Weight**: 33–64 lb (15–29 kg) [est.]
- **Coat**: Medium length, not or only slightly wavy, dense, close lying, water repellent
- **Colors**: Brown-white or brown roan with brown patches, brown mantle, or brown ticking
- **Other Names**: Kleiner Münsterländer; Kleiner Münsterländer Vorstehhund; Small Munsterlander Pointer
- **Registries (With Group)**: AKC (FSS: Sporting); CKC (Sporting); FCI (Pointing Dogs); KC (Gundog); UKC (Gun Dog)

History and Personality

The Small Münsterländer originated more than 500 years ago in Münsterländer, the capital of the region of Münster in northwest

Germany. Bird-dog hunting has long been popular there, and hunters were constantly interested in developing versatile hunting dogs who could excel in air scenting and tracking. The Small Münsterländer was the result of crosses of the German Longhaired Pointer to Continental spaniels. They became popular in 19th-century Germany with the common people, who needed a versatile hunting dog capable of bringing home a variety of game. Today, the Small Münsterländer is prized in his native land for his skill in pointing, tracking, and retrieving birds and smaller furry game. It is a rare breed in most other parts of the world.

Münsterländers are happy, outgoing, and obedient dogs with steady temperaments. They are intelligent, capable learners. After a day in the field, these exceptional hunters, who work close and are people oriented, like nothing better than to curl up beside their family. They love people and are easy to socialize.

Exercise, Training, Grooming, and Health

- Münsterländers require plenty of daily exercise and truly revel in outdoor activities. They need places where they can be allowed to run off lead—this should be done in a large, safely confined area.

- Münsterländers live to please and are relatively easy to train. With positive, reward-based methods practiced for just a few minutes several times a day, they learn quickly and retain their lessons. However, they can be stubborn, which helps in hunting pursuits but may pose a challenge to their trainer at times.

- The Münsterländer's coat should be brushed and combed regularly to keep it free of dirt and debris that he will pick up outdoors, with special attention paid to the feathered areas.

- Average life span is 13 to 15 years. Breed health concerns may include hip dysplasia.

Smooth Fox Terrier

Breed Facts

- **Country of Origin**: England
- **Height**: Males no more than 15.5 in (39.5 cm)/females smaller
- **Weight**: Males 16.5–18 lb (7.5–8 kg)/females 15.5–16.5 lb (7–7.5 kg)
- **Coat**: Short, hard, dense, abundant, close lying
- **Colors**: All white or predominantly white with tan, black and tan, or black markings
- **Registries (With Group)**: AKC (Terrier); ANKC (Terriers); CKC (Terriers); FCI (Terriers); KC (Terrier); UKC (Terrier)

History and Personality

An old English breed, the Fox Terrier was used in the 18th century by foxhunters who needed a compact, energetic, bold dog who would go to ground after quarry. The Fox Terrier was bred to be a quick thinker, relying on his instincts rather than orders from his owner. There are two types of Fox Terrier, distinguished by coat: Smooth and Wire. Although coat is the only major difference between them today, authorities believe that the Smooth and Wire probably have different origins. Ancestors of the Smooth are believed to include England's smooth-coated black and tan terrier, the Bull Terrier, and even the Greyhound and Beagle.

Scrappy, plucky, and energetic, the Smooth Fox Terrier is a wonderful, sturdy pet for an active family. He is friendly and alert and enjoys spending time with his people. With proper socialization, he will likely get along well with other dogs, but he should not be unsupervised around smaller pets that he might view as prey, such as birds, hamsters, or rabbits. This gregarious dog is not well suited to being left alone for long periods—he tends to be vocal and may bark a lot.

Exercise, Training, Grooming, and Health

- Because of his compact size, the Smooth Fox Terrier is suitable for city dwellers, although his owner must be willing to devote time to daily long walks or vigorous play sessions to meet this energetic fellow's exercise needs.

- The Smooth Fox Terrier is bright and eager to please, and he adapts to most positive training regimens quickly. He can also be impulsive, however, because he lives to chase and explore.

- The Smooth Fox Terrier requires little grooming other than occasional ear cleaning and nail trims. A quick going-over with a hound glove every week or so will help keep his coat smooth and healthy.

- Average life span is 12 to 15 years. Breed health concerns may include cataracts; congenital heart disease; congenital deafness; distichiasis; glaucoma; Legg-Calve-Perthes disease; primary lens luxation; and skin allergies.

Breed Facts

- **Country of Origin**: Ireland

- **Height**: Males 18–19.5 in (46–49 cm)/females 17–18 in (43–43.5 cm)

- **Weight**: Males 35–45 lb (16–20.5 kg)

- **Coat**: Single coat is soft, silky, gently waved or curled, abundant

- **Colors**: Any shade of wheaten

- **Other Names**: Irish Soft Coated Wheaten Terrier, Soft-Coated Wheaten Terrier, Wheaten Terrier

- **Registries (With Group)**: AKC (Terrier); ANKC (Terriers); CKC (Terriers); FCI (Terriers); KC (Terrier); UKC (Terrier)

History and Personality

In times past, all of the terriers of Ireland were known collectively as Irish Terriers, so it is difficult to know whether ancient references to this strain are about the generic type or specifically about the Soft Coated Wheaten Terrier known today. The Soft Coated Wheaten

Terrier of 200 years ago was a dog of the poor and was so common that few considered him worthy of notice. He worked on the farm, performing the usual terrier task of chasing small animals into burrows and dragging them out. He was also valued for his skill at working cattle, hunting badgers and foxes, and protecting his family.

Alert, friendly, and happy, the Wheaten is often quieter than the smaller terriers. He is headstrong but obedient. He loves kids and is a good companion for them, although he is best with older children; his enthusiasm may overwhelm small children. If socialized early, the Wheaten will get along well with other dogs, but the breed is often incompatible with other smaller animals, including cats. He is intelligent, playful, and curious about what's going on around him. This affectionate dog bonds closely with his family. Because he will bark to signal the approach of a stranger, he makes a good watchdog.

Exercise, Training, Grooming, and Health

- The Wheaten needs a moderate amount of exercise every day, either indoors or out. A long daily walk, supplemented with a daily play session in the yard, will help keep him fit.

- The Wheaten is a strong-minded dog and can be stubborn—he wants to lead, not follow. The Wheaten needs gentle but firm and consistent training. He is quite intelligent, so he is a quick learner.

- The breed's long, silky coat should be brushed or combed every day or two, and he should be bathed at least every other month. He doesn't shed much, and loose hair will be removed as he is combed—if this is not done, his coat will mat.

- Average life span is 12 to 14 years. Breed health concerns may include Addison's disease; protein-losing enteropathy (PLE); protein-losing nephropathy (PLN); and renal dysplasia.

Breed Facts

- **Country of Origin**: Spain

- **Height**: Males 30.5–31.5 in (77–80 cm) minimum/females 28.5–29.5 in (72–75 cm) minimum

- **Weight**: 90–220 lb (41–100 kg) [est.]

- **Coat**: Medium length, smooth, thick, dense

- **Colors**: Immaterial, although yellow, fawn red, black, wolf colored most appreciated

- **Other Names**: Mastín de España; Mastín de Extremadura; Mastín de la Mancha; Mastín de Leon; Mastín Español

- **Registries (With Group)**: AKC (FSS: Working); ANKC (Utility); FCI (Molossoid); UKC (Guardian)

History and Personality

Believed to have descended from the ancient Molosser dog, who existed as far back as 2000 BCE, the Spanish Mastiff shares a similar history to all of the flock-guarding dogs from Spain and Portugal. He has a long history as an excellent flock guardian, a role he continues in today with great fearlessness. He has also been a draft dog, pulling supply carts, and a fiercely efficient guardian of homes, estates, and even munitions during the Spanish Civil War.

This noble giant is aloof, dignified, calm, and intelligent. He is devoted to his family and may politely accept strangers if he has been socialized properly, although he will be wary of them. He can be aggressive toward other dogs. The Spanish Mastiff may be a less-than-ideal pet in urban situations, where his booming voice and massive size could be problematic. He is a wonderful protector of his home and family.

Exercise, Training, Grooming, and Health

- A long daily walk will be sufficient, although he will appreciate a fenced area where he can exercise at his own rate.

- Socializing and training should begin early to ensure a stable and reliable pet. The breed is quite alert and food motivated but can bore easily; training must be consistent and firm but gentle.

- Weekly brushing of his thick coat will help remove dead hair and reduce shedding.

- Average life span is 10 to 11 years. Breed health concerns may include bloat; enostosis; entropion; heart problems; and hip dysplasia.

Breed Facts

- **Country of Origin**: Spain
- **Height**: Males 17.5–19.5 in (44–50 cm)/females 15.5–18 in (40–46 cm)
- **Weight**: Males 39.5–48.5 lb (18–22 kg)/females 31–39.5 lb (14–18 kg)
- **Coat**: Curly, woolly; longer coats may form cords
- **Colors**: Shades of white and black, white and brown; also shades of white, black, chestnut
- **Other Names**: Andalusian Turk; Perro de Agua Español; Turco de Andaluz; Turkish Dog
- **Registries (With Group)**: AKC (FSS: Sporting); FCI (Water Dogs); KC (Gundog); UKC (Gun Dog)

History and Personality

By the 12th century, a woolly-coated dog was being used for herding and water retrieval in Spain. This was undoubtedly an ancestor of the Spanish Water Dog. He is still working in the mountains of southern Spain, both as a retriever and as a tender to flocks of sheep and goats.

Faithful, obedient, and hardworking, the Spanish Water Dog has strong herding, hunting, and guarding instincts. These traits, combined with his inexhaustible energy, mean that he's really happy only when he has a job to do. He is easily trained and adapts well to just about any situation. He can be reserved around strangers.

Exercise, Training, Grooming, and Health

- The breed needs lots of exercise, such as a long walk every day. He thrives when given a job to do.

- The Spanish Water Dog is intelligent and a quick learner, so he takes readily to obedience training. He can be territorial and should be socialized with people and animals from an early age.

- The Spanish Water Dog's coat, which often forms cords, should be permitted to grow naturally and not be combed or brushed. The coat is shaved down once or twice a year.

- Average life span is 10 to 14 years. Breed health concerns may include Addison's disease; allergies; cataracts; exocrine pancreatic insufficiency (EPI); hip dysplasia; hypothyroidism; and progressive retinal atrophy (PRA).

Spinone Italiano

Breed Facts

- **Country of Origin**: Italy

- **Height**: Males 23–27.5 in (58.5–70 cm)/females 22–25.5 in (56–65 cm)

- **Weight**: Males 70–86 lb (31.5–39 kg)/females 62–75 lb (28–34 kg)

- **Coat**: Single coat is flat or slightly crimped, slightly wiry, tough, dense, stiff; beard and mustache

- **Colors**: White, white with orange markings, white with peppered orange, white with brown markings, brown roan with or without brown markings

- **Other Names**: Italian Coarsehaired Pointer; Italian Griffon; Italian Spinone; Italian Wire-Haired Pointing Dog

- **Registries (With Group)**: AKC (Sporting); ANKC (Gundogs); CKC (Sporting); FCI (Pointing Dogs); KC (Gundog); UKC (Gun Dog)

History and Personality

Purely Italian in origin, the Spinone Italiano is an ancient all-purpose gundog. Noted for his superior nose and ultrasoft mouth, he is especially good in heavy cover or cold, wet conditions, where his protective coat serves him well. Today, he is still hunted throughout Piedmont in Italy.

This charming gentleman is calm, affectionate, and easygoing. He can be timid if not socialized as a puppy, but when socialized, he is friendly toward strangers, if sometimes cautious. He quickly bonds with his family and gets along well with children, other dogs, and most other animals, although he may give chase to small ones. As an adult, he is docile but still playful.

Exercise, Training, Grooming, and Health

- A daily walk or jog, some free time outdoors in a fenced-in area, plus a play session or two should take care of his exercise needs.

- The Spinone is intelligent and a fast learner, but he is not always a good performer; he will do what he is told if he sees a reason for it.

- The Spinone requires no more than a weekly brushing to strip out the dead hair.

- Average life span is 12 to 14 years. Breed health concerns may include cerebellar ataxia and hip dysplasia.

Stabyhoun

Breed Facts

- **Country of Origin**: Netherlands
- **Height**: Males 21 in (53 cm)/females 19.5 in (50 cm)
- **Weight**: 40–55 lb (18–25 kg) [est.]
- **Coat**: Long, smooth
- **Colors**: Black, brown, orange, all with white markings
- **Other names**: Beike; Friese Stabij; Frisian Pointing Dog; Stabij; Stabijhoun; Stabyhound
- **Registries (With Group)**: AKC (FSS: Sporting); FCI (Pointing Dogs); UKC (Gun Dog)

History and Personality

This hunting breed hails from the Dutch province of Friesland, where its type has been known since the 1600s. From the beginning, the Stabyhoun's temperament has been of utmost importance because he was expected to fulfill multiple duties as hunter, watchdog, and family pet. His even, devoted character definitely earns the breed its name, which translates as "stand-by-me dog." Excellent at pointing, flushing, and retrieving game, especially ducks and upland birds, the Stabyhoun is as much at home in the field as he is by the family hearth.

In temperament, the Stabyhoun is the essence of "well balanced." He is a good watchdog without being overly aggressive, and although energetic when involved in a job or sport, he is calm and peaceful indoors. He can be a bit reserved with strangers but is loyal to and affectionate with family members. He gets along with other pets as well as humans and is soft and gentle with children. A good all-around dog in almost every situation, the Stabyhoun is an excellent choice for either family pet or working companion dog.

Exercise, Training, Grooming, and Health

- The active Stabyhoun enjoys long daily walks and romps in a fenced yard.

- The Stabyhoun is an agile dog possessing great intelligence and a great desire to please his trainer. He is ideally suited to any sport that employs his outstanding speed, grace, and retrieving ability.

- The Stabyhoun has a low-maintenance coat—a thorough weekly brushing or combing should keep his long, silky hair free of mats and tangles and minimize shedding.

- Average life span is 13 to 14 years. Breed health concerns may include epilepsy and hip dysplasia.

Staffordshire Bull Terrier

Breed Facts

- **Country of Origin**: England
- **Height**: 14–16 in (35.5–40.5 cm)
- **Weight**: Males 28–38 lb (12.5–17 kg)/females 24–34 lb (11–15.5 kg)
- **Coat**: Short, smooth, close
- **Colors**: Red, fawn, white, black, blue, or any of these colors with white; any shade of brindle; any shade of brindle with white
- **Registries (With Group)**: AKC (Terrier); ANKC (Terriers); CKC (Terriers); FCI (Terriers); KC (Terrier); UKC (Terrier)

History and Personality

The Staffordshire Bull Terrier ("Staffy Bull") descends from early Greek mastiff-type dogs called Molossians, who found their way into fighting arenas throughout the Roman Empire. Developed from bull and terrier types, the Staffy Bull's ancestors were originally used by butchers to manage bulls and by hunters to help catch and hold wild boars and other game. In England, these tasks evolved to become the sports of bull- and bearbaiting, which was later replaced by dogfighting. By the 1930s, dogfighting had thankfully been outlawed and fanciers worked to mold the breed into a show dog and companion.

This breed is well known for its gentle, playful temperament. Animated and clever, he enjoys a good game. He loves his family, especially children, and has even been nicknamed the "Nanny Dog" because of his devotion to them. The Staffy Bull can be aggressive toward other dogs and animals, although he may be able to live with them if well socialized from puppyhood.

Exercise, Training, Grooming, and Health

- The breed's energy reserve and great stamina mean that he requires quite a bit of exercise to maintain his muscular body.

- The Staffy Bull is highly intelligent, although he has a tendency toward stubbornness and independence, traits that can prove challenging to his trainer. However, he is quick to pick up commands and responds well when trained gently but firmly.

- The Staffordshire Bull Terrier's smooth, short hair is easily maintained a few times a week with a grooming mitt.

- Average life span is 12 to 14 years. Breed health concerns may include cataracts; congenital deafness; elbow dysplasia; heart problems; hip dysplasia; hypothyroidism; L-2-hydroxyglutaric aciduria (L-2-HGA); patellar luxation; and skin allergies.

Standard Schnauzer

Breed Facts

- **Country of Origin**: Germany
- **Height**: Males 17.5–22 in (45–48 cm)/females 17–21 in (43–46 cm)
- **Weight**: 31–44 lb (14–20 kg)
- **Coat**: Double coat with hard, wiry, tight, very thick outercoat and soft, close, dense undercoat; beard
- **Colors**: Pepper and salt, pure black
- **Other Names**: Mittelschnauzer; Schnauzer
- **Registries (With Group)**: AKC (Working); ANKC (Utility); CKC (Working); FCI (Pinscher and Schnauzer); KC (Utility); UKC (Guardian)

History and Personality

Schnauzers have been popular farm dogs in Germany for centuries. They were hardworking, tough dogs who eradicated vermin but were also good family companions. Sizes ranged because there was no set type, and the larger dogs were used to pull carts, guard livestock, and hunt pests. The smaller dogs were used as general vermin exterminators. Known at one time as the Wirehaired Pinscher, the Standard Schnauzer is the oldest of the three Schnauzer breeds, which also include the Miniature and Giant Schnauzers.

This spirited, loyal, and intelligent companion excels at hunting, tracking, retrieving, guarding, and competitive obedience. He even delights in performing tricks for an appreciative audience. He loves children and will protect his family with his own life if necessary. The Schnauzer is an even-tempered, friendly, and dependable member of the family.

Exercise, Training, Grooming, and Health

- This energetic breed requires ample exercise, including multiple long walks, daily romps and play off lead.

- The Standard Schnauzer is intelligent and learns quickly, although he may sometimes want to do things his way.

- The Standard Schnauzer sheds only minimally and requires little grooming other than daily brushing of the longer furnishings. A purely pet Schnauzer can be clipped instead of stripped.

- Average life span is 13 to 16 years. Breed health concerns may include cataracts; follicular dermatitis; and hip dysplasia.

Sussex Spaniel

Breed Facts

- **Country of Origin**: England
- **Height**: 13–16 in (33–41 cm)|males 14–16 in (35.5–40.5 cm) [CKC]/females 13–15 in (33–38 cm)
- **Weight**: 35–50.5 lb (16–23 kg)|males 45 lb (20.5 kg) or more/ females 40 lb (18 kg) or more [CKC]
- **Coat**: Flat or slightly waved, abundant; feathering
- **Colors**: Rich golden liver
- **Registries (With Group)**: AKC (Sporting); ANKC (Gundogs); CKC (Sporting); FCI (Flushing Dogs); KC (Gundog); UKC (Gun Dog)

History and Personality

The Sussex Spaniel is named after his place of origin: Sussex, England. He was bred to be a small-game hunter—a slow but steady worker who could persevere in all kinds of conditions. It is believed that the breed was developed by crossing spaniels with hounds, which would attest to its fine nose, heavy-skinned appearance, and urge to give tongue when on scent. The Sussex is also strong and sturdy, and his general appearance of massiveness and compactness is one of the most important considerations in defining his breed type.

The Sussex Spaniel is easygoing and friendly, but he can be slow to warm up to people at times. However, he is attached to his family and will follow them around everywhere. He is excellent with children and other animals. The Sussex can be a bit more territorial than the other spaniels, and he likes to bark.

Exercise, Training, Grooming, and Health

- The Sussex doesn't need a lot of exercise, but he will enjoy a daily walk and playtime in the yard. The breed has a lower energy level than some other spaniels.

- A basically happy-go-lucky dog, the Sussex has been known to assert himself, so it is important to begin working with him from early puppyhood, socializing him to everything to bring out the best in him. He learns quickly and is eager to please his owner.

- The Sussex's soft coat requires regular brushing and will need to be trimmed around the ears and feet. His ears will need to be cleaned regularly and because he is a low dog, his stomach and legs need extra attention, too. His large features include droopy flews and eyelids, which necessitate frequent attention.

- Average life span is 12 to 14 years. Breed health concerns may include congenital deafness; ear infections; eye problems; hypothyroidism; patent ductus arteriosus (PDA); prostate disease; pulmonary stenosis; and tetralogy of fallot (TOF).

Breed Facts

- **Country of Origin**: Sweden

- **Height**: Males 17.5–20 in (45–51 cm)/females 15.5–18 in (40–46 cm)

- **Weight**: 33–44 lb (15–20 kg) [est.]

- **Coat**: Double coat with weather-resistant, standoff outercoat and finely curled, dense undercoat; neck ruff

- **Colors**: Black, liver; white markings|also brown [ANKC]|also bear brown, black and brown in combination [KC]

- **Other Names**: Lapinkoira; Lapland Spitz; Lapplandska Spets; Lapplandska Spetz; Suomenlapinkoira; Svensk Lapphund; Swedish Lappspitz

- **Registries (With Group)**: AKC (FSS: Herding); ANKC (Working); FCI (Spitz and Primitive); KC (Pastoral); UKC (Northern)

History and Personality

The Swedish Lapphund is an ancient spitz-type dog who originated in Lapland, an area that includes parts of northern Norway, Sweden,

Finland, and northwestern Russia. The breed was used by the semi-nomadic Sami tribe, who lived in the region, to hunt reindeer and for protection. When the tribes began to settle, the function of these Laponian dogs changed from hunting reindeer to herding them, and they were used that way for centuries, until the need for reindeer herding began to disappear. Eventually, the Laponian dogs diverged into three different breeds: the Swedish Lapphund, the Finnish Lapphund, and the Lapinporokoïra. Today, he is not an active herding dog, although he still retains those instincts.

The Swedish Lapphund is a versatile dog who is quick to learn and eager to work. He enjoys participating in outdoor adventures—in his native country, the Swedish Lapphund is called to service in the areas of herding and tracking as well as competitive obedience and agility. As is true with many Nordic breeds, he is a barker, and training is necessary to curb this instinct.

Exercise, Training, Grooming, and Health

- Sufficient exercise is critical for the overall well-being of the Swedish Lapphund; without it, he may develop bad habits.

- The Swedish Lapphund is extremely trainable, and he learns best when taught with positive methods.

- The Lapphund's thick double coat sheds, and he should be brushed regularly to help minimize this.

- Average life span is 12 to 15 years. Breed health concerns may include epilepsy; hip dysplasia; and progressive retinal atrophy (PRA).

Breed Facts

- **Country of Origin**: Sweden

- **Height**: Males 12.5–14 in (31.5–35.5 cm)/females 11.5–13 in (29–33 cm)|12–14 in (30.5–35.5 cm) [UKC]

- **Weight**: 20–35 lb (9–16 kg)

- **Coat**: Double coat with medium-length, harsh, tight, close, water-repellent outercoat and woolly, soft, dense undercoat

- **Colors**: Steel gray, grayish brown, grayish yellow, reddish yellow, reddish brown; may have white markings|also black sable with lighter shading [UKC]

- **Other Names**: Schwedischer Schäferspitz; Swedish Cattledog; Swedish Cattle Dog; Västgötaspets; Viking Dog; Westgotenspitz

- **Registries (With Group)**: AKC (Herding); ANKC (Working); CKC (Herding); FCI (Spitz and Primitive); KC (Pastoral); UKC (Herding)

History and Personality

For centuries the Swedish Vallhund has happily served as a hardworking multipurpose farm dog in the west of Sweden. He was adept not only at cattle droving but also as a watchdog and ratter. His numbers began to dwindle by the 1930s, but a dedicated breeder named Count Björn von Rosen was able to rally other fans to work toward preserving this sturdy native son.

The clever and plucky Vallhund is a natural showoff and does not hesitate to vocalize his pure happiness in being alive. He is even-tempered, watchful, energetic, fearless, and alert. Affectionate and intelligent, he makes a wonderful companion. The Vallhund does well with children and other pets when properly socialized.

Exercise, Training, Grooming, and Health

- The Vallhund is naturally active and requires moderate exercise. A brisk walk at least once a day will help keep him physically and mentally fit.

- Extremely responsive, bright, and devoted, he takes to training readily.

- Weekly brushing with a firm bristle brush will help remove dead hair. Daily brushing may be required during periods of seasonal shedding.

- Average life span is 13 to 15 years. Breed health concerns may include cryptorchidism; hip dysplasia; patellar luxation; and renal dysplasia.

Thai Ridgeback

Breed Facts

- **Country of Origin**: Thailand
- **Height**: Males 22–26 in (56–66 cm)/females 20–24 in (51–61 cm)
- **Weight**: 51–75 lb (23–34 kg) [est.]
- **Coat**: Short, smooth; ridge formed by hair growing in opposite direction to rest of coat
- **Colors**: Red, black, blue, light fawn (Isabella)
- **Other Names**: Mah Thai Lung Ahn; Thai Ridgeback Dog
- **Registries (With Group)**: AKC (FSS: Hound); FCI (Spitz and Primitive); UKC (Sighthound & Pariah)

History and Personality

The Thai Ridgeback is an ancient breed from Thailand. For a long time this breed was known as the "cart-following dog" but is now called the Thai Ridgeback after his country of origin and the distinctive way that hair along his back grows in the opposite direction from the rest of the fur. His fierce nature served him well accompanying carts along winding roads, but he was also an able hunter, used to hunt and eradicate vermin from farms—including cobras. Archaeological writings about the Thai Ridgeback date back some 350 years. Because of the isolation in which he spent most of his existence, he has not had the opportunity to crossbreed, so he is true to his heritage.

The Thai Ridgeback is a devoted family member, fiercely loyal to his people and territorial in nature. He can be aloof when meeting strangers and needs socialization to get along with other dogs and cats. He has a strong prey drive, so small pets must be kept away from him. This natural watchdog is active and alert and always on the lookout for anything threatening or worth hunting.

Exercise, Training, Grooming, and Health

- The Thai Ridgeback is an active dog who is forever curious. To satisfy his physical and mental needs, he requires regular exercise in the form of long walks or anything that allows him to explore at length.

- Independent minded and resourceful, he needs a creative but firm trainer to keep his attention on his lessons and to reinforce the rules. Socialization from puppyhood is essential.

- The Thai Ridgeback's dense, short coat is kept tidy and clean with occasional brushing.

- Average life span is 12 to 16 years. Breed health concerns may include dermoid sinus.

Tibetan Mastiff

Breed Facts

- **Country of Origin**: China (Tibet Region)
- **Height**: Males 26 in (66 cm) minimum/females 24 in (61 cm) minimum
- **Weight**: Males 100–160 lb (45.5–72.5 kg) or more/females 75–120 lb (34–54.5 kg) or more
- **Coat**: Double coat with long, straight, thick, coarse outercoat and heavy, soft undercoat (winter) or sparse undercoat (warmer months)
- **Colors**: Rich black with or without tan markings, blue with or without tan markings, shades of gold|also brown [AKC][UKC]
- **Other Names**: Do-Khyi
- **Registries (With Group)**: AKC (Working); ANKC (Utility); CKC (Working); FCI (Molossoid); KC (Working); UKC (Guardian)

History and Personality

The Tibetan Mastiff is an ancient breed that is considered the forebear of many large flock guards and mastiff-type dogs known today. For many centuries, the Tibetan Mastiff was raised in his native land to be a fierce protector of homes and of whole villages if necessary. Tibet was closed to Westerners for many years, isolating the modern development of the Tibetan Mastiff. In the 20th century it was fanciers in the United Kingdom who refined and kept the Tibetan Mastiff alive. There are few specimens in Tibet and the Himalayas even today, and those are usually used as flock guards, protecting livestock and their masters against wolves and other predators.

A large, intimidating dog who takes his job of guardian seriously, the Tibetan Mastiff also has a soft and companionable side. He is absolutely devoted to his family and will not hesitate to protect them; he will also guard his property and whatever he considers his territory. He is gentle and affectionate with the children in his family. The Tibetan Mastiff is independent minded and self-reliant, used to making his own decisions. Because of this, consisting training and socialization are essential. He is naturally aloof with strangers.

Exercise, Training, Grooming, and Health

- The Tibetan Mastiff will enjoy many opportunities to get outside, and he can withstand all kinds of weather. He needs space and is amazingly agile when it comes to escaping from confining areas. He can be active outdoors but typically settles down inside.

- The Tibetan Mastiff is intelligent and tuned in to his owner. However, he is an independent thinker and a large dog, so training him requires respect and understanding. Socializing him is an absolute necessity so that his protective instincts do not get out of control.

- The Tibetan Mastiff's thick double coat demands regular attention. It should be brushed and combed regularly to keep shedding under control, and during shedding season, he may need to be gone over every day.

- Average life span is 13 to 16 years. Breed health concerns may include hip dysplasia; skin problems; and thyroid problems.

Breed Facts

- **Country of Origin**: China (Tibet Region)

- **Height**: Approx. 10 in (25.5 cm)

- **Weight**: 9–15 lb (4–7 kg)

- **Coat**: Double coat with silky outercoat and fine, dense undercoat

- **Colors**: All colors and combinations of colors acceptable

- **Registries (With Group)**: AKC (Non-Sporting); ANKC (Toys); CKC (Non-Sporting); FCI (Companion and Toy); KC (Utility); UKC (Companion)

History and Personality

The Tibetan Spaniel was fostered and loved in the monasteries of Tibet for many centuries. Monks carried these little dogs under their flowing robes in the winter, with both benefiting from the additional warmth. Legend has it the spaniels turned the prayer wheels for the monks in addition to serving as alarms—barking at a stranger's approach. Like the Lhasas, whom the lamas also favored, Tibetan Spaniels were thought to bring good luck.

Tibetan Spaniels ("Tibbies" to their fanciers) are made for companionship. Affectionate and adoring of their owners, they are eager to please. These intelligent and playful dogs wish to be the center of attention at all times. Naturally suspicious of strangers, they warm up slowly to nonfamily members. Tibetan Spaniels are not overly active indoors, but they do make fine watchdogs, alerting their family to any unusual activity.

Exercise, Training, Grooming, and Health

- Playful and spry, the Tibetan Spaniel does not need a lot of exercise but enjoys exploring the great outdoors with his family. He loves to play and gladly engages in games with anyone who shows interest.

- Tibbies enjoy being part of the household. To that end, they will pay attention and be interested in things that seem to benefit their role in the home, and this is the motivation that can yield great results in training. Going through drills with little enthusiasm will cause him to lose interest.

- The Tibetan Spaniel is an average shedder who experiences a heavy seasonal shed. During most of the year, he needs just occasional brushing and combing; during his seasonal shed, he requires daily attention.

- Average life span is 14 years. Breed health concerns may include portosystemic shunts and progressive retinal atrophy (PRA).

Breed Facts

- **Country of Origin**: China (Tibet Region)
- **Height**: Males 14–16 in (35.5–40.5 cm)/females slightly smaller
- **Weight**: 18–30 lb (8–13.5 kg)
- **Coat**: Double coat with long, wavy or straight, fine, profuse outercoat and soft, woolly undercoat
- **Colors**: Any color or combination of colors|but no chocolate, liver [ANKC][FCI][KC]
- **Other Names**: Dhoki Apso
- **Registries (With Group)**: AKC (Non-Sporting); ANKC (Non Sporting); CKC (Non-Sporting); FCI (Companion and Toy); KC (Utility); UKC (Companion)

History and Personality

The Tibetan Terrier (who is not really a terrier but actually a herding dog) may very well be the progenitor of most of the Tibetan breeds, including the Lhasa Apso and the Shih Tzu. Over time, the sheepherding and flock-guarding dogs who served the hardworking people of Tibet developed their own identities through their work, and two in particular emerged: the Tibetan Mastiff, for guarding, and the Tibetan Terrier, for herding. Tibetan Terriers also provided a first line of defense, often alerting the Tibetan Mastiffs to the sign of intruders in a village or on a farm.

The Tibetan Terrier is adaptive to his family, accommodating those with more easygoing lifestyles as well as those who are more active. He is typically outgoing and friendly, although he can be reserved with strangers. Protective of his family, he makes an excellent watchdog; his protectiveness can manifest as territorial behavior with other dogs, so socialization is recommended from puppyhood. He likes to bark.

Exercise, Training, Grooming, and Health

- The medium-sized Tibetan Terrier is content to spend as much time exercising as his owner desires, which can be a lot or a little.

- The Tibetan Terrier learns quickly and wants to please but does have an independent, stubborn streak.

- To prevent tangles or mats, he must be brushed and combed frequently and the hair on his face and feet needs to be kept neat and trimmed. Many owners prefer to keep their Tibetan Terriers clipped to make grooming easier.

- Average life span is 12 to 16 years. Breed health concerns may include canine neuronal ceroid-lipofuscinosis (NCL); cataracts; hip dysplasia; hypothyroidism; patellar luxation; primary lens luxation; and progressive retinal atrophy (PRA).

Tosa

Breed Facts

- **Country of Origin**: Japan
- **Height**: Males 23.5 in (60 cm) minimum/females 21.5 in (55 cm) minimum
- **Weight**: 100–200 lb (45–91 kg) [est.]
- **Coat**: Short, straight, dense, tight lying
- **Colors**: Black, brindle, fawn, red; may have white markings|also apricot [FCI]|also brown [UKC]
- **Other Names**: Japanese Mastiff; Tosa Inu; Tosa Ken
- **Registries (With Group)**: AKC (FSS: Working); FCI (Molossoid); UKC (Guardian)

History and Personality

Tosas were bred as the ultimate fighting dogs in Japan, where dog fighting has long been a national pastime. The breed originated in the Tosa, Kochi Prefecture, where dog fights were large, ceremonial occasions. The dogs were paraded to the rings dressed in elaborate robes, barely held in check by men who held the thick, white ropes that went around their necks. When Japan's national isolation policy lifted in 1854, dog breeds from the West were brought into the country. The Tosas were bred with Mastiffs, Great Danes, Bulldogs, and Saint Bernards, leading to the type that is recognized today. Because of his formidable fighting heritage, he is banned in some countries.

Although the Tosa can make a fine companion when properly handled, anyone who wants to live with this breed must understand that he was bred to give no ground; he attacks head-on. He was also bred to be quiet, and unless he's alerting his owner to something, he is silent. He is massive, but for his size he is also agile and athletic. The Tosa requires an experienced owner capable of physically handling a large, powerful dog—the consequences of not being able to control him could be injurious to other dogs, animals, and people. On the other hand, he is absolutely loyal and wants nothing more than to serve his family wholeheartedly.

Exercise, Training, Grooming, and Health

- The Tosa doesn't require a lot of exercise, but without several walks a day, he will become restless and bored.

- Being highly tuned into the wishes of his owner, the Tosa is a quick study and fairly easy to train. Because he is a large, formidable, and strong dog, he needs an owner/trainer who will not let him come up with his own rules and who understands and respects his power. This is a surprisingly sensitive breed, and harsh methods should never be used. Socialization from puppyhood is critical.

- The Tosa's short, dense coat is easy to keep neat with occasional brushing or rubbing with a hound glove. The wrinkles on his face and neck must be kept clean, and although it isn't excessive, he will drool after drinking and when hot or excited.

- Average life span is 10 to 12 years. Breed health concerns may include bloat; elbow dysplasia; hip dysplasia; and progressive retinal atrophy (PRA).

Toy Fox Terrier

Breed Facts

- **Country of Origin**: United States
- **Height**: 8.5–11.5 in (21.5–29 cm)
- **Weight**: Males 16–18 lb (7.5–8 kg)/females 15–17 lb (7–7.5 kg)|3.5–7 lb (1.5–3 kg) [UKC]
- **Coat**: Short, straight, flat, hard, abundant, smooth, satiny; neck ruff
- **Colors**: Tricolor (black, tan, white); white, chocolate, and tan; white and tan; white and black
- **Other Names**: American Toy Terrier; AmerToy
- **Registries (With Group)**: AKC (Toy); CKC (Toys); UKC (Terrier)

History and Personality

An all-American breed, the Toy Fox Terrier was developed in the United States by breeders who crossed the Smooth Fox Terrier with several toy breeds, including the Italian Greyhound, Chihuahua,

Miniature Pinscher, and Manchester Terrier. The breed's creators were looking to combine the game terrier instincts with the more manageable size and characteristics of the toy breeds. The Toy Fox Terrier is able to work and go to ground and participate in earthdog trials like most terriers and still curl up in his owner's lap at the end of the day.

He is gregarious and friendly, always ready to play and participate in whatever activity in which the household is engaged. He has been described as almost clown-like, wanting to entertain and amuse those around him. Athletic and sturdy for a small dog, he retains the hunting instincts of a terrier and will go after small animals in the garden. Despite his readiness to romp, he also enjoys settling into laps and will quickly quiet down. He can be barky.

Exercise, Training, Grooming, and Health

- The effervescent Toy Fox Terrier keenly enjoys going for walks and being taken anywhere his family wants to go.

- With a great willingness to please and desire to participate, the Toy Fox Terrier is a pleasure to train.

- Going over him with a warm, damp cloth and occasionally rubbing him with a hound glove to stimulate his skin will keep him looking and feeling his best.

- Average life span is 12 to 14 years. Breed health concerns may include Legg-Calve-Perthes disease; patellar luxation; and von Willebrand disease.

Treeing Tennessee Brindle

Breed Facts

- **Country of Origin**: United States
- **Height**: 16–24 in (40.5–61 cm) [est.]
- **Weight**: 30–45 lb (13.5–20.5 kg) [est.]
- **Coat**: Short, smooth, soft, dense [est.]
- **Colors**: Black, brindle; brindle trim; white markings
- **Other Names**: Tennessee Treeing Brindle
- **Registries (With Group)**: AKC (FSS: Hound)

History an d Personality

Hunters and settlers in the southern US worked with small brindle hounds for generations. They didn't have a name for them then—they just knew that these unpretentious dogs were fine open trailers and superb locators of raccoons and squirrels yet very companionable with men and other dogs. It was the Reverend Earl Phillips from Tennessee whose fascination with and passion for the brindled curs led him to eventually formalize, name, and organize the breed. The hunting characteristics of the Treeing Tennessee Brindle are much like the other coonhound breeds, with ample nose for trailing game, a coarse chop mouth, and a fine treeing ability for all types of game.

Treeing Tennessee Brindles are fast and courageous hunters, and as companions, are intelligent, affectionate, and easygoing. Their admirers say that these dogs have "heart and try" in abundance. They are naturally happy, bold, confident, and inquisitive. He is particularly sensitive to neglect or abuse, and breeders warn that care must be taken in training not to destroy his heart which, as they say, "You can take out, but you can *never* put back!"

Exercise, Training, Grooming, and Health

- Anyone keeping a Brindle as a companion and not a hunter must provide some kind of access to an open space in which he can use his nose at will.

- When it comes to hunt training, he picks up what he needs to know seemingly without direction. As for other kinds of training, patience, persistence, and a positive attitude will get results—harsh methods will not.

- He simply needs to be brushed every so often and occasionally rubbed all over with a nubbed hound glove.

- Average life span is 11 to 15 years. There are no reported breed-specific health concerns.

Treeing Walker Coonhound

Breed Facts

- **Country of Origin**: United States
- **Height**: Males 22–27 in (56–68.5 cm)/females 20–25 in (51–63.5 cm)
- **Weight**: 50–70 lb (22.5–31.5 kg) [est.]
- **Coat**: Smooth, fine, glossy, dense enough for protection
- **Colors**: Tricolor (white, black, tan)
- **Other Names**: Treeing Walker
- **Registries (With Group)**: AKC (FSS); UKC (Scenthound)

History and Personality

English Foxhounds were brought to America with the earliest settlers. These hounds formed the backbone of the "Virginia hounds," who were a strain that became popular in the South in the 1700s. These Virginia hounds begat the Walker Foxhounds, who in turn begat the Treeing Walker Coonhounds. The breed's qualities include a hot nose; sensibility on the trail; a clear, bugling voice with a steady, clear chop when changing over at a tree; a wide range; the ability to quickly locate the quarry; superb endurance; and the instinct to leave a track if a stronger scent was detected. As night hunts became more and more popular, the Treeing Walker, with his speed and abilities, was recognized as a winning hound with whom to work—and still is today.

The Treeing Walker Coonhound is not only a fine hunting companion, but he is also a sensible and kind family companion. Still, plenty of exercise and a chance to hunt are necessary to allow this breed to shine. He gets along well with children and other dogs and delights in lounging around the house after a hard night at the hunt. He is intelligent, energetic, affectionate, and confident.

Exercise, Training, Grooming, and Health

- He has been bred for speed and endurance, and his athleticism necessitates that he have an outlet for his energy and power.

- This is a large dog with a strong desire to hunt, and his nose will always come before any obedience requests. Still, he is intelligent and eager to please, so with consistent training he can become a fine family companion.

- The Treeing Walker Coonhound's short, hard coat needs only to be brushed and rubbed down occasionally for him to look his best.

- Average life span is 11 to 13 years. There are no reported breed-specific health concerns.

Breed Facts

- **Country of Origin**: Hungary

- **Height**: Males 22–25 in (56–64 cm)/females 21–23.5 in (53.5–60 cm)

- **Weight**: 44–66 lb (20–30 kg)

- **Coat**: Single coat is short, smooth, dense, close lying

- **Colors**: Shades of golden rust

- **Other Names**: Hungarian Pointer; Hungarian Shorthaired Pointing Dog; Hungarian Vizsla; Magyar Vizsla; Rövidszörü Magyar Vizsla

- **Registries (With Group)**: AKC (Sporting); ANKC (Gundogs); CKC (Sporting); FCI (Pointing Dogs); KC (Gundog); UKC (Gun Dog)

History and Personality

The Vizsla's ancestors were hunters and companions for the Magyar, a nomadic tribe that eventually settled in what is now known as Hungary. He is believed to be descended from the ancient

Transylvanian Hound and the now-extinct Turkish yellow dog. Later, the German Shorthaired Pointer and Pointer were added. The Vizsla is most associated with the Puszta region in Hungary, a central area with diverse agriculture and a variety of game. Life in this vast terrain helped in creating a dog with a superior nose and hunting ability suited to all weather extremes.

The Vizsla's talents are many; he is a proven tracker, retriever, pointer, agility and obedience competitor, and a striking show dog. If not sufficiently exercised or stimulated his naturally energetic nature may lead him to indulge in destructive behaviors. Ignoring this need is not fair to the noble Vizsla, who is at heart a highly sociable and demonstrative dog. When raised properly, he is excellent with children who are old enough to manage his high energy.

Exercise, Training, Grooming, and Health

- Vizslas are lively, athletic dogs who thrive on exercise—preferably being allowed to hunt over large areas.

- The Vizsla is a multitalented and trainable animal, although as a high-energy dog he is easily distracted.

- The Vizsla's short, smooth coat is easy to keep clean with a hound glove and a soft brush.

- Average life span is 11 to15 years. Breed health concerns may include allergies; ectropion; entropion; epilepsy; hip dysplasia; hypothyroidism; progressive retinal atrophy (PRA); sebaceous adenitis (SA); and von Willebrand disease.

Breed Facts

- **Country of Origin**: Germany
- **Height**: Males 23–27.5 in (59–70 cm)/females 22.5–25.5 in (57–65 cm)
- **Weight**: Males 66–88 lb (30–40 kg)/females 55–77 lb (25–35 kg)
- **Coat**: Two varieties—*shorthaired* has short, strong, very dense, smooth-lying outercoat and no or sparse undercoat/*longhaired* has long, flat or slightly wavy, soft outercoat and may or may not have undercoat|one variety—short, smooth, sleek [AKC][UKC]
- **Colors**: Solid color in shades of mouse gray to silver-gray
- **Other Names**: Weimaraner Vorstehhund
- **Registries (With Group)**: AKC (Sporting); ANKC (Gundogs); CKC (Sporting); FCI (Pointing Dogs); KC (Gundog); UKC (Gun Dog)

History and Personality

This elegant breed was developed in Germany and was a favorite at the court of Weimar, in east–central Germany. Originally called the Weimar Pointer, he was used to track and hunt large game such as bears, wolves, and big cats. As the large game populations decreased, wing shooting became most popular, and the then-large and houndy Weimaraner was crossed with bird dogs to bring in bird-hunting abilities. Soon hunters working with the breed developed the dog who is admired today as an all-around gundog capable of locating and bringing in game.

The Weimaraner is a talented, friendly, obedient, alert, high-energy dog. He was bred to handle tough situations, and he doesn't back down easily. Effusively affectionate with his family and those he knows, he can be aloof and suspicious with strangers. The strong and athletic Weimaraner needs lots of outdoor exercise but is not an outdoor dog, craving regular attention from his people.

Exercise, Training, Grooming, and Health

- The Weimaraner thrives on exercise, and if he doesn't get enough of it, will become bored and restless and resort to destructive behavior.

- This is a breed that requires a persistent and patient trainer who understands that he learns quickly and bores easily.

- The shorthaired Weimaraner is kept clean with an occasional brushing or rubdown with a hound glove. The longhaired Weimaraner should be brushed and combed weekly to keep his fine coat free from knots and debris.

- Average life span is 10 to 12 years. Breed health concerns may include bloat; elbow dysplasia; hip dysplasia; hypertrophic osteodystrophy (HOD); and von Willebrand disease.

Welsh Springer Spaniel

Breed Facts

- **Country of Origin**: Wales
- **Height**: Males 18–19 in (45.5–48.5 cm)/females 17–18 in (43–45.5 cm)
- **Weight**: 35–45 lb (16–20.5 kg)
- **Coat**: Straight, flat, soft, silky, waterproof, weatherproof; moderate feathering
- **Colors**: Rich red and white; any pattern is acceptable
- **Registries (With Group)**: AKC (Sporting); ANKC (Gundogs); CKC (Sporting); FCI (Flushing Dogs); KC (Gundog); UKC (Gun Dog)

History and Personality

This distinctive Welsh breed harks back to the red-and-white hunting dogs who populated the British Isles for millennia. He shares his history with his close relatives—the English Cocker Spaniel and English Springer Spaniel. At one time all of the spaniels were called simply "cockers" or "cocking spaniels," and they were interbred for the sole purpose of achieving a hardy, close-working gundog. Eventually, the springers and cockers were separated, and from there the Welsh and English breeds were further differentiated. The Welsh Springer differs from the English Springer in size, appearance, and coloring. He is shorter, has smaller-sized but higher-set ears, a more tapered head, and the hallmark red-and-white coat. A natural flushing spaniel, he is a keen and tireless worker and is particularly good in water.

The Welsh Springer Spaniel is a good-natured companion who is amenable to spending his time equally in the great outdoors and curled up by the fire. An unspoiled breed, he retains the hunting instincts that have been bred into him for centuries—bird sense that finds, springs, and retrieves game. He has plenty of stamina and can stay out all day, yet when he comes inside with his family, he is quick to settle down.

Exercise, Training, Grooming, and Health

- For a Welsh Springer Spaniel to be truly happy, he'll need to get out into the great outdoors as much as possible.

- The Welsh Springer Spaniel shares the tractable nature of springers and cockers in general, so he is an agreeable dog to train.

- The Welsh Springer Spaniel's silky coat needs brushing and combing every few days.

- Average life span is 12 to 15 years. Breed health concerns may include epilepsy and hip dysplasia.

Welsh Terrier

Breed Facts

- **Country of Origin**: Wales
- **Height**: Males 15–15.5 in (38–39.5 cm)/females smaller|not exceeding 15.5 in (39.5 cm) [ANKC][FCI][KC]
- **Weight**: 20–21 lb (9–9.5 kg)
- **Coat**: Double coat with hard, wiry, dense outercoat and short, soft undercoat
- **Colors**: Black and tan, black grizzle and tan
- **Registries (With Group)**: AKC (Terrier); ANKC (Terriers); CKC (Terriers); FCI (Terriers); KC (Terrier); UKC (Terrier)

History and Personality

Many of today's terriers can be traced back to the old black-and-tan Broken-Coated Terrier (or Old English Terrier) of northern England. The terriers were prized for their abilities to hunt otters, foxes, and badgers one-on-one by cornering them in their dens, and to hunt in packs for other game. Environment helped define hunting style, and the Welsh hunters bred a dog with longer legs and a broader body. All Old English Terriers were shown under the same classification until 1888. It was then that a dog named Dick Turpin shook things up. He was winning so much that the English wanted him categorized as English, but the Welsh wanted him recorded as a true Welsh Terrier. The Kennel Club (KC) sided with the Welsh, and Dick Turpin became a foundation sire for the breed people know today.

The Welsh Terrier's compact, sturdy exterior hides a genuinely affable dog who relishes time spent with his nearest and dearest. This handsome fellow makes a fine travel companion, as he's curious, friendly, and easy to get around with. But the Welsh Terrier is all terrier, and if challenged, will be hard put to resist. For this reason he makes a great watchdog—and a dog for whom socialization from puppyhood is necessary.

Exercise, Training, Grooming, and Health

- The Welsh Terrier doesn't require a great deal of exercise several walks a day should suffice.

- He is an intelligent and talented dog but is independent minded and somewhat easily distracted. Training sessions should be kept positive and short for best results.

- About four times a year, the Welsh Terrier should be professionally groomed by hand-stripping his coat to keep it from becoming shaggy.

- Average life span is 13 to 15 years. Breed health concerns may include epilepsy; glaucoma; skin problems; and thyroid problems.

West Highland White Terrier

Breed Facts

- **Country of Origin**: Scotland
- **Height**: Males 11 in (28 cm)/females 10 in (25.5 cm)|11 in (28 cm) [ANKC][FCI][KC][UKC]
- **Weight**: 15–22 lb (7–10 kg) [est.]
- **Coat**: Double coat with straight, harsh outercoat and short, soft, close undercoat
- **Colors**: White
- **Registries (With Group)**: AKC (Terrier); ANKC (Terriers); CKC (Terriers); FCI (Terriers); KC (Terrier); UKC (Terrier)

History and Personality

Rough-coated terriers have existed in Scotland for hundreds of years. White-colored pups were selected from these generic terriers to form the West Highland White Terrier ("Westie"). Their distinctive all-white coats made them easy to see in the Scottish countryside, and they have been popular there for more than 300 years. Like all of the other terriers, the Westie was used for vermin control.

The West Highland White Terrier has an adorable face and charming personality, but he is still a no-nonsense terrier. The breed is hardy, devoted, and spunky, exhibiting typical terrier tendencies: sturdiness, alarm barking, digging, cock-of-the-walk strutting, and one-upmanship with other dogs. But this dog is not as volatile as some of the others in the terrier group. In fact, the Westie standard warns against excessive pugnacity.

Exercise, Training, Grooming, and Health

- The Westie is happy to accompany anyone who's going out on an adventure, whether it be a stroll through the neighborhood or to a soccer game.

- The West Highland White Terrier is one of the easiest terriers to train. He is eager to please and responsive.

- The Westie has a wash-and-wear coat that quickly comes clean of dirt and mud with a simple brushing and combing. He is not a shedder, but his thick coat needs to be hand-stripped several times a year to keep it from becoming shaggy.

- Average life span is 12 to 14 years. Breed health concerns may include copper toxicosis; globoid cell leukodystrophy; Legg-Calve-Perthes disease; pulmonary fibrosis; skin problems; and white shaker dog syndrome.

Breed Facts

- **Country of Origin**: Great Britain
- **Height**: Males 18.5–22 in (47–56 cm)/females 17–21 in (44–53.5 cm)
- **Weight**: 25–40 lb (11.5–18 kg) [est.]
- **Coat**: Short, smooth, firm, close
- **Registries (With Group)**: AKC (Hound); ANKC (Hounds); CKC (Hounds); FCI (Sighthounds); KC (Hound); UKC (Sighthound & Pariah)

History and Personality

The Whippet was developed fairly recently—in the 1800s. A Greyhound in miniature, he is the fastest domesticated animal for his size, capable of speeds up to 35 miles per hour (56.5 kph). He was fashioned from "snapdogs"—dogs who were used as sport by gamblers who would bet on how many rabbits they could chase and kill in an enclosed area over a set amount of time. Many snapdogs were Greyhound-Terrier crosses: While terriers were noted rat killers, they were no match for the fast rabbits, and Greyhounds and other large sighthounds were too cumbersome to work in the small areas where snapdogging took place. Eventually, the "sport" was banned, and bettors turned to placing wages on speed animals. The fleet breed that emerged from the snapdog pits and was further refined to run over greater distances is the Whippet.

The Whippet is an elegant, easygoing, adaptable breed. Although focused and intense while running or participating in sporting events, at home he is gentle and affectionate, always ready to curl up on the couch for a snooze. He is very attached to his owners but in general is friendly and trusting with strangers. Calm and steady, he does well with children and other dogs but may chase small animals. He should be kept on leash unless he's in a securely fenced area.

Exercise, Training, Grooming, and Health

- Although the Whippet is capable of great bursts of speed, he doesn't need to sprint every day to keep him in shape or happy.

- He is intelligent and independent minded. He will need to have things repeated, and shouldn't be expected to work or perform like a retriever.

- Clean and tidy dogs, Whippets are naturally neat. They are helped by an occasional brushing or going-over with a hound glove.

- Average life span is 13 to 15 years. Breed health concerns may include eye problems.

Breed Facts

- **Country of Origin**: England
- **Height**: Males no more than 15.5 in (39.5 cm)/females smaller
- **Weight**: Males 18 lb (8 kg)/females smaller
- **Coat**: Double coat with very wiry, hard, dense outercoat and soft, dense undercoat
- **Colors**: Predominantly white with black, black and tan, or tan markings
- **Registries (With Group)**: AKC (Terrier); ANKC (Terriers); CKC (Terriers); FCI (Terriers); KC (Terrier); UKC (Terrier)

History and Personality

An old English breed, the Fox Terrier was used in the 18th century by foxhunters who needed a compact, energetic, bold dog who would go to ground after quarry. The Fox Terrier was bred to be a quick thinker, relying on his instincts rather than orders from his owner. There are two types of Fox Terrier, distinguished by coat: Wire and

Smooth. Although coat is the only major difference between them today, authorities believe that the Smooth and Wire probably have very different origins. The Wire is believed to have descended from the rough-coated black and tan terrier of Wales.

Outgoing, energetic, and self-assured, the Wire Fox Terrier is a wonderful, sturdy pet for an active family. He is alert and curious and needs attention from his family. Although he is confident and friendly with strangers, he does have a tendency to be protective of his owners. With proper socialization he can get along well with other dogs, but he should not be unsupervised around smaller pets. He tends to be vocal and may bark a lot.

Exercise, Training, Grooming, and Health

- The Wire Fox Terrier needs daily exercise and the chance to explore outdoors.

- The feisty Wire can be a handful to train, but he's never boring. He is a smart dog and will bore quickly, and he is also easily distracted.

- A Wire who is hand-stripped and tidied up by a professional several times a year will only need occasional brushing. His wire coat is practically nonshedding.

- Average life span is 12 to 15 years. Breed health concerns may include cataracts; deafness; distichiasis; glaucoma; Legg-Calve-Perthes disease; lens luxation; and skin allergies.

Wirehaired Pointing Griffon

Breed Facts

- **Country of Origin**: France
- **Height**: Males 21.5–24 in (54.5–61 cm)/females 19.5–22 in (49.5–56 cm)
- **Weight**: 50–60 lb (23–27 kg) [est.]
- **Coat**: Double coat with medium-length, straight, harsh, coarse outercoat and fine, thick, downy undercoat; mustache
- **Colors**: Steel gray with liver brown patches, liver roan, liver, liver and white, orange and white
- **Other Names**: French Wire-Haired Korthals Pointing Griffon; Griffon d'Arrêt à Poil dur Korthals; Korthals Griffon
- **Registries (With Group)**: AKC (Sporting); CKC (Sporting); FCI (Pointing Dogs); KC (Gundog); UKC (Gun Dog)

History and Personality

This versatile breed was created by Dutchman Edward K. Korthals in the 1870s. He wanted to create a close-working, hardy, walking hunter's gundog. Korthals's basic stock started with a griffon-type female named "Mouche," and he crossed in other griffons for coat, love of water, and intelligence. Experts speculate that he used various setters, pointers, or spaniels for pointing ability and air scenting. This multipurpose breed was also bred to retrieve in water and on land.

The Wirehaired Pointing Griffon ("Griff") is a wonderful companion for those who love the outdoors. Good natured and affable, he thrives on long walks through all kinds of environments and in all kinds of weather. Indoors, he is a mellow dog who wants to spend time with and be near his family. The Griff is great with children—he is patient yet playful, a large, solid dog with a stable disposition.

Exercise, Training, Grooming, and Health

- Daily exercise is necessary for this sporting dog. If not being used for the hunt, he'll need at least a 20-minute romp in a field or other outdoor area.

- Bred to work close to the hunter and be a truly all-purpose dog, the Griff is easy to train. He is respectful and responsive, quickly picking up what is expected of him.

- He has a harsh coat that comes clean easily with occasional brushing, and he is naturally low shedding.

- Average life span is 10 to 12 years. Breed health concerns may include hip dysplasia.

Breed Facts

- **Country of Origin**: Mexico

- **Varieties**: Standard, Miniature, Toy

- **Height**: *Standard*: 17.5–23.5 in (25.5–35.5 cm); *Miniature*: 13.75–18 in (35–45.5 cm); *Toy*: 10–14 in (25.5–35.5 cm)

- **Weight**: *Standard*: 20–31 lb (9–14 kg) [est.]; *Miniature*: 13–22 lb (6–10 kg) [est.]; *Toy*: 9–18 lb (4–8 kg) [est.]

- **Coat**: Two varieties—*hairless* has total lack of hair on the body, although short, coarse, thick hairs on forehead and back of neck/ *coated* has hair all over the body|one variety—hairless [KC]

- **Colors**: Hairless range from black to gray, red, liver, bronze, to golden yellow; particolors occur, including white patches/ coated can have any color or combination of colors|any color combination allowed [UKC]

- **Other Names**: Mexican Coated Dog; Mexican Hairless Dog; Perro sin Pelo Mexicano; Tepeizeuintli; Xoloitzcuintli; Xoloitzquintle

- **Registries (With Group)**: AKC (FSS: Non-Sporting); CKC (Non-Sporting); FCI (Spitz and Primitive); KC (Utility); UKC (Sighthound & Pariah)

Origin and History

The Xoloitzcuintle ("Xolo") is one of the world's oldest and rarest breeds. Known as the first dog of the Americas, its ancestors accompanied the first migrations of people across the Bering Strait more than 15,000 years ago onto the lands that are now the continents of North, South, and Central America. Artifacts such as clay and ceramic effigies found in the tombs of the Aztec, Mayan, Zapoteca, and Colima Indian tribes dating back 3,000 years show that today's Xolos remain almost unchanged from their ancient cousins. Aside from their value as pets, food, and sacrificial offerings, these dogs were also highly prized by the Aztecs for their curative and mystical powers. None of the varieties of Xoloitzcuintle are particularly large, and all three share the same breed standard except for size.

Serving as guardians for millennia, the Xolo is suspicious of strangers and can be aloof when first meeting them. For his family, though, he has nothing but affection, and he is supremely loyal. Cheerful, attentive, and alert, he is a great companion and watchdog. He is generally calm and quiet in the home, although he will spring into action if he detects or perceives danger or a distraction. He does not bark frequently, so when he does, he should be heeded. The Xolo has been described as a big dog in a small body, and he is no pushover. He needs direction and fair leadership to understand his role in the family.

Exercise, Training, Grooming, and Health

- Although he may appear fragile to some, the Xoloitzcuintle is a hardy and sturdy dog who is up for exercise of all kinds. The Xolo should wear a sweater outdoors to protect him from being chilled, even in just cool weather.

- Naturally in tune with their caregivers, Xolos are easy to train.

- The hairless Xoloitzcuintle is relatively easy to groom. Dark-colored Xolos have the hardiest skin, and lighter-colored ones may require extra care. Sunscreen is necessary when spending time outdoors. The coated variety needs regular brushing and combing.

- Average life span is 15 to 20 years. There are no reported breed-specific health concerns.

Yorkshire Terrier

Breed Facts

- **Country of Origin**: England
- **Height**: 6–7 in (15–18 cm) [est.]
- **Weight**: No more than 7 lb (3 kg)
- **Coat**: Moderately long, straight, silky, glossy, fine
- **Colors**: Steel blue and tan
- **Registries (With Group)**: AKC (Toy); ANKC (Toys); CKC (Toys); FCI (Terriers); KC (Toy); UKC (Companion)

History and Personality

The first Yorkshire Terrier on record is Huddersfeld Ben, acknowledged to be the foundation sire of the breed. Ben was born in 1865 and hailed from the county of Yorkshire in northern England, from which the breed's name comes. This rugged region was notorious for its hardworking coal miners and mill workers, who needed these tough little dogs to keep vermin under control in the mines and textile mills. Yorkshires were initially much bigger dogs, but as their reputation as good-looking and reliable working dogs spread, they quickly became more popular as companion pets for high society. As a result, they were bred smaller and smaller.

The Yorkshire Terrier is a charming dog. Although small in size, his heart and personality are large. The Yorkie has a playful side, too, and can be mischievous and lovable all at the same time. An energetic and exuberant companion, he is still a true terrier—feisty, fearless, and ready to take on the world. Tenacious in defending his territory, this brave and loyal little dog will let his family know about any perceived danger long before they may be aware of it.

Exercise, Training, Grooming, and Health

- The Yorkshire Terrier gets his exercise by going everywhere with his owners.

- The ever-attentive Yorkie will gladly perform for rewards and positive feedback, although he can be stubborn. Lessons need to be kept simple and short and repeated often. He can be difficult to housetrain.

- A Yorkie kept in full coat must be brushed and combed every day to prevent tangles. Many owners often prefer to keep the coat clipped, which makes grooming much easier—although it will still require regular brushing.

- Average life span is 12 to 15 years. Breed health concerns may include bladder stones; cataracts; collapsing trachea; distichiasis; hypoglycemia; hypoplasia of dens; keratitis; Legg-Calve-Perthes disease; patellar luxation; portosystemic shunts; and retinal dysplasia.

Resources

Breed Clubs and Registries

AMERICAN KENNEL CLUB (AKC)
AKC Customer Care
8051 Arco Corporate Drive, Suite 100
Raleigh, NC 27617-3390
Telephone: 919.233.9767
Website: www.akc.org

AMERICAN RARE BREED ASSOCIATION (ARBA)
9921 Frank Tippett Road
Cheltenham MD 20623
Telephone: 301-868-5718
Fax: 301-868-6409
Website: www.arba.org

AUSTRALIAN NATIONAL KENNEL COUNCIL (ANKC)
www.ankc.org.au

CANADIAN KENNEL CLUB (CKC)
Canadian registry of purebred dogs.
200 Ronson Drive, Suite 400
Etobicoke, Ontario
M9W 5Z9
Canada
www.ckc.ca

FÉDÉRATION CYNOLOGIQUE INTERNATIONALE (FCI)
Place Albert 1er, 13
B-6530 Thuin
Belgium
Phone: 32.71.59.12.38
Fax: 32.71.59.22.29
www.fci.be

THE KENNEL CLUB (KC)
1-5 Clarges Street
Piccadilly, London W1J 8AB
England
Phone: 0870 606 6750
Fax: 020 7518 1058
www.thekennelclub.org.uk

UNITED KENNEL CLUB (UKC)
100 East Kilgore Road
Kalamazoo MI 49002-5584
Phone: 269-343-9020
Fax: 269-343-7037
www.ukcdogs.com
www.ukpetsitter.co.uk

Rescue Organizations and Animal Welfare Groups

AMERICAN HUMANE ASSOCIATION (AHA)
63 Inverness Drive East
Englewood, CO 80112
Telephone: (303) 792-9900
Fax: 792-5333
www.americanhumane.org

AMERICAN SOCIETY FOR THE PREVENTION OF CRUELTY TO ANIMALS (ASPCA)
424 E. 92nd Street
New York, NY 10128-6804
Telephone: (212) 876-7700
www.aspca.org

HUMANE SOCIETY OF CANADA (HSC)
Telephone: (800) 641-5463
E-Mail: info@humanesociety.com
www.humanesociety.com

The Humane Society of the United States (HSUS)
2100 L Street, NW
Washington DC 20037
Telephone: (202) 452-1100
www.hsus.org

Royal Society for the Prevention of Cruelty to Animals (RSPCA)
RSPCA Enquiries Service
Wilberforce Way, Southwater,
Horsham, West Sussex RH13 9RS
United Kingdom
Telephone: 0870 3335 999
Fax: 0870 7530 284
www.rspca.org.uk

Therapy
Delta Society
875 124th Ave, NE, Suite 101
Bellevue, WA 98005
Telephone: (425) 679-5500
Fax: (425) 679-5539
E-Mail: info@DeltaSociety.org
www.deltasociety.org

Therapy Dogs Inc.
P.O. Box 20227
Cheyenne, WY 82003
Telephone: (877) 843-7364
Fax: (307) 638-2079
E-Mail: therapydogsinc@
qwestoffice.net
www.therapydogs.com

Therapy Dogs International (TDI)
88 Bartley Road
Flanders, NJ 07836
Telephone: (973) 252-9800
Fax: (973) 252-7171
E-Mail: tdi@gti.net
www.tdi-dog.org

Training
Association of Pet Dog Trainers (APDT)
150 Executive Center Drive Box 35
Greenville, SC 29615
Telephone: (800) PET-DOGS
Fax: (864) 331-0767
E-Mail: information@apdt.com
www.apdt.com

National Association of Dog Obedience Instructors (NADOI)
PMB 369
729 Grapevine Hwy.
Hurst, TX 76054-2085
www.nadoi.org

International Association of Animal Behavior Consultants (IAABC)
565 Callery Road
Cranberry Township, PA 16066
E-Mail: info@iaabc.org
www.iaabc.org

THE INTERNATIONAL ASSOCIATION OF CANINE PROFESSIONALS (IACP)
P.O. Box 560156
Montverde, FL 34756
Telephone: (877) THE IACP
E-Mail: iacpadmin@mindspring.com
www.dogpro.org

Veterinary and Health Resources

ACADEMY OF VETERINARY HOMEOPATHY (AVH)
P.O. Box 9280
Wilmington, DE 19809
Telephone: (866) 652-1590
Fax: (866) 652-1590
www.theavh.org

AMERICAN ACADEMY OF VETERINARY ACUPUNCTURE (AAVA)
P.O. Box 1058
Glastonbury, CT 06033
Telephone: (860) 632-9911
Fax: (860) 659-8772
www.aava.org

AMERICAN ANIMAL HOSPITAL ASSOCIATION (AAHA)
12575 W. Bayaud Ave.
Lakewood, CO 80228
Telephone: (303) 986-2800
Fax: (303) 986-1700
E-Mail: info@aahanet.org
www.aahanet.org/index.cfm

AMERICAN COLLEGE OF VETERINARY INTERNAL MEDICINE (ACVIM)
1997 Wadsworth Blvd., Suite A
Lakewood, CO 80214-5293
Telephone: (800) 245-9081
Fax: (303) 231-0880
Email: ACVIM@ACVIM.org
www.acvim.org

AMERICAN COLLEGE OF VETERINARY OPHTHALMOLOGISTS (ACVO)
P.O. Box 1311
Meridian, ID 83860
Telephone: (208) 466-7624
Fax: (208) 466-7693
E-Mail: office09@acvo.com
www.acvo.com

AMERICAN HOLISTIC VETERINARY MEDICAL ASSOCIATION (AHVMA)
2218 Old Emmorton Road
Bel Air, MD 21015
Telephone: (410) 569-0795
Fax: (410) 569-2346
E-Mail: office@ahvma.org
www.ahvma.org

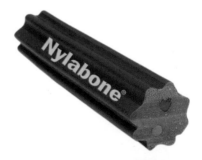

AMERICAN VETERINARY MEDICAL ASSOCIATION (AVMA)
1931 North Meacham Road, Suite 100
Schaumburg, IL 60173-4360
Telephone: (847) 925-8070
Fax: (847) 925-1329
E-Mail: avmainfo@avma.org
www.avma.org

ASPCA ANIMAL POISON CONTROL CENTER
Telephone: (888) 426-4435
www.aspca.org

AUSTRALIAN VETERINARY ASSOCIATION (AVA)
Unit 40
6 Herbert Street
St. Leonards NSW 2065
Telephone: 02 9431 5000
Fax: 02 9437 9068
E-Mail: members@ava.com.au
http://avacms.eseries.hengesystems.com.au/AM/Template.cfm?Section=Home

BRITISH VETERINARY ASSOCIATION (BVA)
7 Mansfield Street
London
W1G 9NQ
Telephone: 0207 636 6541
Fax: 0207 908 6349
E-Mail: bvahq@bva.co.uk
www.bva.co.uk

CANADIAN VETERINARY MEDICAL ASSOCIATION (CVMA)
339 Booth Street
Ottawa, ON
K1R 7K1
Tel: (613) 236-1162
Fax: (613) 236-9681
E-Mail: admin@cvma-acmv.org
www.canadianveterinarians.net

CANINE EYE REGISTRATION FOUNDATION (CERF)
VMDB/CERF
1717 Philo Rd
P O Box 3007
Urbana, IL 61803-3007
Telephone: (217) 693-4800
Fax: (217) 693-4801
E-Mail: CERF@vmbd.org
www.vmdb.org

ORTHOPEDIC FOUNDATION FOR ANIMALS (OFA)
2300 E Nifong Boulevard
Columbus, MO 65201-3806
Telephone: (573) 442-0418
Fax: (573) 875-5073
Email: ofa@offa.org
www.offa.org

Websites
www.nylabone.com
www.tfh.com

Index

Index

Index

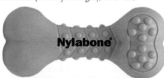

Index

Index

Photo Credits

Contributing Photographers (Courtesy of Shutterstock):
WizData, Inc., Dan Briski, Racheal Grazias, Tina Rencelj, Justyna Furmancyzk, John Lumb, Patricia Marroquin, Artur Zinatullin, Daniel Hughes, Dwight Lyman, Anyka, L Higgins, Tad Denson, Joy Brown, Mike Rogal, E. Spek, Tommy Maenhout, Waldemar Dabrowski, Anyka, Eric Isselee, Claudia Steininger, Lisa A. Svara, Tomasz Szymanski, Jerzy, Richard L. Paul, wojciechpusz, Laila Kazakevica, Brian Rome, Judy Ben Joud, Annette Shaff, Cynoclub, BORIEL Pavel, Marianne Fisher, Randy C. Horne, Velora, Utekhina Anna, Natalia V Guseva, K. Kolygo, Rolf Klebsattel, Dina Magnat, Andreas Gradin, Quayside, ncn18, WilleeCole, Linn Currie, Lakatos Sandor, Natalia V Guseva, eleana, Vladimir Gramagin, Sergey Lavrentev, Amy Myers, Sue C, Yan Wen, Connie Wade, argo74, vgm, Sally Wallis, Lobke Peers, Lenkadan, Nikolai Pozdeev, Paul Shlykov, Toloubaev Stanislav, Dalek, Paul Shlykov, Jambostrock, Svetlana Valoueva, AnetaPics, Vitaly Titov & Maria SideInikova

All other photographs courtesy of Isabelle Francais and TFH Archives.